Parent Power

A Guide to Your Child's Success

Parent Power

A Guide to Your Child's Success

Bonnie Williamson

Dynamic Teaching
Company

Parent Power

A Guide to Your Child's Success

By Bonnie Williamson

Published by: Dynamic Teaching Company
Post Office Box 276711
Sacramento, CA 95827
(916) 351-1912

First printing 1997

Printed in the United States of America
Cover design by Pearl and Associates
Illustrations by Jeff VanKanegan

Publisher's Cataloging in Publication
(Prepared by Quality Books Inc.)

Williamson, Bonnie
    Parent power : a guide to your child's success /
Bonnie Williamson
    p. cm.
    Includes index.
    Preassigned LCCN: 96-85895
    ISBN 0-937899-43-7

    1. Education—Parent participation. 2. Parent and child.
3. Home and school. I. Title.

LB1048.5.W55 1997   649'.68
                                                       QBI96-40266

To my nieces and nephews – Ron, Sharon, Patty, Kathleen and Jim –
for inviting me to share in their growing-up years, I give my love.

Other Books By Bonnie Williamson

A First-Year Teacher's Guidebook for Success

Classroom Management: A Guidebook for Success

101 Ways to Put Pizazz into Your Teaching

Acknowledgements

My sincere thanks to Lynn Pribus and Kathy Hoff, my editors for taking my words and making them "sing." I thank the rest of the "book team," Robert Howard, Debbie Timothy and Frank Meder, as well.

I also express my appreciation to Mary Alexander, Bonnie Allen, Jeff Bartley, Carolyn Bennett, Ginney Connor, Diane Duncan, Dave Fiscus, Pat Holzknecht, Pat Moore-Howard, Pete Kazak, Wanda Shironaka, Anna Severin and Sister Cora. These teachers' expertise in specific subjects provided me with outstanding information and encouragement as I was writing this book.

Contents

Author's Note

Please come sit in my back yard and join me for a cup of coffee. We can visit while looking out at the large oak trees — trees over a hundred years old. They require little care, but this is not true of children. Our children require large amounts of our time and I've found that while some people provide that time, others do not.

I've been a teacher for thirty years and have taught students from kindergarten through sixth grade. Some of my students achieved great success while others never reached their potential. The one thing which appears to most accurately indicate their future success is the amount of time parents or care givers are willing to spend to help them achieve a good education.

Getting an education is like climbing a ladder. Children do this one rung at a time and no rung should be missed. At school, with thirty-one students (or more), I'm not always able to spend as much time on each skill as I'd like. This is where some parents really make a difference. They make the time at home.

Also, some days certain students appear happy, but the next day, or month, they fall apart. This is an example of a time when parents and teachers must work together because some problems take a team effort to solve. I want to show you how to do that.

As we sit and visit, let me share with you from my years of experience and show you how you can help your child be more successful in school.

Bonnie Williamson
Sacramento, California

Parent Involvement
You Can Make A Real Difference

"I feel parental involvement is an important part of the child's learning process. The parent, child and teacher are a team and each team member plays an important role in this procedure. The parent's role includes sending the child to school in a positive way, making sure the child is prepared to learn each day and reinforcing skills and concepts taught by the teacher at school."

Elois Henderson, Sixth-Grade Teacher, Dayton Public Schools, Dayton, Ohio

You are your child's first teacher and play a greater role than the teachers at school. As a parent or care giver, you are the most important factor in your child's future success in school. This is indeed an awesome task, but it should also be considered a privilege.

3

Since you are such an important person in your youngster's life, here are some things you can do as an involved parent.

BE AN EXAMPLE

Reading. Be a reader and let your child see you read. You want to set an example, so read for yourself as well as having the child hear you read for him/her. Turn off the television and read with your child. Announce that this is your special time together.

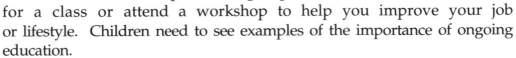

Go to the library and bring home books, magazines and tapes for both of you to enjoy. Your youngster will see how important reading is to you and will want to copy what you're doing.

Your education. Continue your own education. When possible, sign up for a class or attend a workshop to help you improve your job or lifestyle. Children need to see examples of the importance of ongoing education.

Educational resources. Have educational resources available around the house and use them. These might include encyclopedias, a world globe, atlas, shelves of books, tapes, CDs and even a computer. Using these resources establishes an example to your child of the importance of expanding his/her world.

PARENT TIP: **From time to time, sets of encyclopedias can be purchased fairly inexpensively at grocery stores. You usually need to buy a nominal amount of groceries and pay an additional few dollars for each book. I've used these books in my classroom and have been pleased with the information provided. Garage sales and flea markets are good sources for used encyclopedias.**

SUPPORT SCHOOL RULES

Rules and procedures. Every school has rules, discipline procedures and goals. It's very important for parents to support them.

Usually at the beginning of each school year, a list of rules and procedures is sent home. Arrange a time when you can sit down with your child to review them. Read them aloud and ask, "What do you think this means?" Or, "Why do you think they have a rule about not throwing food in the school cafeteria?" Or, "Why shouldn't you call other students names?"

Home and classroom rules. Talk about home rules such as no television while doing homework, or coming home promptly at six o'clock for dinner each night. Discuss why we have one set of rules at home and a different set at school. Compare your family size, perhaps five members, with school where the classroom family could number twenty-five or thirty students, or even more. Ask, "Why should classrooms have rules?" Or, "Do all the students in class behave, or do some of them create problems for others?"

Also, talk to your child about the consequences of breaking school rules. Say, "What happens when you call others names or throw food in the cafeteria? What are the consequences?"

As you discuss the rules together, your child will understand that you know the rules and expect they will be followed and obeyed. Talk about how students who follow the rules help create an atmosphere where the teacher can teach and students can learn.

BE AVAILABLE

Thirty years ago when I started teaching, I had many parent volunteers. These days, many more mothers have gone back to work, there are more single-parent families and some parents speak limited English. Often, I don't have many parents in my classroom but I'm always excited and pleased to see them.

Parent helpers. Remember, each school will vary in needs and in what activities, such as fund raisers, it promotes. There are numerous ways you can help the teacher during the year.

- Chaperone a field trip with your child's class.

CAUTION: If you're asked to drive a car, see the principal first to be sure this is allowed. If you go, make sure that you have at least the minimum amount of insurance required by the school district. Do not leave yourself open to a lawsuit.

- Participate in a bake sale by making cupcakes or cookies. Check with the teacher to be sure the school allows parents to send home-baked goods for sales. Some do not.
- Help your child's classroom raise money by collecting empty aluminum cans. Take the cans to the recycling station.
- Be a room parent.
- Tell the teacher you'll be a classroom speaker. You may be a nurse, an artist or a fisherman. Be willing to share your talents or special knowledge with others.
- Help once a week, or even once a month, at school in reading, math or science.
- Arrange to help on the day when sales are being held.
- Take papers home to grade at night.
- Volunteer to tutor a child in reading once a week.
- Tell the teacher you'll make telephone calls prior to the next field trip or class party.

- Build a holder for Sno Cones for the next carnival.
- Purchase plastic pipe and volunteer to make hoops for the physical education program at school.

Today we need parents more than ever as helpers in our schools. One of the ways you can show your child you care is to be there. Even if your time is limited, teachers appreciate parents willing to grade papers at home, go on a field trip or volunteer to help at a school carnival or other function.

Field trips. Depending upon the destination and the age of the students, at least one adult is needed for every ten students. This is especially true in the kindergarten-primary grades. You are needed.

Work closely with the teacher so you know what is expected from you and the students. By working together, you'll help provide a much more worthwhile learning experience for the children, for you and the teacher. Volunteer as often as you can.

Even if you work, more companies are responding to parents' needs to be involved in their children's schools. Take some personal or vacation time to accompany students on a field trip, and you will really impress your child with your commitment.

Room parent. It's exciting to be a room parent. You'll work with students during the happy times such as holiday parties and get to know your child's classmates better. Teachers use their room parents in various ways. The teacher should meet with you early in the year and explain what you will need to do.

PARENT TIP: **Feel free to make suggestions about things you would like to do. Parents have wonderful ideas and most teachers are interested in working with them. One year a parent prepared homemade ice cream for our Christmas party. My students were ecstatic and so was I. You are unique; speak up and let the teacher know what kinds of things you'd be most comfortable helping with.**

Your talents. I have little background in music and often felt inadequate to teach it to my students. But one year a parent with musical experience offered to teach music each week to my students. She brought in a guitar and autoharp. She taught music theory for the first ten minutes of each lesson and followed it with an exhilarating "sing-along." My students looked forward to her visits and, believe me, so did I. Let your child's teacher know early in the year about any talents you'd like to share with the class such as those in art, music or science, or even crafts or special physical activities.

School library. With so many financial cutbacks in education, many schools no longer have a full-time librarian. Hundreds of fascinating books sit on dusty shelves because no one is there to keep the library open.

You might consider volunteering for a few hours a week to work in the library. What a worthwhile gift you'd give all those children hoping for an opportunity to read some of those books!

Teacher's helper. Classrooms are frequently packed with children, many in need of individual help from the teacher. Bright and beautiful bulletin boards enhance the introduction of new lessons or serve as an enrichment for lessons already introduced. It would be a real help to a teacher and class to sometimes put up a new bulletin board.

PARENT TIP: **Less money is available today for school supplies. If you have large pieces of fabric, you can take the yardage to share with the teacher. Fabrics can be used in place of expensive bulletin board paper to make a room look happy and inviting.**

Classroom observation. From time to time, write or call the teacher and ask to observe in the classroom. Not only will you be more informed, but your child will understand that you feel school is important. Remember, you're not there to evaluate the teacher but to find out what is happening on a day-to-day basis.

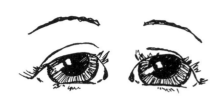

ATTEND MEETINGS

PTA. At many schools, attendance at PTA meetings has dropped off drastically but some reasons are valid. In many areas, parents just don't feel safe going out at night.

Now that more parents work, they have less time to attend meetings, day or night. Also, as children get older, they often don't want their parents to attend school meetings. In the latter case, PTA notices seldom get home.

If you meet with the teacher early in the year, you can ask when a PTA meeting will be held. If possible, be there.

PARENT TIP: **Since school schedules are often filled with many activities, it is wise to either purchase or make a daily journal. Preprinted journals are often expensive, so consider making your own by purchasing an inexpensive nine-by-seven-inch binder with lined paper at your local grocery store. Go through the binder and mark each page with the date in sequence for the next three months. At the first of each month, enter all school meetings for each of your children on the correct date. You may prefer to purchase a large calendar for the kitchen and record all meetings on the appropriate days.**

Parent meetings.   More and more schools are offering meetings to coach parents on how to work with their children. Sometimes these are held during the day and open with coffee and donuts and a time to visit with other parents as well as the teacher. Take advantage of these meetings.

Parents are frequently asked at the beginning of the year to select topics they would like discussed during the school year. Guest authorities present information on subjects such as "How to Help Your Child Read."   In some areas, the police are asked to talk about gang activity and how to protect your child from gangs.

In my chapter titled, "Help Bilingual Students Be Successful In School," I discuss meetings for limited-English parents. I hope you'll read it even if your child doesn't come from a bilingual home. By being aware of the needs of bilingual or non-English-speaking adults, you'll be more informed about changes going on in our culture and can help your youngster to be better prepared for the future as well.

Advisory meetings.   Many school districts receive additional funds from federal and state agencies to help needy children. In order to meet some of the requirements for these funds, an advisory council must be established. Parents are needed to serve on the board. If possible, volunteer to serve at least one year.

You'll learn much more about your school's programs and, at times, will be invited to attend meetings with parents from other schools. You can enjoy talking to other parents while becoming more informed about programs in their districts.

Back-To-School Night.   One of the most important meetings you can attend each year is this one held soon after school opens. Make every effort to attend this critical meeting for you and your child, as it sets the tone for the whole school year.

Teachers usually give a brief talk which includes an overview of what will be covered during the school year.   Textbooks will be displayed along with any computers or other special school aids the classroom might have.

There is time at the end of the talk for parents to ask general questions about the class and planned curriculum. Be prepared. The questions you ask will also certainly help other parents attending the meeting, but keep in mind this is <u>not</u> the time to ask specific questions about your own child.

You might want a clear definition of the homework rules for the classroom, information on field trips and a preview of items to be brought to school for art or science or other activities.

At the meeting you may be given a small handout with academic goals for students in your child's grade. If you do not have this important handout, look at "Academic Goals" in the Resources section of this book. Feel free to make a copy of the grade levels you need.

PARENT TIP: **Post the "Academic Goals For Students" pages on your refrigerator. Refer to it all year long and use it as a checklist to be sure each rung of the academic ladder is being achieved by your child.**

Open House. The final big meeting for the school year is usually this event which is a gigantic SHOW AND TELL. Teachers and students spend days in preparation, decorating their classrooms with art, history and language projects.

PARENT TIP: **Before going to Open House, sit down with your child and make a simple checklist. Ask, "What should I look for?" Where in the room can I see your language and math papers? Do you have** an art project you want me to see? Where is it?" Often classrooms get very crowded and your student will be disappointed if you don't get to see all the work he/she has done.

Generally, no formal meeting is held for this special occasion. Instead, parents, students, grandparents and other relatives are welcome to attend. Children enjoy going with their parents to this meeting. If possible afterward, take your child out for a favorite treat. This says, "You are really special, and I'm proud of you."

PARENT TIP: **Take a small camera with you. Have your child stand next to his/her art work, for example, and take a picture. Take a picture of your youngster and the teacher and of your child sitting at his/her desk. Place these pictures in a scrapbook marked with the appropriate year. Save space for sample handwriting, math and a list of books read. You'll provide your child with a visual journey through an important year in school.**

NOTE: While your being involved at your youngster's school does not mean your child will get special treatment, it <u>can</u> make a difference if problems arise. You'll be more familiar with the people and resources there, and it's simply human nature that when you are involved and helping, the school staff will want to help you.

In this chapter, I've told you about the many ways you can become part of your child's education. This can develop a strong, positive relationship between your home and your youngster's school. Enjoy each year to the fullest.

Prepare Your Child For Preschool

"As adults we master new things with difficulty such as a foreign language, computer skills or a song. Little children can master many things almost without any conscious effort. Give them love, attention, security and conversation, and they will amaze you!"

Jean Reitmeier, Preschool Teacher, Pilgrim Lutheran School, Beaverton, Oregon

Brandon, my niece's energetic three-year-old, sits in his car seat counting pine trees as his mother drives along a mountain road. He yells out, "One tree, two trees, three, four...."

Later Brandon holds up three fingers to show his age and a wooden block with the letter "B" indicating the first letter of his name.

Brandon's parents have spent much time talking, encouraging and working with their young son. As the youngster eagerly reaches out to learn more about his expanding world, it's obvious his parents' efforts have succeeded.

"Jump start" your toddler for success. Recent studies described by Sharon Begley in *Newsweek* magazine (February 19, 1996) tell how you can help your youngster become successful in school and life.

At birth, your baby will have trillions of neurons (I call them "spark plugs") in his brain. Some will already be functioning, while others will be waiting to be turned on.

Millions of these spark plugs come equipped with their own timelines and await your input. It is critical that you begin working with your baby early, often by four months. Without input, neurons die.

Talk to your baby, read aloud, play games, laugh, play music and clap. Your interactions will activate the spark plugs so they come alive.

Language. The more words and sounds your child hears early, the sooner she will learn language. I know this is true. When one little six-year-old entered my classroom, he could barely speak. I learned his cocaine-addicted mother had usually left him home alone while she "worked the street." Since he heard little language in his critical early years, his speech spark plugs were barely active.

Math and music. Math spark plugs are beside the music plugs. Play Mozart as you teach your child to count, to copy patterns and to draw geometric figures. Children learn math more quickly while listening to music.

Emotions. Show your happiest emotions when your child pets the cat, rolls a ball or takes first steps. This will activate positive emotions and help your child to be excited about life.

Open windows. The windows of opportunity for motor development, emotional control, vision, social attachment, math, vocabulary and second language have limited access and can only be opened during their special timelines. Use those early years wisely.

For activity ideas see Lewis Sparling's book, *Learningames*.

Encourage your child to be creative. Have a box of "things" such as building blocks and plastic dishes and let the youngster play freely. Provide old clothes, hats, and pieces of fabric in a box for your child to play dress up and encourage imaginative play.

Help your child become aware of colors and textures and to see the beauty of the world around him/her. Your home, street and community will become your child's "learning" world and you'll provide the materials and encouragement to explore.

Touching and feeling. Children enjoy touching things. Sensory awareness, the sense of touching, needs to be developed in your child, because it is the most basic foundation for helping him/her develop thinking skills. Provide your youngster with many opportunities to touch and feel. Fill a basket, for example, with sample fabrics such as velvet, satin, corduroy, chenille, denim and cotton. Add samples of lace, edgings, thread and yarn and ribbons in a variety of colors.

Put ten items like a dime, a toy truck, a pencil and a spoon in a paper bag. Have your child identify each by touch.

Place the cat on your lap and help your child feel the fur. Talk about how it feels and the color of the fur. He/she can also listen to the "purring" and feel the "vibrations" if the cat's "motor is running."

Walk outside and put your arms around the trunk of a tree. Say to your child, "Feel the bark. How does it feel?" Have your child close his/her eyes and move from sunlight to shadow.

Looking around. Take your child outside and point out shapes of leaves, raindrops on the sidewalk or snow on a flower. Talk about the beauty of a row of corn stalks, vines on a wall and acorns on a pathway. Watch the shadow of a building move during the day. Show how your own shadows move as you move.

Sounds and smells. Start early to call your child's attention to the songs of different birds, and the sounds of a brook, a siren, a motorcycle or a truck. The smell of bread baking, a fire in the fireplace and a fresh fall breeze will add to your child's awareness of the sensory world all around.

Sorting. Sorting is an activity to organize your child's mind while putting things together which go together. Children need experiences in organizing their minds and their lives. Provide them with a variety of opportunities to sort items.

One popular category is buttons in various sizes and colors and numbers of holes. My mother saved hundreds for me to use with my students. They particularly enjoyed touching and sorting the very old buttons in the box. Ask your child's grandmother for buttons. Have your child sort them by color, or size or number of holes. Say, "Show me the buttons with two holes. Show me the buttons with four holes. Show me all the white buttons, or red or blue. Show me the round ones. Show me the square ones." Other items for sorting include macaroni shapes, nails, screws, spools, rocks, coins, toy soldiers, doll clothes, books, and dominoes.

Field trips. When a child actually sees a zoo animal or a fire truck, the animal and truck are much more meaningful than when simply seen on television or as a picture on a flash card. Whether routine or planned, field trips can broaden and enlarge your child's firsthand experiences and emphasize using the senses. These trips can be as simple as a walk

around your neighborhood to watch construction workers building a house or repairing a roof. Family outings and vacations, trips to a large city or a rural area can also enlarge a child's personal library of experience. Other field trips which children enjoy are visits to the library, a bakery, a candy factory, a fire station or a body-and-fender shop.

Jeff, one of the youngsters at my inner-city school, was thrilled to hear the story of the *Three Little Bears* but he could not figure out exactly what a bear was until we took him to the zoo. He jumped up and down yelling, "Look, Teacher, it's a bear! It's a <u>real</u> bear just like in the story." For Jeff, taking a field trip made that story come alive.

One of my favorite field trips with my nieces and nephews was a trip to a candy factory. Can't you imagine their excitement when they smelled the candy cooking as we entered the building? Their eyes grew LARGE as they watched hundreds of candy bars moving along an assembly line. It was a thrill for me to share in their excitement during this trip.

Some other enjoyable trips for preschoolers are to visit a pet store, a petting zoo or a farm or watch neighborhood sports activities such as youth soccer or a high school track meet.

PARENT TIP: **After you return from a field trip, ask your child to dictate a few sentences about what you saw. Then help your child draw a picture about the trip. This might be a bridge, a barn or a rainbow. Have your young artist autograph the picture and post it along with the story where the family can see and appreciate the work.**

Brandon shares his artwork with me while I'm writing this chapter. He drew a picture of his smiling face and some rocks and pebbles he remembered from his back yard. The picture hangs above my computer, reminding me of that happy and exuberant three-year-old.

On the road. When you drive around your community, talk to your child. As you approach a corner say, "We are turning left now." Bend your body to the left and your child will bend left as well. This is a great way to teach your child "left" and "right."

As you approach a miles-per-hour sign say, "It says we can go 35 miles an hour here. See the 3 and the 5? That means 35 miles an hour."

Give your child a pencil and pad to put down a mark every time you see a red car. When you get home, count the number of red cars you saw.

Letter recognition. Your youngster needs to see numbers, letters and shapes over and over again in order to recall them when presented in school. Many children watch "Sesame Street" and the letters on the TV screen. You need to provide them opportunities to recognize letters in everyday life. For example, when you drive to the store, say, "We're going to the Supermarket to shop. See the big 'S' on the sign over the store?"

As you drive say, "There's an 'S' in STOP at the stop sign." Take out the newspaper and point out letters that begin with "S." If your child's name is Sidney, say, "Sidney, your name begins with an 'S' and also has the letter 'y' that goes down in it. Your name has a letter with a little dot above too. We call that letter an 'i.'" Print your child's name and have your child touch each letter. Children love to see their names in print.

PARENT TIP: **Don't push your child to write his/her name. Your child will let you know when he/she is ready. This is the time to expose your youngster to letters and numbers. When your child does express**

an interest, write out the name in clear capital letters which can be copied.

CAUTION: Be sure your child holds the pencil correctly. This means the pencil rests on the third finger and is controlled by the pointer finger and the thumb. The pencil rests in the "V" between the thumb and pointer finger. Have your youngster hold the pencil at the edge where it is cut (where the paint begins). It can take first-grade teachers a year to retrain a youngster to hold a pencil the right way, because it's very difficult to break a bad habit.

If you have a computer, look for software for Preschool-Kindergarten students. I've used programs where my kindergartners click the mouse on, for example, a "C." Then the picture of a cat appears and they click on the cat which is followed by the word "cat" and they type the word. Children enjoy working on the computer and they stay motivated. See the chapter on "Computer-Wise Kids" for outstanding software programs.

Another way to help your child learn about numbers and letters is to purchase a drip pan at an automotive parts store. This will serve as a magnetic board if you make or buy letters and numbers with magnets on the back. Magnets may be purchased at hardware stores in strips with adhesive on the back. Cut to the size of the numbers and letters you are using. Attach the drip pan to a wall, fence or shed and show your child how to stick numbers and letters on the metal sheet.

Speaking. "When talking to your child," says Preschool Teacher, Jean Reitmeier, "speak slowly and distinctly to help your child develop good speech habits."

She also recommends that as often as you can, kneel or sit on the floor so you can carry on a conversation with your child at eye level. These are the times to ask questions such as, "What can your eyes see today? Your ears hear? Your nose smell? Your tongue taste? Your hands feel?"

Physical activities. It's also important during these preschool years that your youngster has plenty of opportunities for physical exercise with various levels of activity.

The following are some sample activities:

- Build a sandbox for your child and supply it with pie, cake and muffin tins for scooping sand, building tunnels and making mountains.
- Build a sand volcano. Help your child mound up sand and make a depression for a volcano. Pour two teaspoons of baking soda into the depression with one-fourth cup of vinegar. Then add some red food coloring to make the event even more dramatic.
- Have plenty of crayons, pens and large pads of paper for your child to use while developing fine motor skills.
- Arrange water activities for your child to use out-of-doors or in the bathtub. In good weather, take a baby washtub outside. If you don't have one, buy one at a thrift store. Provide measuring spoons, squirt bottles, plastic cups and dishes and measuring cups with spouts for pouring. Put in a dash of liquid soap and food coloring for additional interest.
- As you ride your bicycle around the neighborhood, have your child go along on a tricycle or bicycle. As you ride say, "Watch for cars coming out of driveways." When you pass signs, point out the beginning letters and talk about the colors. Ask if the signs have large or small letters.
- A tire swing makes a wonderful gift for a child. Construct one with chains or ropes and a tire and teach your child how to swing.

HINT: This is also the time to provide your youngster with opportunities to play with other children. They can play house, build a bridge with blocks or pretend they are truck drivers. This gives your child the opportunity for give and take with other children. The child also verbalizes ideas such as "Let's play fireman.

Let's fill the bucket with water." This interplay helps your child move out into a larger world of peers.

Learning through exploration. Children need to explore to develop language. Exploring and experimenting, trial and error, observing, interacting with people and objects and seeking conclusions to problems are all valuable components to learning.

Parents have told me they placed a card table in the living room and covered it with a sheet or blanket. Their child, sometimes with a playmate, spent a great deal of time each day building and rebuilding a "blanket house" while using language to "act" the parts of a parent, a mail carrier and a storekeeper.

PARENT TIP: **When children enter school, they will meet many different adults and children in their own peer group. By providing your child with opportunities to interact with others from an early age, you'll help your youngster fit into the classroom better.**

Children learn about math, science and social studies through meaningful activities such as measuring, cooking or working with wood. One way is to have a small tub available for corn meal and one for rice. Provide your child with an old strainer. Let your youngster pour the corn meal and rice through the strainer. He/she will discover that the rice stays and the corn meal comes out. Children love doing this.

Finger painting is always fun and is especially nice when you can do it outdoors. Use an old waterproof card table and a can of shaving cream. Your child will enjoy covering the table top with shaving cream and then "drawing" in the foam. Finger painting with shaving cream can also be done on the side of the bathtub or the shower. For variety add food coloring.

Place an easel outdoors and let your child finger paint on the easel or on a fence or shed wall. A large shirt buttoned down the back makes a great substitute painter's smock.

PARENT TIP: **Another outdoor idea for general play activities is to use an old counter top. Attach one side to a fence, shed or garage. Make sure the curved lip is on the side where the child will be standing. Cut several round holes in the lip and add cups filled with tempera for painting. Also, save old dried-out felt pens and make water available for your child for dipping pens and drawing. The old pens will be revived to use again.**

    Chalkboards.   Since writing on a chalkboard helps children develop large muscles, encourage writing this way.   Buy white and colored chalk.   If you don't have a chalkboard, you can purchase plywood and special chalkboard spray paint to make your own the size you wish.   Show your child how to season the board by turning a piece of chalk on its side and rubbing it all over the chalkboard.   Then erase and it is ready to use.

    Also show your child how to use an eraser correctly.   Chalk dust is not to be blown at other people; nor is the eraser to be banged against the house or tossed at other people.   These are gentle lessons which will help your child learn how to get along well in school.

    Chalk may also be used on sidewalks.   Have your children draw pictures to greet friends or relatives coming to visit.   You can help write names.   The chalk washes off easily with water.

    HINT: Some children are allergic to chalk dust.   If this is the case in your home, buy a dry-wipe board which can be purchased at a discount store.   Provide dry colored markers and an eraser for your child.

    Colors.   Recognition of colors is important for children.   Knowing colors helps them learn to read.   They will know that apples are red, grass is green and the sky is blue.   When your youngster writes a story and uses colors, he/she will know what the colors look like.   Not only should your child know the basic colors of red, green and blue but also colors like pink and peach.   As you walk about the neighborhood, point out that trees are green, some flowers are yellow and sidewalks are gray.

Bookstores carry children's books on colors and some libraries have a special section for books about them. Some may encourage you to mix food colors together to form new colors or perform other interesting experiments.

Play "I Spy" and say, "I spy something with my eye that is red"; then have your child guess the item.

Point out that your one child is wearing a green dress and your other child a blue shirt, while Mom is wearing a purple apron. Dad's glasses have brown rims and he is wearing a red necktie.

Shapes. By the time children enter first grade, they should know shapes. Cut a small square, rectangle, circle and triangle from wood or heavy cardboard. Give them to your child to trace the shapes on the chalkboard. Talk about their names.

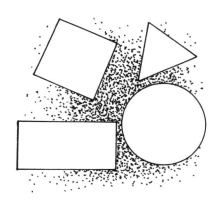

As you walk about the house say, "Look, the television is square, the plate is round and the birdhouse is a triangle." Always look for ways to alert your child to shapes.

Scissors. Kindergarten teachers are seeing more and more children who have never held a pair of scissors in their hands. It takes these children weeks to feel comfortable using them. Give your child a head start in their use under your supervision. Preschool teachers say one good brand of rounded-point scissors is Fiskars™ made for either left-handed or right-handed youngsters; they can be purchased at fabric shops.

Your child will enjoy cutting out pictures from old catalogs, magazines, sample wallpaper books and throw-away ads that come in the mail. Have a "hunting party," where you name an item for your child to find and cut out. Talk about each item. You can also make a counting book with one picture of a stove, two pictures of telephones and three pictures of flowers. Glue these onto pieces of paper and fasten together into a book.

Numbers. Find an old calendar, preferably a large one. Help your child cut out the squares with the numbers inside. You can also make a set of numbers out of old three-by-five index cards. Have your child place on the table, for example, the square with the "10." Ask, "Can you show me the number that goes <u>before</u> number ten?" Say, "Show me the number that comes <u>after</u> number ten."

Position words. In order for your child to function well in everyday life, it's important to know and understand words such as under, over, up, down, beside, before, after, in, out and through. Constantly talk to your child. Say as you drive, "We are driving <u>over</u> a bridge. We are now <u>on</u> the bridge. We are <u>off</u> the bridge."

Take your child to the zoo and say, "Look at the hippopotamus. He has his eyes <u>out</u> of the water." Say, "See, the birds are flying <u>up</u> in the sky." Or, "There's a squirrel <u>on</u> the roof." Remember, lots of teaching is not formal; it's just you and your child, but learning can be exciting.

An obstacle course. Set up a card table and say, "Go <u>under</u> the card table." Put out two chairs and say, "Walk <u>between</u> the chairs." Place a rope on the floor and say, "Walk <u>beside</u> the rope."

HINT: Use a large refrigerator carton or other big cardboard box for your child to crawl through. Use it in an obstacle course as a way of teaching "through the tunnel." Around the house say, "Go <u>through</u> the door." Or, "Now you're <u>in</u> the hall."

Math. To help your child develop math concepts such as counting, have him/her help you set the table. Say, "We have five coming for dinner tonight. How many forks do we need? How many plates? How many chairs? How many glasses?"

Say, "You must be really thirsty. You're having your second glass of milk."

When you play ball outside, say, "How many balls did we bring out here? You have one and I brought two. How many?"

Your child can view fish either at home or sometimes in town. Where I bought my car, there's a large aquarium where children gather to talk about the number of fish, their colors and what they are doing.

Consider having a fish bowl or aquarium in your home and have your child observe as you place your fish into the bowl. You can count together.

Say, "Here is one orange fish.

Now I'm putting in a silver fish.

How many fish so far?" Two.

"This time I'm putting in one blue fish.

Now we are putting in a black fish.

How many fish do we have altogether?

Yes, we have four fish in our bowl."

Through observation, listening and counting, your child will begin to understand numbers.

CAUTION: It's very important to allow your child to develop at his/her own pace. Simply let him/her enjoy life by providing a variety of experiences. Your child will pick up the ABCs and numbers while hearing you read and while watching television. You should provide input and guidance without pushing. A good book to read is *The Hurried Child* by David Elkind.

Overparenting. Many of us know parents who overparent. Often they are from the baby boomer generation and they take child rearing VERY SERIOUSLY. Having the brightest, most precocious child around is a status symbol. Fortunately, most children survive their parents and turn out fine. It's good to encourage your youngster, but pressuring can backfire. Just remember, you can make all kinds of mistakes, but so long as you love and accept your children, they'll do well.

Prepare Your Child For Kindergarten

"Provide your youngster with opportunities to interact with other children. If at all possible, have your child attend a preschool. Studies have shown that children who attend preschool do much better in kindergarten."

Lisa Golden, Kindergarten teacher, Hal Henard Elementary School, Greenville, Tennessee

For many children, kindergarten means buying new shoes, clothes and a lunch pail. It may even mean riding on the big yellow school bus. The event is a wonderful adventure in a big new world for some. For others, it can become a terrifying experience.

Several months before your child starts school for the first time, you need to begin talking in a positive way about the coming new adventure. School is where the child prepares for the future. School is also the place where children learn new things and make new friends. It is a place where they start to learn letters and numbers and sing songs and draw pictures if they haven't already learned some of these things at home or in preschool.

There are skills you can teach your child to ease the transition from home to school. If your child does not attend preschool, you'll need to spend extra time preparing for kindergarten.

Getting dressed. You need to teach your child to be independent, and an important part is to be able to get dressed alone. Choose clothes which are easy to get into and out of when they go to the bathroom. I particularly appreciate parents who teach their little boys how to zip and unzip their pants. When you shop, select clothes that are suitable for sitting on the floor and active play. It also helps to buy pull-over tops, pull-on bottoms and shoes with Velcro™ sticky fasteners. Choose boots, rainwear and snow clothes that are easy to put on. It's a good idea to label clothes and shoes with your child's name.

PARENT TIP: **Children should not wear dress-up shoes to school. Often these have slippery soles and the shoes frequently come off easily, causing children to slip or fall. Also, for safety's sake provide your child with covered-toe shoes rather than sandals.**

Getting-along skills. As your child moves from the small home or-day-care world into the larger school world, it's important for them to understand responsibilities and good manners. Teach your child to be responsible for personal belongings. Expect your child to help with household chores from an early age. Children should be able to use a sponge to wipe a table, for instance. Also help your youngster learn to share toys and take turns. Emphasize that knowing these "getting-along" skills will help your child make new friends.

Letting go. Most teachers recall children coming to school the first day shaking with fear. These youngsters had never been away from home without their parents before. Helping your children develop social and emotional skills so they will be prepared to enter kindergarten is part of learning.

If your child is not in day care or preschool, it's crucial to provide the experience of going places without you. Your child should be used to visiting friends or relatives alone. Help form a parent-cooperative group for baby-sitting so you can begin to separate from your child.

Prepare ahead. More and more schools are holding get-acquainted days for incoming students to see their new school. These might include an all-school family potluck picnic or a chance to eat in the school cafeteria with other students before school recesses for vacation the previous semester.

Prepare your child ahead of time by visiting school on a weekend when it is quiet. Look around the playground, peek inside the windows. Explain to your child that during the school day many boys and girls

will be there and it will be noisy with so many people talking and having fun.

If at all possible, visit the school again the week before school starts. Have your child meet the school secretary, the nurse, the principal and custodian. Check with the school secretary to be sure your child's forms and records are on file. In most states your child must have a physical exam, immunizations, proof of birth and proof of residence.

Visit the teacher. Usually, the teacher will be working in the classroom before school opens. Stop by <u>briefly</u> and introduce your child to the teacher and let your youngster spend a few minutes looking around the classroom.

Most teachers are delighted that parents are interested enough to come to the school and don't mind spending a few minutes getting acquainted. If you will be able to help during the year, tell the teacher you are a willing volunteer and emphasize your commitment to be part of the child/teacher/parent learning team. I have found some of my best parent-volunteers during these unscheduled "drop-ins."

Behavior needs. Lots of children who start kindergarten just aren't ready. Teachers must spend time preparing such children to learn instead of being able to simply begin teaching.

From my own experience and from talking to many teachers over the years, I believe the two biggest problems are lack of responsibility and lack of self-discipline.

Perhaps the most important thing is to be able to sit still for at <u>least</u> five or six minutes at a time. Susan Schlossberg and Karen Van Wormer, team kindergarten teachers in California, point out that the distraction of children running around seriously impairs the learning process. They also see many children who are not able to take turns and yell out answers during class.

Knowing ABCs. Kindergarten teachers appreciate children coming to school knowing their ABCs and knowing the beginning letter of their first names. Recognizing at least some colors and shapes will also be helpful for your child's first days of school.

Bilingual parents. Please read my chapter on "Meeting The Needs Of Bilingual Students." Also, I've found it is so helpful to have older brothers and sisters work with their younger siblings on the alphabet, shapes and colors before school begins.

I've worked with many children from bilingual homes and many enter school with few skills. See if your area has "Twilight Schools" where your child can receive tutoring to prepare him/her for school. These sessions are free and often held right at the school at the end of the school day.

INFORMATION FOR NEW KINDERGARTNERS

Attendance. Make sure your child attends school every day and arrives on time. Most children who attend school regularly do well. Those who do not, do poorly. Model for your child the importance of timely attendance by being on time yourself for church, the dentist or the doctor.

Absence and early release. Always write absence excuses when your child is sick and sign your child out at the office for early release. Schools must follow certain rules and show when and why children are absent. By following school rules, you'll have fewer telephone calls from the school office.

Show and Tell. I have found that Show and Tell can be one of the most exciting events for a kindergartner to experience. Most children enjoy showing and telling about a toy, a rock or a book in class.

At many schools, kindergarten teachers ask that children participate regularly. Have practice sessions at home or let your child do a trial run for friends or family. Have your child pick out a toy or book and stand in front of the group and tell about the object.

Volunteers. Most teachers need helpers in the classroom. During the first week of school, fill out the form your child brings home and, if at all possible, be a helper.

If you work and cannot help on a regular basis, consider volunteering for field trips. When children go to the zoo or a dairy, they need several adults to help make the experience move along smoothly. I've always appreciated parents who were willing to take an hour or two to help me take children for drinks or the bathroom or help get them on the bus.

Snacks. When children enter school, their stomachs are on "Summer-time" eating schedules. Be sure your child has a good breakfast and provide a piece of fruit or small sandwich for the first few weeks of school. I always keep graham crackers in a cupboard for children who forget or come from homes where they don't have money for extra treats, but not all teachers do this.

Rest and nutrition. Studies show that children do better in school if they have gotten a good night's sleep and have eaten a good breakfast and lunch. Most kindergartners should have at least ten hours of sleep each night. By sixth grade it decreases to at least eight hours.

PARENT TIP: **The greatest gift you can give each morning is to have your child leave home with a happy feeling. Don't yell or scold. The tone you set at the front door is the feeling the child will take to the classroom that day.**

Self-reliance. Please help your child learn to take proper care of belongings such as coats and lunch boxes. Buying your child a backpack to carry papers, notes and snacks would be very helpful.

I believe that the practical skills you teach preschoolers about keeping track of things carry over into all the school years. I've always appreciated children who have been trained to hang up their jackets, place their lunch pails on the shelf and keep their desks tidy enough so they can find things.

Name and address. Your child should be able to recite his/her full name, address and phone number. This is important for your child to know in case of an emergency. Children who ride the bus must be able to tell the bus driver where they live and should be able to recognize the correct bus stop.

Bilingual parents. Please have an older brother or sister ride with your kindergartner each day for the first week of school. Kindergartners have come to my class speaking little English, afraid of teachers and bus drivers and not knowing where to get off the bus. In order to quell their fears, it would be helpful to have an older family member ride with the child and point out where to get off when going home.

To and from school. Instruct your child to go directly to and from school and not play along the way. Discuss the importance of never talking to strangers or accepting rides from people they don't know.

At dismissal time, pick up your child on time. Being left for a long time after everyone else has gone is upsetting to any child. I've watched far too many kindergartners sit in the office and scream and cry for their parents who were as much as two hours late picking them up. Such children feel abandoned, unloved and become fearful about coming to school.

When you tell a child you'll pick him/her up at a specific time, be on time. Otherwise, arrange for another family member or close friend to pick up your child, but be sure and call the school to alert the office that another person will be there. School office clerks are reluctant, and with good reason, to have anyone but a parent take a child home. Arrangements for a change in pickup must be cleared with the office first.

Kindergarten. Prior to the "big day," talk with your child about what he/she will wear and take to school. Some children come loaded with binders, large pencil boxes, a watch and a radio. All too often, by the end of the first day, some of these items have disappeared and the child erupts in tears. Limit the number of things your child takes to school.

In kindergarten and in the following grades, your child will benefit from and appreciate your interest. In return, you'll be a proud parent knowing you've done a great job.

Each New School Year Is A Whole New Ballgame

"A lot of parents concern themselves with the academic side of preparing their child for school. This is important; however, for the most part schools teach children to read and do mathematics. It's the things that are not as obvious that profoundly affect a child's performance in kindergarten and beyond. Parents have the earliest and best opportunity to teach their children how to get along with others, to value themselves, and to have confidence in themselves and their abilities. These things will not only aid in a child's readiness for school, but also for life."

Pat Facemire, Elementary Counselor, Braxton County Schools, West Virginia

Each new school year is a special event. The first day of school usually means new clothes, a new notebook and a new classroom.

Mark this day as special with some small ceremony that can be the same year after year. (Your kids may snort as they grow older, but they secretly find security in family traditions.) Perhaps your celebration will be a family dinner out the night before or a breakfast including a favorite coffee cake. Or a unique gift-wrapped surprise on the breakfast plate. Whatever you do, give the day some special recognition.

Enthusiasm. With each subsequent year, you'll want to maintain your enthusiasm. Point out how much your youngster has learned already and the wonderful new things to discover this year.

I've found that parents who are enthusiastic about school, books and learning have children who enjoy school. When children enjoy school, they frequently do outstanding work. Your feelings of a joy in learning will be passed on to your child not only in what you say but in how you act toward school.

Routine and organization. Children respond well to routines in the home and at school. As a parent you need to es-tablish a schedule so your child knows when to do homework and chores. Every child, whether in kindergarten or high school, needs to have a designated place for all materials to be returned to school. A "launch pad" near the front door, such as a plastic carton with the child's name on it, is helpful. Everything should be in the box before the child goes to bed the night before. Teachers also appreciate backpacks, which help get books and papers to school clean and dry. Put your child's name <u>inside</u> his/her backpack.

Good nutrition. Children need a good breakfast. Go easy on sugary selections which don't provide "fuel" for the entire morning. Instead choose foods like wheat toast, whole grain cereals and peanut butter. I've had youngsters come to school carrying packages of powdered gelatin dessert which they ate all morning long. This is not a nourishing way to begin a day. It is a long time until lunch, and children cannot concentrate when hungry.

Besides a good breakfast, children need a nutritious lunch. Pack one if the school doesn't provide food or you're not pleased with the selection. (For the first few weeks, you may also wish to send crackers or fruit as a snack if the teacher is willing.)

CAUTION: Through the school years do not allow your child extra money to stop at the store and buy candy, cookies or gum to munch or chew on during the school day. This creates jealousies and "copy cats" in the classroom and it gives children a "sugar high" which doesn't help the learning process.

Sleep. Ample sleep is vital for children in order to grow and to provide the necessary energy to study in school. Children ages five to seven should have at least ten hours of sleep each night.

Those from eight to fourteen need eight hours.

If your child has been going to bed (and getting up) late during vacation, start a week before school begins and insist on bedtime fifteen minutes earlier each night. This will help your youngster's "body clock" grow accustomed to school time.

Television and computer games. Even some of my very young students stay up late at night watching television. More and more youngsters also stay up late playing computer games. The next morning they fall asleep at their desks, often during reading.

Some television is exciting, fun and educational; however, many children watch more than six hours of television each day. This nearly equals the time they spend in school, and studies show that heavy TV watching is clearly tied to a drop in student test scores. Begin early to control the amount of time your child watches television. Instead, have plenty of books available for reading and games to play.

NOTE: Are you aware that the average five-year-old has spent 4,000 hours watching television? The average child by age twelve has seen 8,000 murders on television. Be aware of what your child is watching.

Listening. As your child enters the new world of school, he/she will come home eager to share stories about new friends, the classroom and the teacher. Be there to listen. Don't criticize, complain or belittle. <u>Just listen.</u> This can be done with milk and cookies after school, while riding home together from day care or while you prepare dinner.

To encourage your child, ask an occasional "open-ended" question, one that can't be answered with a simple yes or no. For instance, instead of asking, "Did you have fun in math today?" try asking, "What did you do in math today?"

Responsibility for school attendance. Be sure your child attends school regularly. The attendance patterns established early stay with children through future years. Surveys indicate that students who achieve in school, usually attend regularly. Students who miss school for either long or short periods, often fall behind. That may cause them to get discouraged and begin to give up on school. Don't let this happen.

Some of my students have missed up to forty-five days of school in a year and it is so sad to have them return and discover how far behind they are. More often I've heard parental excuses for a day's absence such as the parent working late, didn't set the alarm or thought the day was Saturday. But in the end, one of your most important jobs as a parent is to see that your child gets to school.

Frequent moves. I know that sometimes you don't have a choice, but according to recent studies, children who move often are 35 percent more likely to fail a grade and 77 percent more likely to have behavioral problems than students who rarely move.

Students have entered my classroom and moved away eleven days later. I've also had students come to me in March after having already moved five times during the year. These are frequently quiet, sad-faced children who have difficulty making friends. Others are arrogant and pick fights and get into trouble the first day in the classroom.

Some children who move often use this as an excuse not to work. I've heard a child say, "I don't have to do my math 'cause we're moving next week."

"A family move," writes Dr. David Wood of the Los Angeles Cedars-Sinai Medical Center "disrupts the routines, relationships and attachments that define the child's world, and almost everything outside the family that is familiar is lost and changes." *(The Journal of the American Medical Association,* September 15, 1993)

If you <u>must</u> move, try to make the change prior to the opening of school so that your child will not be thrown into a new environment needing to make new friends, master new rules and procedures and work with a new teacher in the middle of a year.

Your school attitude.   "Your attitude toward education will be reflected in how your child feels about school," says Dr. Bonnie Allen, Superintendent of Latrobe School District in California. "If you have a positive attitude toward school, then your child will see school as being important. Not always fun, perhaps, but a good place to learn and to grow."

Emotional bumps.   Children need to arrive at school rested, relaxed and happy. More and more families are being shattered by divorce, job losses, problems with drugs and other serious family problems. If your family is experiencing rocky times, it's essential that you and the school work together to help your child. Talk it over with the teacher. In serious situations, ask if a counselor is available to counsel your youngster.

Remember that each school year, you and your student will be starting on an exciting new adventure. Enjoy every day and every year of the trip.

Homework – An Important Ingredient In Learning

"If you don't understand what your child's homework assignment is about, it's critical for you to contact the teacher. When your child is little, you may have to be there all the time. As children grow older they need to work independently, but they still have to know they can come to you for help at any time."

Sue Toolen, First-Grade Teacher, Pershing Elementary School, Orangevale, California

Perhaps no school topic is more controversial than homework. Some parents expect their children to have it every night. Others say, "Don't send any home. I don't have time to help my child."

This places teachers right smack in the middle! Some students desperately need to do homework and yet not all parents are willing to cooperate.

A number of schools and school districts have now set guidelines or rules regarding homework. Many districts even spell out what nights work must go home.

In addition, weekly folders for students to take home have become an increasingly popular way to monitor homework. These folders are usually bright colors with inside pockets for graded homework, spelling words and math facts. Also, teachers send home letters updating parents on what is going on in the classroom. By checking the weekly folder, parents and teachers can act as a team to keep track of the flow of work between school and home.

Remember that homework is for your child, not for you. The joint effort between parents and teacher makes the child responsible for homework, not the parent.

WHY HOMEWORK?

There are four important reasons for students to work at home.
- To reinforce the skills they've already learned (the most important)
- To encourage students to be prepared for the lessons the following day
- To teach responsibility
- To promote learning and thinking

At the start of each year, be sure you know what days your child will have homework and how much time should be spent each night. Ask about any ongoing weekly homework assignments. Also, find out early about big projects so these can be worked into the homework schedule ahead of time.

Setting up a routine. In order for homework to get done on a daily basis, a time schedule must be established day after day and month after month. Children find time to play soccer after school, visit a friend, or go to the store. You need to establish a time when they do homework.

A calendar is a useful tool. Purchase or design a calendar with large squares which you can use for writing times for homework and other activities.

PARENT TIP: **Mid-January is a good time to look for discounted calendars for that year. Sometimes by shopping after Christmas, you'll find good buys at discount and stationery stores.**

At the first of each month, sit down with your youngster, and fill in the calendar. Write the times for sports activities, club meetings, music lessons, church activities and other meetings.

Now look over the calendar and decide on the best hours each day to do homework. If your child is a primary student, schedule at least twenty to thirty minutes each night. For students in grades four to six, set aside from forty to sixty minutes. Studies indicate that American first-graders average only fourteen minutes of homework each night and hate it. Japanese students spend thirty-five minutes and love it. We need to improve on the amount of time for homework and increase our children's interest in doing it.

HINT: You may also provide your child with a small notebook to keep track of homework assignments.

Depending upon the grade level and individual ability of your child, you may occasionally need to re-evaluate the time he/she spends on home-work. If the child is bringing home notes regarding incomplete work and poor grades, you'll probably need to increase the time. Then, too, the usual time may not be enough, particularly on longer projects, and you can decide together to change the schedule to reflect this.

On the other hand, if your child is completing all work and doing it well and accurately, you may be able to reduce homework time.

Your child, or you, may use either a timer or a clock to keep track of the time spent doing homework. I suggest you obtain a large clock, perhaps with a decorated face, and hang it near the child's desk so the youngster can be responsible for keeping track of the time. The child, using a "sticky note," could jot down the beginning and ending times. Ideally, a duplicate note should be posted on the outside of the bedroom door for you.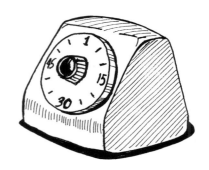

Encourage your child to make a sign for the bedroom door which might read, "Stay Out! Genius at Work!"

THE PLACE

Selecting the right place for your youngster to work is important. The special workplace might be at the kitchen or dining room table, but I recommend a quiet place to work. Consider setting aside a corner in the child's room as an "office."

How do you make a "personal office"? The office might be in the child's room or even in a corner of the parents' room if several children share a bedroom.

Mark off the spot with a small area rug or use masking tape. In my classroom, I've had good results using masking tape as a way of setting aside "offices" for some of my more "active" students. These students are to stay in their "offices" and other students are to stay out and it really works! Also, students feel much more important when they have their own personal offices.

If your youngster doesn't have a desk or chair, visit garage sales or flea markets. Many great bargains are available. Sometimes churches, park districts or community centers have parking lot sales. School districts often sell older chairs and desks at a discounted price. You can help your child paint used furniture any color of the rainbow and the entire project can become a long-lasting learning experience. Be sure you also provide good light for reading.

PARENT TIP: **Install a 4-by-8-foot Marlite™ board (sometimes called showerboard) in your child's room. Depending upon available space, you can place it either vertically or horizontally on a wall near the desk. The board, along with felt pens and an eraser, can be used to practice spelling words and write math facts and vocabulary words. By providing your youngster with several colors of pens, you'll help make homework more fun. You can even write an occasional message like "Good job on your math," or "A smart kid works here."**

GETTING ORGANIZED

Once your child's "office" is established, you can help him/her get organized. Provide pencils, erasers, paper, ruler, compass and

crayons. If the desk doesn't have drawers, use a supply box. You'll also need colorful file folders, "in" and "out" trays and pencils and pencil holder. If there's space, provide a bulletin board.

Many schools have computer labs. If so, your child may be used to a computer for writing assignments. If you have a home computer, set up rules and be sure your student has his/her personal disks that don't need to be shared.

Also, you can now purchase CDs holding an entire encyclopedia. Consider buying one as a gift for the whole family. On-line services, such as CompuServe, also have encyclopedias available.

Check with the dealer where you purchased your computer encyclopedia regarding updates. Some companies, upon the initial purchase, put your name into their database and will notify you when upgrades become available. By being in the database, you'll be able to purchase the upgrades at a discount.

Additional resources. In addition to an encyclopedia, primary children should have your state map and a United States map to post on their walls. Intermediate students need United States and World maps.

Paperback dictionaries are inexpensive. Older students will appreciate a Thesaurus when writing their reports.

Have multiplication tables for your child to use when doing math. If one is not available, feel free to make a copy of the one in the Resources section in the back of this book.

HINT: Your child may bring home information from a book club about books, maps and other resources which can be ordered. Look at these carefully as they often have good materials at a discounted price.

THE TIME

This is the area where power struggles can develop between parent and child. Children have a hundred excuses for not having time to do homework. I've heard a lot of different ones over the years.

"I had to play soccer last night and I was too tired when I got home."

"We went to my aunt's house and didn't get home until real late."

"My mother had to take my little brother to the hospital 'cause he was coughing bad. I went along and we had to stay all night."

PARENT TIP: **Sometimes true family emergencies do arise. In that case, let the teacher know. Otherwise, do not set an example of lying by writing excuses for unfinished homework. You'll be setting up a pattern of tolerating incomplete work.**

Between parent and child. Children need to understand that homework is <u>their</u> job, not yours. They also need to know that even when they do not have homework assigned at school, they go to their desk and work. This might be reading a book, memorizing math facts or doing research on a paper to turn in later.

Sit down at the start of each school year to review the homework rules at your house. There are several reasonable guidelines for homework time.

- No use of the telephone
- No television
- No visitors or visiting
- No radios, stereos or computer games

As a parent, you are in the leadership role. Establishing clear-cut rules says, "I am in charge." What you are doing now is helping your child develop good study habits which will carry over to junior high, senior high and college years. Studies indicate that successful students know how to study. You must remember that you, as a parent, have the power to get the behavior you want from your child.

Whenever needed, it's important to consistently give firm messages such as:

- You're going to school every day. Studies indicate that students who attend school daily are much more successful in school.
- You're going to learn and behave in school and I expect you to always do your very best.
- Your homework will be neat, tidy and readable.
- Your homework will be monitored daily.

Children must understand that homework is not something done <u>after</u> soccer, TV, or talking to friends on the telephone.

When you ask your child, "Where is your homework?" and the child says, "I finished it at school," say, "Let me see it." Also, be sure your child knows what to do and how to do it. This might mean spending time helping him/ her understand how to use a dictionary or the encyclopedia. If you aren't sure the child knows what to do, have the youngster tell you. That way you can determine if he/she truly understands what is expected.

You must set firm guidelines for your child and show him/her you expect them to be followed. In this way you're ensuring that your youngster will develop strong skills and knowledge in all areas before moving up to the next rung on the academic ladder.

Between parent and teacher. If problems develop, contact the teacher immediately.

Your child's teacher should keep the communication lines open between the school and home. You should be kept informed of any present or potential problems as soon as possible. Deficiency notices or comments about the possibility of retention should come early in the school year.

In turn, if problems develop at school, your child needs to be aware of the ongoing relationship between you and the school. This team effort can serve as a powerful influence upon your youngster's schoolwork. Use it.

One of my students whom I'll call Ryan, refused to do homework and misbehaved in class as well. I suggested to his parents that we make a three-way contract with the school, the parents and Ryan. The parents told me what Ryan really enjoyed was riding his dirt bike each weekend.

We all sat down to discuss his failure to do homework. The terms of a contract were agreed upon, and we all signed it. In the contract, Ryan agreed to take home a note each day saying whether or not he had behaved and turned in homework. If he collected five "Happy Notes" during the week, he could ride the bike that weekend. If not, he couldn't.

His parents were as delighted as I was when he began to do his homework faithfully. His behavior also improved so he almost always got to ride the bike.

PARENT TIP: **If your child begins to neglect homework, you'll need to repeat your discussion about its importance. Suggest your child write out the appropriate statement for clarity. "When I do my homework and behave, I have time to ride my bike." Or, "If I misbehave and don't do my homework, I don't have time to ride my bike." This could be posted on the youngster's bulletin board as a daily reminder.**

Consequences for not doing daily work. Sit down with your child and talk about the consequences for not doing homework. This might be not watching television for a certain number of hours or not being allowed to use the telephone or play with friends. You and your child must set the guidelines <u>before</u> the problem occurs.

If your child has developed a pattern about not bringing home school assignments, go to the teacher early in the year. This is the time to establish a connection between you, the teacher and youngster. Have the child sit in with you as you talk with the teacher. Make the youngster aware that it is his/her responsibility to bring home all assignments each day. To not do so will result in loss of privileges.

By establishing rules and procedures when your youngster is in elementary school, you'll model responsibility. You can then begin to let your teen assume responsibilities for homework in junior high school.

PARENT TIP: **A simple way to keep track of daily homework is to purchase a small notebook especially designed for assignments. This will give you a personal check-off list each night to be sure the work is done. Determine with your child ahead of time the consequences for not bringing the notebook home each night.**

SINGLE PARENTS OR PARENTS WHO WORK

Some parents' schedules make it very difficult to find time to help their child with homework. Parents who work are not always at home to assist. Here are some suggestions to help you decide the best way to get your child to do homework.

Study halls. Some schools provide after-school or night-time study halls where children can go to be supervised while doing homework. Often the supervisor is a teacher on the staff but in some cases, college students are employed.

In one of my inner-city schools, I saw two college football players tutoring young students in reading and math after school. Many of these youngsters came from homes without a male role model. It was a joy to watch those youngsters beam at their male helpers. I also noticed

that they often worked far harder for those tutors than for me. Check to see if you have such a study hall in your school district.

HINT: Some school districts now have telephone hotlines with homework assignments and even tutors to help children with questions regarding reading and math.

Reading and spelling. Have your child sit at the kitchen counter and dictate into a tape recorder the spelling words for the week. After each word, ask your child to slowly spell the word while looking at the spelling list. Later, after dinner, you can listen to the word dictation and spelling together to check for errors.

PARENT TIP: **Studies indicate that children need to hear, see or vocalize each spelling word, math fact or vocabulary word twenty-six times correctly before it is imprinted upon the brain. If they make an error during the twenty-six times, they must go through the process hundreds of times before a correction is made in the brain. Be sure your child does it <u>right</u> the first twenty-six times.**

Homework with a friend. Consider having your child share homework time with a friend. Arrange with a nearby neighbor or the mother of a friend of your child to swap homework time. Parents can sometimes take turns providing supervision in their homes. Stress though, this is not a play time.

Get up early to do homework. Each child has a different body cycle and some do their best work early in the morning. If this is true with your child, provide the youngster with an alarm clock to get up early and do the work before breakfast. Sit with your child at breakfast and look over the work to be sure it is done neatly and completely.

Homework supervised by a care giver. If your child is in day care, you may discuss whether the care giver can provide supervision for the child's homework. If so, be sure the care giver understands your rules for homework and the consequences for the child not doing it. You'll need some sort of chart or notebook for the care giver to record the length of time worked and what was covered. You'll know then if more work needs to be done at home under your supervision.

PARENT TIP: **One of the most important items for your child to have is a box in a specific place (ideally by the door) for homework, books, lunch money or forms to be signed and returned to school. Each child in the family should have an individual box.**

Remind your child that every night when homework is finished and papers signed, all "going-to-school" materials must be placed in the box. The box should be located in a place where your child can see it when leaving for school each morning.

MOTIVATION

In order to continue climbing the academic ladder, children need praise and encouragement. Some youngsters require much more than others. You'll need to sit down with your child and talk about goals and achievement of success in school. Explain to your child how one skill builds upon another.

Talk with your child about the "Academic Skills" for his/her grade level found in Resources in the back of this book. For example, in Language Arts for second grade, a child must know how to punctuate ends of sentences and write out abbreviations and dates. Also, help your child understand that by achieving success in Language Arts in second grade, the youngster is preparing to do well in writing essays in third, fourth, and fifth grades and beyond.

Your child might need to have a success chart and earn stickers for encouragement as homework is completed. Some children can "live by praise alone," but others cannot. You must determine the needs of your particular child.

For some children, a special night out with a parent, a sleepover with a friend or extra time playing a computer game will be good motivation. Just as employees are rewarded by pay bonuses or extra time off, students will "work" toward recognition and rewards.

HINT: Again, you may need to set aside a time to remind your child about consequences for not getting work done. Remind your child that being responsible for his/her homework means a sleepover, extra time to play or a visit with a friend.

To Motivate Your Child:

- Encourage your youngster and help him/her to know and meet school homework deadlines.
- Provide your child with a success attitude and successful experiences.

- Affirm your belief in your child by providing a "can-do" attitude. Many children, both at home and at school say "I can't do that," when given an assignment or project. They frequently give up before they try.

HINT: If your child tends to give up when doing homework or a class project, help break the assignment into smaller pieces. Say, "Tonight you can do this much and tomorrow night do this."

By encouraging your child with these small steps, you'll help your youngster develop a "can-do" attitude toward life.

ONGOING SUCCESS

From time to time, you'll need to stop and re-evaluate the progress being made. Say to your child, "How are you doing? Are you getting everything in on time? Any big projects coming along that I should know about? Do I need to take you to the library some night to pick up extra resources?"

Ask yourself:

- Have I established a strong, ongoing homework pattern?
- Is my youngster becoming more responsible for schoolwork?
- Am I seeing an improvement in work habits?
- Can I let up now and to what extent?

If the answers are "Yes," you've done a great job. Keep in mind that children need to know you're in their corner. You must believe that your youngster can learn and be successful in this life. What a treasure to give a child!

In this chapter, you've learned about the importance of instilling good study habits in your child. This is a step-by-step activity beginning with a special place, a special time and available resources. Remember, you the parent are the critical person in this ongoing process. Do your best and be willing to reach out for help, if needed, along the way.

Develop Successful Readers Preschool-Kindergarten

"Kindergarten is a special place where parents and school together are partners in learning. What can you do to help?

Create a curiosity in your child. Have a special place where your child has access to crayons, markers, paper, scissors, notebooks, and drawing pads. Have your child help you write out a grocery list. Look for shapes such as circles and triangles at the toy store. Name the colors on a car trip. Let your child pick out books at the library. Read to your child every day. Give your child responsibilities at home like helping set the table or matching socks in the laundry.

Children who have these experiences will feel secure in their new environment. They will be ready to assume responsibilities at school and be able to verbally share their knowledge."

Brenda Greenshields, Kindergarten Teacher, John F. Ward Elementary School,
Houston, Texas

One of my earliest memories is of my Great-aunt Mae holding me on her lap as she turned the pages of a magazine, pointed at a picture and said, "barn," "cow" or "cat."

Each afternoon when my mother left to do the grocery shopping, Aunt Mae would go through the same ritual. She taught me to recognize pictures and words. To this day, I have an ongoing love affair with reading which has opened up my life to worlds of adventure, intrigue, love, romance and wonder. This is a life-long gift to give a child.

Why your child should read. Reading is the golden key to your child's future and it is critical to success in school. All schoolwork depends upon the ability to read.

Reading helps us entertain and educate ourselves by comprehending books, magazines and newspapers. In our high-technology world today, reading is vital to understand computer manuals; learn to set up modems, VCRs, CDs and other household appliances; understand and apply car and other equipment manuals' diagnostic and repair techniques; and to learn how to install and run complex industrial equipment.

Reading will eventually help your youngster get a job. He/she must be able to read to complete a job application and on most jobs, people must be able to read to survive.

Provide time during your child's early years to read together and to simply enjoy reading for fun and pleasure, which in time, will be transferred over to reading for understanding elements in the work world.

PARENT TIP: **Magazines are a wonderful gift for a child because they encourage reading and become personal possessions. If a grandparent or other relative or friend wants a birthday gift idea, suggest a subscription. Three magazines for young children are** *Chickadee, Ladybug* **and** *Sesame Street Magazine.*

PRESCHOOL READING — AGES THREE AND FOUR

Read aloud from the time your child is born. Hearing your voice while nestling in your arms gives your baby a warm, secure feeling. As a result, reading will become an enjoyable, comfortable experience. Even if other people say, "That baby doesn't understand a word you're saying," keep reading.

Model reading. Let your child watch you read books, magazines and newspapers. Children will do what their parents model for them.

When the mail arrives, sit with your child and read your letters. "Donate" some of the suitable junk mail for him/her to "read."

When reading aloud, become an actor. Make the sounds of thunder, the shrill sound of a siren, or the bark of a dog. Children love this.

Ask questions. After you finish reading a book ask, for example, "What did Mr. Pig wear? Where did he live? What happened to Mr. Pig?" Children enjoy having a part in the stories being read and this will encourage the development of reading comprehension.

Make tapes. I give my preschool nieces and nephews books as gifts and include an audio tape of me reading the book aloud. I begin by reading the title of the book, author and illustrator. This will help

them later when they go to school and
report about books and authors.

As I read, I "ham it up," by
changing my voice to fit the animal or
the character in the story. I love to do
this and they love hearing it.

At night when they go to bed and listen to me reading the story,
they can start and stop the tape by themselves. I suggested to their
parents that they put green dots on the "Start" buttons of the cassette
players for their children and red dots for "Stop." Try this at your
house.

Visit your library. Be a frequent visitor to your local library.
Introduce your child to the children's librarian. Ask when story time
will be conducted and take your child. Help your youngster get a
library card and then take a walking tour of the children's area so you
can find books of interest. If your library has a computer-catalog system,
type in a title of a favorite book and show how to locate it. Show also
how to find other information. Begin now to teach your preschooler to
become an independent reader and researcher.

CAUTION: Do not push your child. Simply make books, resource
people and information available. All children have their own time to
grow, to talk and to read.

Ask questions. When you come to a stop sign say, "What does
that word say?" Or, when you come to a railroad crossing say, "What
does that sign say?" You are teaching
words, and words lead to reading.

Encourage your child to write.
When you sit down each week to write
your grocery list, have a pencil and paper
available for your preschooler. Dictate
slowly what you plan to buy and while
you make your list, let your youngster
write a list in "scribble writing." (See
more about "scribble writing" in the
Preschool-Kindergarten chapter on writing.)

Buy books. Children at this age enjoy books about home, the farm, cars, trucks and animals. They also enjoy riddles, guessing books and nursery rhymes. Provide your child with a wide variety of books to enjoy.

While it's fine to borrow library books, it's wonderful for children to have their own libraries. Suggest books as gifts from friends and relatives. When children have gift money, take them to a bookstore to make their own choices. Also watch for used books at garage sales or organize a neighborhood book swap.

On page 79-80, you'll find a list of outstanding books for your child to read.

Books and tapes. To teach your child nursery rhymes and lullabies, go to your local bookstore and purchase *Wee Sing — Nursery Rhymes and Lullabies.* The audio cassette tape is an hour long and there's a 64-page illustrated booklet for your child to follow along. It is filled with out-standing songs, including "Over In The Meadow," one of my students' all-time favorites.

Ask your children's librarian for other suggestions. These days, many libraries have books and tapes which you can check out.

Provide a place for books. Arrange a shelf or box in your child's room for books. Have him/her help arrange this "library."

PARENT TIP: **As a first-grade teacher, I needed a bookshelf and didn't have a suitable one in my room. I found a wobbly (but inexpensive) bookcase at a garage sale. After some simple repairs and a coat of paint, I took it to school. My students enjoyed going to the book-shelf for books when they finished doing their regular seatwork.**

Read to your child. Preschoolers enjoy hearing the same book over and over, so choose books you can enjoy, too. In time, your child will memorize the story and can even tell you the ending. Read a story or a short book before your youngster goes to bed at night. This is a pleasant way to end a day with some quiet time together.

Teach your child to love words. At ages three and four, children develop a love of words. Their vocabulary is exploding. They enjoy the discovery of words and will take one and make it into a silly, rhyming word. They will sing words, change words and mimic them. Your youngster can now put words into sentences such as, "I don't want a nap." or, "The cat ran away."

Questions. Pete Seeger used to sing a wonderful song about children. The first line of the chorus went "Why, oh why, oh why, oh why?" (And the second line was, "Why, oh why, oh why?") Sound familiar? Get books of amazing facts, books that ask and answer questions. With a growing knowledge of words, your youngster wants to know why birds sing, why trains run on tracks and why the sun goes to sleep at night. As you answer these questions, your child is acquiring more knowledge of words.

Make a book. An unforgettable gift you can give your child is his/her very own book. When you feel your child is ready with words say, "Let's make a book for Andrew."

Take paper and ask Andrew to propose a subject. He might say, "I want to write a book about Roscoe the mouse."

"What do you want to say on the first page?" you ask.

Andrew says, "Roscoe was a mouse." Write this one sentence as a model for him, using both upper and lower case letters.

"What should we say on the next page?" you then ask.

"Roscoe lived in a little house," Andrew may say. Write this also. Continue to the end of this story.

Ask Andrew to illustrate each page with your help. Use a piece of construction paper to make a cover for the book. It should have this "author's" name on the cover and might say something like *Andrew's Book About Roscoe Mouse.*

Find a small picture of Andrew and paste it on the front of the book. A picture of a mouse for the inside would be an additional treat. Have Andrew place the book on his bookshelf as part of his reading collection.

How to encourage your preschooler to read. You may want to post this reminder list for yourself:

- Make books available.
- Model reading for your child.
- Read to your preschooler every day.
- Answer your child's questions.
- Provide time for your youngster to talk while you listen.
- Write a book together.
- Don't push your child into reading.

THE KINDERGARTEN CHILD

Not all children walk at the same time or talk at the same age. Nor should they all go to school at age five. Five is not a magic age. One child may have just turned five, while another is nearly six. Some children, especially those small for their age, may not be mature enough and are not yet ready to move into the school world.

There's a real tendency to want to hustle a child into kindergarten, especially if you're involved in day care with its expense and complications. However, a child who isn't quite ready, one who is physically younger, less strong and less coordinated may have trouble excelling.

If you question whether your child is ready to start school, go and discuss your concerns with the teacher. If your youngster appears not to be ready for kindergarten, perhaps he/she should go to preschool, nursery school or stay home another year. This is particularly true of little boys. Some boys do much better if they're a little older to enter kindergarten.

PARENT TIP: **During my years as a resource teacher, several parents asked me if I felt their children were ready for school. I spent time with each parent and child and sometimes suggested they wait a year.**

I'm pleased to say that when these children came back later, they were at the top of their classes. Not only were they academically ready, they were prepared socially and emotionally, as well.

Testing. My district has a simple test for students during the first month of school. They are asked to name shapes such as a square, rectangle, triangle and circle; identify colors such as yellow, green, red, brown, white, purple, black, blue, pink and orange; and identify the numbers from one to ten.

They are also asked to describe what is going on while they view a picture of children in a park. Some say, "Swing" when looking at the picture, while others say, "The boy swings." This question helps the teacher learn which children have a strong word vocabulary and which do not. Many children, particularly from other countries, need extra help from aides to handle kindergarten work.

Children aren't expected to score 100 percent on the test, but those who have some acquaintance with shapes, colors, numbers and letters do much better in kindergarten than those entering with no background. Those without this knowledge must play "catch-up" all through kindergarten and often into first and second grade.

PARENT TIP: **One way to help your child prepare for reading is to set aside time in your family to play games. Turn off the television and play "Brain Quest," a game for kindergartners which can be purchased at toy stores or your local bookstore. Three hundred questions with colorful answers are printed on enlarged bookmark-type cards held**

What number comes after 6 ?

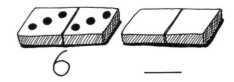

6 _____

together by a large brad. Questions range from alphabet puzzles and Mother Goose to "What's wrong with this picture?" drawings. While playing this game, your children will be learning letters and words, patterns and shapes plus logic and thinking skills. Enjoy this game often as a family.

SUGGESTIONS: Games like "Twenty Questions" and "I Spy" provide good learning experience and fun whether you play at home or in the car. When playing "Twenty Questions," one person thinks of something and identifies it to others as animal, vegetable, mineral or a combination. Other players take turns asking questions which can only be answered by "yes" or "no." If the item can't be identified within twenty questions, the person who thought of it tells what it is and then thinks of another. The person who guesses it gets to think of the next item.

In "I Spy," one person chooses an object and says, for example, "I spy something brown that begins with an R." The other players guess and are answered with either a "yes" or "no" until someone identifies the object.

Bookworm game. Use either tagboard or heavy construction paper to make this reading game based upon some of the words in your child's favorite book. The board should be about 18 by 12 inches. Draw a bookworm, divide it into twelve 1 1/2-inch segments and number each section.

Help your child color the bookworm different colors. With a dark felt pen, number the segments and write a word from a favorite reading book in each segment.

Use an over-sized die and show your youngster how to throw it and count the dots on the faces. Move a small object from "Start" to, for example, segment number three. Your child must be able to say the word or his/her playing piece cannot remain on number three.

Make several of these boards and keep them handy for play. (You could also photocopy several "blank" bookworms to fill in with new words.)

Read to your kindergartner. Continue to read to your youngster for at least ten to fifteen minutes each day. You can often purchase books at discount stores or your local grocery store but take the time to visit a bookstore, too. Note the colorful children's books available. If your kindergartner is studying "Colors" at school, ask for a book about colors.

Become familiar with the children's section at your local library. Many have special shelves for color-and-shape books and for *Reading Rainbow* books. If you use a bookmobile, you may want to request books a week early.

The Disney Company has many books, some with companion tapes, for young children. A series titled, *Thomas The Tank Engine And Friends* also combines books to read aloud with tapes. Children at this age enjoy books about animals such as dogs, cats and farm animals. They need to hear written language spoken aloud over and over in order to read well.

Your child's attention span. When reading, be aware when your youngster begins to become restless. That's time to stop reading. You want this to always be an enjoyable activity in your child's life.

Help your child practice "reading" a book. At age two or three, your youngster begins to turn pages in a book. Then the book is "read" to you by looking at the pictures. By this time, many children are "reading" the story, as they have it memorized. As your youngster gets older, he/she might begin to pick out a few of the words and be able to read these. Be a strong cheering section for your child and encourage this reading.

HINT: Help your child move along on a page in the book from left to right. To facilitate this skill, provide a paper marker to place under the sentence. It is also acceptable at this stage for children to use a finger as a marker.

Reading projects. We've talked about making a book together. You can also encourage a "journal" after a field trip like a visit to the zoo. As you write, have your child dictate the story and then draw pictures to illustrate what you've written.

When your child is invited to a birthday party, help make a birthday card to take. Your youngster will enjoy presenting a personalized greeting to a friend.

When you write to a relative or friend, ask if your child would like to add a sentence or two at the bottom of the letter. Or encourage dictation of a post card or letter with pictures to a grandparent.

Help your child write invitations to birthday, Christmas or family parties. When possible, help illustrate the invitation and add glitter for special occasions.

PARENT TIP: **Begin to point out signs and help your youngster read them. I recently observed a young mother with her daughter on the first day of school. Before leaving, she walked the girl to the restroom and together they stood there with their fingers tracing the letters for "Girl" and "Boy" so her daughter would know which restroom to use. A most caring mother, indeed.**

Make a child's dictionary. Help your kindergartner fold pages of paper into a small spelling dictionary. Pick out words with special meaning for your youngster and write them. Look up the meanings of the words and write a brief phrase about each one.

Use brightly colored construction paper and have your child place an illustration on the front. Help write a title using the child's name. This might be *"Michelle's Spelling Dictionary."*

As your child moves toward first grade, continue to encourage reading, drawing and talking. Provide magnetic letters to use on the refrigerator for making words. Help your kindergartner write his/her name. In time he or she will begin to recognize the correct sequence of letters and read it back to you. Always be the cheerleader as your youngster marches into first grade.

Develop Successful Readers Grades One-Three

"Success in reading is the result of a partnership between the child, home and the school. Youngsters need to read to others and with others, to share what they read and to read independently. Without interaction among the student, the teacher, the parents, and fellow students, the student has only a limited opportunity for success."

Julie Thomsen, Third-Grade Teacher, North Ward Elementary School,
McCook, Nebraska

GRADE ONE

Entering first grade is an exciting time for children. Many of them know some of their classmates from kindergarten. They also know letters of the alphabet, many colors and shapes. But most of all, they love books and they come to school excited about reading.

Many children at this age enjoy books about animals, bugs and birds. Take your child to your neighborhood library often to pick out books. Also, check with the school to see if books from school libraries can be brought home.

HINT: Be sure to keep a box by the front door with your child's name on the side and place library books which are due in the box. Many schools now have fewer financial resources to hire a librarian and volunteers can come only a few days each week. To cut down on their work, return books on time.

Your first grader will also enjoy word games. These could include guessing games, "Hang Man" or "Bingo" played with customized cards. Using the vocabulary words from your child's reader to play "Bingo," will help your child learn the words while playing a game.

Child-size reading resources. Primary children seem to prefer either very large or very small books. They particularly like tiny books about 3 by 4 inches. Look at your grocery store or local bookstores for these. Many are simple riddle books which primary children can read. They also enjoy small books with silly drawings and sayings.

Writing. At this age, your child will be eager to print words. Many children can now use both upper-case and lower-case letters correctly. But they still need paper with lines.

Provide your child with paper for writing a story about a field trip, a story about a neighbor's cat or a letter to Grandma.

PARENT TIP: **Many schools supply their students with monthly copies of either** *Scholastic Magazine* **or** *Weekly Reader*. **When you attend the Back-To-School Night at your child's school, ask the teacher if one of these outstanding magazines will be available. Due to financial problems, many schools can purchase only one set for each grade. The teacher then must pass these on to the other teachers. If so, your child might not be able to bring a copy home. The magazines have wonderful pictures, stories and fun-reading games to play and puzzles to do.**

Join a book club. Many teachers make order forms available from a variety of book clubs such as Troll Book Club in Mahwah, New Jersey. If possible, have the summer selections of the book club sent to your home for your youngster to enjoy.

Computer time. Students love to work with computers, even at ages five and six. I had one little girl who was most proficient on the keyboard, typing out "cat" or "dog" while sucking the thumb of her left hand.

If you have a computer, make it available to your child, but give firm instructions on how to treat the computer and the keyboard.

HINT: In Resources at the back of this book, you'll see a computer keyboard picture which you may enlarge and copy for your child to use to become acquainted with key locations. Have your youngster color the keys of his/her first name, the Enter key and Backspace key. Let your child play on the paper keyboard to become better acquainted with the keys before beginning to use a real keyboard.

By using the computer, your child will begin to know his/her letters and numbers and can make up simple words such as "frog" or "house" or "stove" to type.

PARENT TIP: **Many children come to school after being baby-sat by television for many years. More and more, teachers are trying to teach children who can sit quietly for only a few minutes and cannot listen** or follow directions. They are so used to seeing a picture <u>move</u> that they simply won't look at a printed page for any length of time.

As parents, be aware of how much time your child watches television. More and more studies indicate that too much time in front of the TV is definitely harmful to school achievement.

GRADE TWO

I always enjoyed teaching second grade, because these students like to read and are usually good listeners. They also love to please. This makes a most enjoyable classroom environment which is also conducive to learning. In addition, second graders are becoming more independent and want to do more things without help.

Reading. At age seven, children enjoy reading alone but still at times, want you to read them a story, especially at bedtime. Continue to do this, as it will help your child become a good reader.

Second graders, in particular, enjoy stories about dinosaurs; some of them are also beginning to read comic books. Continue to make books available at home and take your youngster to the library.

PARENT TIP: **Hold a book swap on your driveway each month. If you have a specific day, for instance the first Saturday of the month, the neighborhood children will remember. Invite them to bring books to swap. This will provide all the children with an ongoing and inexpensive supply of different books to read.**

Make a bookmark. Each time my students enter a new reader, I help them make a bookmark to go along with the new title. Use colorful construction paper and cut out a marker about 7 by 1 1/2 inches.

If your child is reading a book about a dog, encourage drawing a picture of a dog or pasting a dog picture or sticker at the top. Have your child write his/her name on the back.

The marker can be used for two purposes. It's not only a place marker but can also be used to move under sentences to help your child read. Since children at this age still have problems tracking with their eyes, a marker can be a big help.

Games for readers. "Brain Quest™" for second graders is similar to the adult "Trivial Pursuit™" and is an outstanding way to encourage children to read and follow directions. The cards are easy for small hands and the game can be played alone or with another child.

A question is asked on one card and the answer is found on another. All cards have outstanding colored drawings and are easy to read.

"Trivial Pursuit™" has a game for juniors, ages seven to ten. The board is colorful and categories range from Nature to Stories and Songs.

Language arts task cards called "Grope 'n Group™" are available at most Parent-Teacher Bookstores by grade levels. The inexpensive cards consist of words used in most readers and will be helpful to seven-year-olds. In fact, they are available for many levels of readers.

Children at this age enjoy doing crossword puzzles. "Crossword Task™" cards are also available at Parent-Teacher Bookstores. These illustrated cards were devised and tested by teachers in their classrooms.

The cards are plastic-coated and can be used with a crayon or washable felt pen. Answers are given on the back of each card.

Fun books to read. Children at this age still enjoy reading tiny books such as *Stop the Watch* riddle books and silly sayings. At bookstores look for unusual books such as this one which asks a child "to stand on your right foot." The book comes with an attached stop watch so your youngster can record the length of time he/she stands on the right foot.

Continue to provide your child with stories on tapes to listen to during the day or when going to bed at night.

Writing. Encourage your child to continue writing. A pen pal, grandparents or a summer-camp friend make good recipients for letters and will usually thrill your youngster with letters in response.

HINT: I kept a small basket on my desk with slips of paper about 2 by 2 inches for me to write words which children said they needed for story writing. At this age, it is difficult to get students to use the dictionary, as they are not secure with how words are spelled. You can do the same thing at home.

GRADE THREE

By grade three, both boys and girls enjoy reading books with riddles, jokes or rhymes. They are eager to share what they are reading with others in the classroom and on the playground.

If the teacher still has "Show and Tell," they ask to tell a favorite joke or riddle. After one is told, someone else always wants to "do one better" with another.

Girls begin to ask for mystery books while boys are more interested in books on sports. They enjoy reading at this age and can usually figure out words themselves without help.

CAUTION: If your child is still having problems with reading, be sure to discuss the problem with the teacher. If your child's vision has not been checked recently, ask if the nurse could do this the next time she comes to the school.

If reading problems continue, ask if a resource specialist is available to have your child tested for possible difficulties which would interfere with reading ability.

Fun books to read. Children enjoy reading comic books and I often set aside a time to read them on Fridays. In order to have a good supply of these books, I found a store where I could purchase a wide selection of used comic books. I was able to reach some students only through the reading of comic books. They are fine to read but I was always careful about the material inside. I never brought anything violent or unwholesome into the classroom.

If your child is interested in reading comic books, consider finding such a store in your town so you'll have a ready supply available. However, be sure you know what is coming home.

Hobbies. Children at this age read about hobbies they enjoy. As an example, bookstores carry a supply of rather unusual books for children this age. One book titled, *The Bug Book* comes inside a bug-holding bottle with holes for air. Inside the book are delightful drawings of bugs along with easy-to-read information on how to catch, identify and care for the creepy crawlers.

Other available books include an endless supply of topics from whales and spiders to rocks and rockets.

Writing. Children at this age enjoy writing. They can stay on the line and their writing has improved a great deal from second grade. I found that my girls, in particular, liked to put hearts instead of dots on top of "i's" and start each sentence with a fancy letter.

This is an age where children like to write notes to their friends and will write short letters to children they've met during camp or while visiting out-of-town. Encourage your child to write by providing appealing stationery and an easy-to-read dictionary.

Games to play. Many games to enhance reading are available at your Parent-Teacher Bookstore. A number of stores now set aside an entire section for parents, and some bookstore managers offer workshops for parents.

The "Crossword Task™" game is available by reading levels and has fifteen illustrated crossword puzzles for children to use. Children at this age enjoy puzzles both at home and in the car. They can use either a crayon or a washable felt pen.

Reading ability. By the end of third grade, your child should be able to read a story and identify the characters, the setting and the time of the story. Your youngster should also be able to distinguish between a fact and opinion in a story.

Children need to be encouraged, but not pushed, to continue to read as they will soon enter the intermediate grades. It is in these grades where they will be reading for information and need to be proficient readers.

Develop Succesful Readers Grades Four-Six

"Successful readers are 'captured' rather than created. One delightful way to do this is by reading aloud. Read the first of a series of books and be sure to have the sequels. Or else read the beginning of a book and stop just before the climax. Another way is to read aloud books that relate to areas of study. Read about amazing pets when your child is studying mammals, or read about life in a Japanese fishing village while your child is studying Asia."

Rachel Patten, Fifth-Grade Teacher, Santiam Christian School, Corvallis, Oregon

In the intermediate segment of grade school, students read for information. They use reading as a way to learn. During grades four, five, and six your child will spend a great deal of time not only reading, but also using a dictionary, an encyclopedia and an atlas. Be sure these are available in your home if at all possible.

GRADE FOUR

The reluctant reader. At this age and beyond, some children begin to turn off to reading, causing great concern to both parents and teachers. To get a child interested again, give the reading a purpose. A good example, though older than fourth grade, was when Dave's mother was upset when he stopped reading; however, this youngster was fascinated by cars and was repairing an actual engine in their garage. She bought a car manual for him and before long he had read it from cover to cover.

If your child has lost interest in reading, don't push. Instead, find an interest or hobby and a book to go along with it. Also, ask other children your youngster's age to tell you what they're reading. Find an easy, but enticing, book and leave it for your child to find.

While fourth-grade boys are often no longer interested in reading, many girls show a great interest in mystery and adventure stories. Both boys and girls usually like to read comics.

PARENT TIP: **The fourth grade is a critical reading year for your child. If he/she enters without good reading skills and is below grade level,** you <u>must</u> take action. Your child is an at-risk student who may drop out of school by junior or senior high. These youngsters begin to show signs of "dropping out" mentally and emotionally when they sense they are behind the others in their class. This is the time to begin to work regularly with your child at home on reading, look for a tutor or send him or her to summer school. This is a crucial grade and you need to watch for academic problems.

GRADE FIVE

Some fifth graders read constantly, while others are not interested. The readers choose books about horses or dogs or biographies of famous people. Often these are people they see on television or videos.

NOTE: One of the most requested books by my fifth graders was the *Guinness Book of Records*. Students sat as a group while one read and the others made comments about the scores. Try to have this book available at home.

Magazines. Youngsters at this age enjoy reading magazines such as *Ranger Rick* and *Sports Illustrated for Kids*. If these are not in your home, see if you can check them out of the school or local library each month.

HINT: At this age, your fifth grader is capable of reading aloud to younger siblings and will enjoy a book which is easy to read. Tap into this energy and enthusiasm for reading.

Writing. In fifth grade, your child will be required to write a number of reports. Keep in touch with the teacher so you're aware when these reports are due. From time to time, check on the work to be sure it is being neatly written and is grammatically correct.

HINT: If you have a computer and the teacher approves, have your child write the reports on the computer. Children enjoy the ability to produce neat work and the ease of correcting mistakes.

GRADE SIX

Again, these students are reading more and more for information. They are required to write reports, letters and projects. Also, many schools have computer labs where students write simple stories and place them in book covers. If you have a computer, your child has even more chances to do neat work and edit right on the screen.

Some children at this age will read the comics or sports section in a newspaper. Make these available for them.

Reading for a purpose. A great deal of reading now will be done for a purpose. If your child is interested in soccer or dancing, he/she may suddenly be interested in finding a book for more information. A child who likes to collect sports cards will read them and share with others.

HINT: A good magazine for a youngster interested in sports is *Collector's Sportslook*. It contains detailed information on baseball, basketball, football and hockey.

Some children at this time will begin to read easy, general-interest magazines such as *Reader's Digest*. Comics are still important and should also be available.

Read a mat. Parent-Teacher Bookstores carry reading place mats to be used at the table, but they could be put on a wall near your child's study area. One mat has colorful pictures of the flags of forty-five countries with the names of each country printed below. Another has a map of the world with all the countries, oceans and islands labeled. A third shows South America with all the countries names alongside, including the Islands of the Caribbean.

Games for intermediate students. "Brain Quest™" is available for all intermediate ages as well as "Grope 'n Group™" language cards. Part of being a good reader is learning to follow directions, and games like "Monopoly™," "Clue™" and checkers provide this practice for your youngster.

In this chapter, I've provided a number of ways to not only help your child learn to read but to continue to be a good reader. You, as the parent, know your child best. Pick and choose what you feel will turn him or her into a lifelong reader.

OUTSTANDING BOOKS FOR CHILDREN

Here is a list, by ages of some of my all-time favorite books. I've also included suggestions by Jim Trelease in his book, *The New Read-Aloud Handbook*; books from *The New York Times Parent's Guide To The Best Books For Children* by Eden Ross Lipson, Children's Book Editor; and *Choosing Books for Kids* by Joanne Oppenheim, Barbara Brenner and Betty Boegehold. Although these books are listed in a particular age group, many are appropriate also for older or younger categories.

PRESCHOOLERS — AGES THREE AND FOUR

Abiyoyo by Pete Seeger
Alphabears: An ABC Book by Kathleen Hague
Big Sister and Little Sister by Charlotte Zolotow
Blueberries for Sal by Robert McCloskey
The Carrot Seed by Ruth Krauss
Changes, Changes by Pat Hutchins
Curious George by H. A. Rey
Is It Red? Is It Yellow? Is It Blue? by Tana Hoban
Make Way for Ducklings by Robert McCloskey
The Napping House by Audrey Wood

KINDERGARTEN — AGE FIVE

The Cat in the Hat by Dr. Seuss
Corduroy by Don Freeman
Danny and the Dinosaur by Syd Hoff
Little Bear by Else Minarik
Madeline by Ludwig Bemelmans
Millions of Cats by Wanda Gag
Nutshell Library by Maurice Sendak
Red Riding Hood retold by Beatrice Schenk de Regniers
The Story of Holly and Ivy by Rumer Godden
The Tale of Peter Rabbit by Beatrix Potter

PRIMARY STUDENTS — AGES SIX AND SEVEN

Anatole by Eve Titus
Bear's Picture by Manus Pinkwater
Benji by Joan Lexau
Blackberries in the Dark by Mavis Jukes
Friends by Helen Heine

Gregory, the Terrible Eater by Mitchell Sharmat
Hurray for Pippa by Betty Boegehold
A Lion to Guard Us by Clyde Bulla
My Father's Dragon by Ruth Gannett
The Polar Express by Chris Van Allsburg

PRIMARY STUDENTS — AGES EIGHT AND NINE

Charlotte's Web by E. B. White
The Cricket in Times Square by George Selden
Dominic by William Steig
James and the Giant Peach by Roald Dahl
The Lion, the Witch, and the Wardrobe by C. S. Lewis
Little House Series by Laura Ingalls Wilder
Pearl's Promise by Frank Asch
Ramona by Beverly Cleary
Sarah, Plain and Tall by Patricia MacLachlan
The Velveteen Rabbit by Margery Williams
The Witch of Fourth Street by Myron Levoy

INTERMEDIATE STUDENTS — AGES TEN, ELEVEN AND TWELVE

A Book for Jordan by Marcia Newfield
Call It Courage by Armstrong Sperry
Confessions of a Prime Time Kid by Mark Harris
From the Mixed-up Files of Mrs. Basil Frankweiler by E. L. Konigsburg
Island of the Blue Dolphins by Scott O'Dell
My Side of the Mountain by Jean George
Path of the Pale Horse by Paul Fleischman
Roll of Thunder, Hear My Cry by Mildred Taylor
Sing Down the Moon by Scott O'Dell
Thank You, Jackie Robinson by Barbara Cohen
The Twenty-one Balloons by William Pene Du Bois
A Wrinkle in Time by Madeleine L'Engle

Make Math Count Preschool

"To help your preschooler succeed in math, you'll need to introduce your youngster to colors and counting. You can do this by talking about the color of cars as you drive around; count the number of steps as you walk from the school parking lot to the classroom and count dishes and silverware as the child sets the table. Make math a daily happening at your house."

Joanne Rykonen, Preschool Teacher, Phillips-Osborne School, Painesville, Ohio.

Justin, an active, almost-three-year-old, is learning his colors and how to count while looking at the colorful stars on his "Potty Chart" posted on the bathroom door. Justin's mother is eager to get him potty-trained so she can enroll him in preschool. She took a large piece of construction paper and made a graph.

Justin earns a red star each time he remembers to go to the bathroom on his own and a blue star for washing his hands. He gazes up at the big graph with his name at the top while saying, "One red star, two red stars and one, two, three blue stars."

As he walks around the neighborhood with his Grandma, Justin can count the number of blue birds singing, green trees in the park and number and colors of the leaves he picks up from the ground.

As your youngster moves out into the community, use yards, parks and playgrounds as places for your child to begin to understand that math is all around us.

Why math is important. We need math all our lives. We pay bills, do income taxes and estimate the driving time to Grandma's house. We measure ingredients as we cook, fabric as we sew and lumber as we build a shelf.

As parents of a preschooler you need to serve more as a guide and facilitator than a teacher. At the ages of three and four, children need to spend more time observing and interacting with people than in formal learning situations.

This is the time to provide your child with blocks and puzzles and opportunities to measure sand or water. Have your child help you cook and observe how you measure and set the timer and the temperature on the oven.

When you provide stimulating materials for your child to enjoy, you are furnishing opportunities to explore. As you observe your child, you'll see the beginning of understanding of concepts. If children enjoy what they are doing, they become even more motivated to learn.

An overview of preschool math. To understand math concepts your child needs a wide range of activities, a variety of materials, and a time to discuss observations and discoveries. As a parent you can enjoy the experience of helping your child begin to understand math. Be aware of the many opportunities during your child's day for its incidental learning.

Your child discovers math patterns through active investigation and manipulation of real objects and materials. You need to be alert to everyday experiences, pointing out apartment numbers, the number of buttons on the car radio and the fact that certain lids fit certain pans.

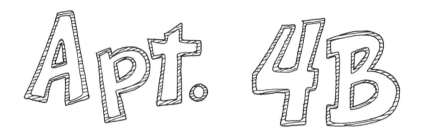

Use your young child's natural curiosity to bring math into daily life. As your youngster stacks wooden blocks, steps over a stool and eats off a round plate, he/she is discovering the descriptive word "tall," the space word "over" and "round," the name for a shape. Watch your child play and say, "You just built a <u>tall</u> stack of blocks." Or, "Show me how you can step <u>over</u> the stool." Say, "You're eating off a <u>round</u> plate this morning." As you match words with objects, your child will begin to learn the terms we use in math.

Use concrete materials. Children this age aren't ready for paper-and-pencil activities yet. Instead this is the time to work with objects found around the house.

PARENT TIP: **Constantly talk with your child when engaged in an activity. Questions might be, "How many blocks do you have in your** right hand?" Or, "Tell me the colors of the blocks in your left hand. "As you drive, "How many letters in that big word on the red Stop sign?" If your child can tell you what he or she is doing, it demonstrates an understanding of the process.

Some items for the preschooler that will help with math are wooden blocks, a sandbox with buckets and cups, egg-size rocks, pencils, crayons, a tub with water, measuring cups and plastic jars.

A few examples of math-related activities for your child are to:

- Stand near you as you follow a recipe. Let your youngster hand you the measuring cup and spoons and count aloud as you measure the ingredients.
- Help you set the table. If five people are eating say, "How many spoons do we need?" If six are eating ask, "How many forks?"

- Play in a sandbox. Say, "How many cups of sand will it take to fill this plastic jar?"
- Sit on the teeter-totter at the park. Say, "Why did you go up in the air when Brian went down?"
- Count as you take walks or go driving. Count trees or red trucks or blue cars.

Talk about things you see around the house. Hold up an apple and a peach. Ask, "What color is this apple?" Or, "What color is the peach?" Say, "Feel the apple and the peach. How are they the same? How are they different?"

Have your youngster sniff an apple and banana and tell how they smell. Ask, "How are they alike? How are they different?"

Children enjoy dressing up. Have a box of old clothes for play. Afterward ask questions such as, "What color was the shirt you wore?" Or, "How did those high heels feel? Did you feel tall?"

Most children love to play with blocks, cars and trucks. Join in as your youngster builds a road and moves a car along the roadway. Later, ask questions and encourage your youngster to describe how the bridge worked and how the cars moved along the road. Ask, "How many blocks held up the bridge? Did you use the long or the short blocks? Why? How did you build your road? Was it a smooth road?"

PARENT TIP: **Set aside a box and fill it with pieces of various types of fabrics such as velvet, corduroy, fur, cotton, nylon, netting, silk, satin, polyester, denim and lace. If you do not have such materials, ask at a fabric store for samples. Encourage your child to play with fabrics. Ask questions such as, "How does the fur feel? The lace? The denim?" You're teaching your child to observe and to note patterns, textures and colors of fabrics.**

Sorting. Sorting is a basic thinking skill that helps children and adults organize and understand their surroundings. We talked about sorting in reading but it also applies in math.

Here are some simple ways for your youngster to learn to sort:
- Encourage laundry-sorting help.
     Say, "Let's put the towels here and the socks there."
     Ask, "How many blue socks or how many red shirts?"
- Put all the cereals together in one place on the shelf.
- Put all soup cans in one place and all cans of vegetables in another.
- All spoons go in one slot in the tray and forks and knives in another.

- Put his or her shirts in one drawer and socks in another.
- When you're waiting in line somewhere, have your child count the short people and the tall people.

Have available for your child a quantity of similar items for sorting. Just a few possibilities are keys, shells, bottle caps, buttons, coins, screws, toy soldiers, miniature plastic dolls or small toy animals.

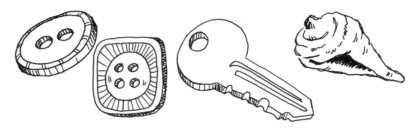

CAUTION: Talk with your child about NOT sticking small things in his or her mouth, eyes, ears or nose. I once heard of a youngster putting a bean in his ear and the bean sprouted! This is a true story. We don't want that to happen or for your child to choke on some object.

There are various ways to sort items. Ask your child to put all the buttons with two holes in one pile and those with four holes in another. All small bottle caps can be put in one row and large ones in another. Your child can also sort by color, shape, size or texture.

Patterning. This is an important skill because it teaches a child the repetition of a sequence. This skill will touch every aspect of your child's life. He or she will begin to observe patterns of leaves, patterns on fabrics, on buildings and on floors and furniture.

For example, the next time you drive by one of the major fast-chicken restaurants, have your child look at the pattern of stripes on the awning. Look for other patterns of stripes.

When you visit the park, look for the way the lawn is cut. Sometimes it's back and forth, or across or on the diagonal. Look at brick houses and walls and sidewalks for a variety of patterns.

As you walk around your neighborhood, look at shrubs. Some are shaped like three balls of leaves from large at the bottom to small on top. Others make a seemingly solid hedge. The following is an example of a simple pattern.

X OO X OO X OO X

Your youngster can be encouraged to make patterns by using keys, pasta, nuts, bolts, buttons and even leaves and small sticks.

I have found that kindergarten children coming to me in the computer lab with some patterning experience do much better on the computer. Many of the lessons deal with duplicating a pattern of animals or other items shown on the screen. Children enjoy doing this but do better with some background experience.

Numbers. While it is important that children be able to count to five, for example, it is even more important that they know what five stands for.

Take a large piece of paper and draw a big "5" on the page. Help your child to slowly count out five buttons to place on the 5. Afterward have your child trace the number with his/her finger, then count fingers. Do this for numbers 1 through 10.

Constantly point out numbers. As you drive, say, "Look at the sign. It says 25 miles per hour. That is a number '2' and a number '5.'" As you read, point out page numbers. Watch the floor numbers on an elevator or the numbers on a school bus.

PARENT TIP: **If your child cannot remember numbers or mixes them up, cut numbers out of fine sandpaper and paste them on a piece of tagboard. Gently take your child's finger and begin to trace the number. Say, "This is number '3.'" Do this several times. Many children need to see, hear and feel numbers in order to remember them.**

Graphing. Graphs are frequently used as a means of picturing information, and children like to make them. In newspapers and magazines point out how often graphs are used to make it easy to compare things from money, to numbers of people or animals to how much rain falls in a month.

To clearly show how a graph "works," create one with your child. For example, make a graph of the pets in your neighborhood. Ask how many dogs, cats, fish or hamsters there are. Decide upon a colored block for each species. If there are three dogs, have your child place three red blocks on the table. If you counted four cats, four blue blocks should be placed next to the red blocks.

FISH   DOGS   CATS

Continue until you've counted all the pets. Then talk about the graph of pets you've made. Say, "What did we find out?" Explain, "We found out that there are three dogs, four cats and two fish. Then say, "How many altogether?" Encourage your child to use describing words such as an orange cat with long hair or a brown dog with a long tail.

Measurement. Young children can learn about measurement by looking at things around them. When you measure yardage, have your child help you. When a family member is building something, have the child help with the measuring.

Ask questions such as, "Which is longer, the knife or spoon?" When you go outside ask, "Look at the shadows from the big tree and the little tree. Which shadow is shorter?"

HINT: I am discovering in the classroom that today more and more children do not know what a ruler is and have no idea how to use it. Also, many of my children have no idea how to hold scissors and have to be taught at school. These are skills they should have acquired at home.

Time and Temperature. You'll begin to talk about time and temperature before your child is introduced to clocks and thermometers. Now is simply an observation time to start learning concepts. The measurement of temperature and the difference between hot and cold can be learned by talking about the proper clothes to wear in winter or summer, comparing pizza and ice cream, or comparing a brick in the sun with one in the shade. Talk about time during the day with questions like, "What do you do before you take your nap each day? What do we do after Daddy comes home?"

Money. By age four, children are eager to learn more about the world around them, especially money. Use this interest to provide your child with hands-on materials to teach money concepts. Some suggestions follow.

As you stand in the check-out line at the grocery store, the movies or a fast-food restaurant, take out some coins to share with your child. Use vocabulary to go along with money such as a *penny*, a *nickel*, a *dime*, a *quarter* and a *dollar*. Talk about the color of money. Have your youngster look at the color of each of those coins and a dollar bill. Explain to your child about values of money.

The next time you are in a line, ask your child to point out the pennies, nickels and dimes in your hand. This teaches the value of specific coins and coin recognition.

Play a game by placing five pennies in a row and eight pennies in a pile. Ask your child which of the two arrangements has more pennies.

HINT: Remember you're simply introducing objects and the vocabulary about money at this time. Help your child enjoy the learning process without any pressure.

Preschoolers learn best in a relaxed, nonstructured atmosphere. This is the time to help your child "notice" the world which, of course, includes a multitude of mathematical concepts.

Language and math. In addition, you need to reinforce words that are math-related. Call attention to sizes and amounts. You can say, "That is a <u>big</u> dog. The tree is <u>tall</u>. The truck is <u>long</u>. You have <u>one</u>, <u>two</u>, <u>three</u> books on your lap."

Preschoolers sometimes find comparisons and relationships a lot of fun. Emphasize the proper words. Say, "The girl is <u>first</u> in line. The

boy is <u>second</u> in line. Their dog is <u>third</u> in line. This bean jar is <u>empty</u>. We have <u>some</u> beans in this jar. That jar is <u>full</u> of beans. The cat is <u>under</u> the table and the dog is <u>around</u> the corner. The bird's cage is hanging <u>over</u> the table. This button is an <u>inch</u> across. This ruler is <u>long</u> and that ruler is <u>short</u>. <u>Yesterday</u> we went to the park. <u>Today</u> we will go to the zoo. <u>Tomorrow</u> we will go to

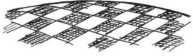

Grandma's house. <u>Today</u> is <u>Monday</u> and <u>tomorrow</u> is <u>Tuesday</u>." Talk about the days of the week. Mark them off on a large calendar and when you plan the sequence of your activities for each day, say them out loud to your child.

PARENT TIP: **Keep in mind that learning may be haphazard. Your child will not learn all math skills right after each other. Don't expect your youngster to progress in math or any other subject in an orderly manner. Don't push. Instead, give praise and enjoy the journey together.**

CHAPTER 10

Make Math Count
Kindergarten-First Grade

"Life can be a puzzle for children and adults, but solving a puzzle is fun and challenging and rewarding. Math can be a puzzle, too. It is so abstract to a six-year-old, that you have to make it real. Bake a cake together and eat some fractions!"

Janet Merle, Elementary Teacher, Parkland Primary School, Greece, New York

Math is different from reading in that it requires a great deal of hands-on activities. In order to provide your child with a good foundation in math, I've grouped kindergarten and first grade into one chapter. This will provide a longer time for your child to explore and discover math before beginning to do large amounts of paper-and-pencil activities.

In this chapter, I'll also give you suggestions on ways you can help your youngster understand the patterns of math. You'll find that most of the materials come from your child's personal world which will be more rewarding and comfortable.

Kindergartners and first graders look forward to school. Often this means new experiences, making new friends and even riding the school bus. This is also the time when children sit in groups and learn about numbers.

Children now are on the first rung of the kindergarten ladder in math. Ideally, your child had the opportunity to go to preschool and you've taken the time to build a strong math foundation as well. If so, your youngster has been learning colors, counting and measurement.

During these early years in school, children are exposed to many concepts in math. They learn these skills while working alone and in groups. As a parent, you'll need to spend time reinforcing what your child is being taught at school. There are a number of things you can do at home and in the neighborhood to help your youngster establish a stronger math foundation.

One-to-one correspondence. You'll need to help your child understand that each object (item) has only one number. For example, put out one yellow car or one chocolate chip cookie or one blue plate.

After your child understands this concept move on to one more. This could be one hat, two hats, or one dog, two dogs. Or one paper clip and one more paper clip. We now have one plus one equals two but this process takes time for a child to internalize. Be patient.

Observation. Continue to provide your child with opportunities to observe the world around him or her.

- Help your youngster see things another way.
    Put three red lima beans (or buttons or pennies) in one cup and two blue (or buttons or nickels) in another.
    Ask, "How many red beans do you have? How many blue beans?"
- Pour all the beans into one cup.
    Ask, "How many beans altogether?"

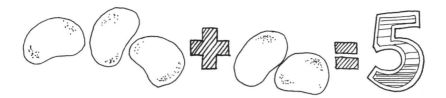

Write out on paper 3 + 2 = 5.
Have your child say the equation with you. Then write it out as 2 + 3 = 5. Say, "We can write this either way and our answer is five."

- Now your youngster is beginning to bring ideas together to make sense out of math. For example, your child has seen and counted beans before but is now putting objects together. He/she can now see that the equation 3 + 2 = 5 can also be written 2 + 3 = 5.

- Help your youngster make a judgment about what he/she already knows. You might say, "Where did those walnuts on the ground come from?" Or, "If you build a tall stack of blocks, what do you suppose might happen?"

PARENT TIP: **Purchase a set of "dominoes," ideally the ones with colored dots. I use these in the classroom and children like to touch those colored dots. Place a pile of dominoes on the table and ask your youngster to pick out the one with three dots on one side and two on the other. Place the domino horizontally in front of your child and ask how many dots there are. Then turn the domino vertically and ask for the total number of dots. Children need to see that the answer is still five.**

Number sense. In order for children to understand computation in math they must understand "number" and what a number stands for. Food is a good place to start.

- "If I have one cookie and you have two cookies, how many do we have altogether?"

- "I have a bag of six cookies. I'll split the cookies with you. How many will you have? How many will I have?"

- Talk about fractions in a simple manner. Say, "You have one cookie so let's share it." Cut it in half and hand it to your child while saying, "You have one-half of the cookie and I have the other half." Later say, "Let's cut this other cookie into thirds and share it with Mr. Chips." Now you've introduced the idea of thirds.

Keep a pad of paper and crayons available. When you talk with your child and read about the number "3" in a story, for example, write a large number "3" on the pad. Hold up the paper for your child to observe. Then ask him or her to write number "3" in the air with an index finger.

Do this over and over. Later, put three beans in your hand and close your hand. Ask your child to guess how many beans you have. Then open your hand and let your child count, "One, two and three." Point out the number "3" each time you see it on TV or as you drive around your community. The magic word here is "observation."

The process is much more important than always getting the right answer. Mistakes do happen but move on and continue talking about numbers.

PARENT TIP: **This is the time to help your child explore, observe and discuss what your youngster sees. Provide many opportunities to observe patterns and allow the child to draw conclusions.**

Mental math. Children love to play guessing games. This natural interest can be used to increase their awareness of numbers. By now you've asked questions such as:

- "What's inside this apple?" Seeds.
- "What's inside this pumpkin?" Seeds.

At Halloween time, since your child already knows there are seeds inside a pumpkin, have him or her guess how <u>many</u> seeds are inside. Then cut it open, rinse and dry the seeds and count. Remember, children like LARGE numbers, so this will be an enjoyable project. Ask about the number of seeds in other fruits such as an apple or pear. Cut open some fruit and together count the number of seeds inside.

HINT: Use apple and pumpkin seeds to make an interesting pattern across the kitchen table. Encourage your child to say, "Two apple seeds and three pumpkin seeds. Four apple seeds and four pumpkin seeds."

Sorting. Sorting continues from preschool. It helps us put things together so they are organized and not hit-or-miss. While sorting, your youngster can begin to see patterns like two holes in one button and four in another. Or, a round button and a square button. Have available keys, colored plastic blocks, tooth picks, plastic jars, lids, checkers or beans. I use lima beans in the classroom. I spray one bag of beans blue and the other red. This is helpful when sorting and also so children can make repeated patterns such as two red beans and one blue bean.

Save egg cartons and have your child place one lima bean in a "hole." Then write the number "1" on a small piece of paper and place it inside the hole with the bean. The next day put two beans in the second hole. Write the number "2" on a slip of paper and place that in the hole. Repeat this process each day until you arrive at the number "10."

HINT: If your child has problems recognizing numbers at any time, purchase fine sandpaper and cut out the numbers from 1 to 10. Take

your child's finger and trace over the numbers.

I have found in the classroom that keeping a box of sandpaper numbers and ABCs is helpful for children having difficulties remembering a particular number or letter of the alphabet. I sit with the child and take his/her finger and trace it gently over the number while saying "7" or "A," "B," or "C."

Shower tiles are good for creating patterns. Go to a discount lumber or paint and tile store and purchase small square tiles in different colors. Children have fun using these when sorting and making patterns.

HINT: Have your child tell you what he or she is doing. For example, "I have three square tiles in my right hand and four blue lima beans in my left hand. Do I have more tiles or beans?" Children might know the number in each hand but they also need to be able to explain the process and the number. This indicates understanding.

Playing cards. Purchase or make large playing cards. I use cards that are 7 3/4 by 4 3/4 inches in my classroom and the children like to work with the large numbers on them.

Fill a small paper cup with pennies and sit with your child as you cover, for example, the three hearts in the middle of the "three-of-hearts" card. Then touch the number "3" at the top of the card and move down and count aloud as you touch each penny. After you model this for your child, help your youngster pick a card and use a penny to cover each of the hearts or diamonds which appears on it. This is a great way to establish one-to-one relationships.

PARENT TIP: **If you have many loose items around the house for sorting, use old shoe boxes for storage. Place the boxes with items inside on a child-level bookshelf for easy use. Label each box with a picture so your child can understand how to find certain items. Labeling helps us organize things.**

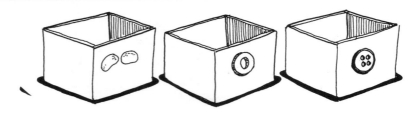

Measurement. In addition to a sandbox, have a tub for water and a number of small and large jars (unbreakable plastic) for filling and pouring. Also, for extra fun, have food coloring.

Go outside if you have a yard and the weather permits, and fill the tub with water. Let your child "explore" pouring a small jar of water into a large jar. Sometimes color the water. Afterward, talk about how many little jars it took to fill a large jar. In the winter, your youngster can do this activity in the bathtub. Provide plastic measuring cups for filling and pouring water.

Use shoes and shoe boxes to measure your child's room. Say, "Your room is twelve shoe boxes across," or "It takes sixteen shoes to cross your room."

Encourage your child to use things around the house for measuring, stacking and counting, and building bridges, long roadways and overpasses. Children like to create their own designs.

HINT: There is no wrong way to explore. Just encourage your child to "do it."

For Halloween, make a costume for your child. While working on this outfit, you'll model for your youngster:

- How to make a tail for an animal costume
- How to make parts of an animal — legs, paws, head and ears
- How to determine the length the costume needs to be to fit
- How to tell what various fabrics feel like, such as furs around the neck or yarn on the tail
- How to use scissors

PARENT TIP: **With newspapers, catalogs and television constantly promoting children's toys, give your child the opportunity to make toys from items found around your house. When children use their own hands to create something, the object has much more meaning than a brightly painted plastic toy purchased at a store. Example: Take an old clean**

sock and help your child make a puppet to illustrate a book you're reading at night.

Geometry. At school, your child will be introduced to geometric shapes. Remember that children enjoy using BIG words, so don't hesitate to label the shapes and solids you'll be talking about.

To help your child understand shapes, use a paper cup to make a cone, small boxes to make a prism and a cube and a paper towel roll to make a cylinder. Use a ball for a sphere.

While you work with these objects ask questions such as, "Which one of these rolls? What could you build with this prism? Which objects can we stack? What toy could you make from two of these shapes?"

Continue to talk with your child about those shapes, as well as a triangle, square, rectangle and circle. If he or she has trouble identifying them, purchase a book of stickers in these shapes.

PARENT TIP: **Food is always an interesting way to help your child understand shapes. You might cut a sandwich into squares, triangles or rectangles. Be sure and use the words to describe the shapes. For example, say, "Today your sandwich is the shape of a triangle. How many sides? Touch the three sides."**

I learned the shape of a triangle early in my life. My mother often cut my sandwich into triangle shapes. As I pulled my sandwich out of my lunch box, my friends were eager to see my "tuna triangles."

HINT: At Parent-Teacher Bookstores and toy stores you can find table place mats designed with a circle showing where the plate should sit, a triangle showing where the napkin goes and another smaller circle for a cup. Large illustrations of the knife, fork and spoon are arranged for placement of silverware. These "Eat-and-Learn" mats are not only colorful, but a good teaching tool as well.

Problem solving. Children need the opportunity to listen to simple stories and then think about what might happen.

Tell a story such as this one to your child. "One day three acorns fell on the ground in the back yard. A squirrel dashed over and picked up two of them and buried them under a bush."

Ask your child, "What might happen to the two buried acorns? What do you think will happen to the third acorn?" Give your child the opportunity to sit quietly and think about these questions before answering.

Watch your child at play. Then ask questions such as "What did you build? How did you build it? Why did you choose to play with the airplane? What did you do first? What did you do next? What is the last thing you did?"

Money managers. By now your youngster should be familiar with a variety of coins. Provide some money which could be used for special treats, for a movie or for shopping at the store; then sometimes let your child decide how to spend it. Children need the opportunity to make their own decisions. Like adults, they learn from mistakes, particularly their own.

The following are helpful experiences your child should have.

- Go to the store with you to observe how you handle money.
- Play a game — "Guess who is on this coin."
- Put your child on a budget when eating out. Say, "Here is $4.00 for your meal tonight. You decide what you want to eat."
- Help pick out and pay for birthday or Christmas gifts for friends and family.

As children learn to understand money and how to use it, they become more comfortable with it.

Time. At school, your kindergartner or first-grader is being introduced to the clock. Many of my students had problems understanding the hour and minute hands. Use paper plates to help your child understand time.

Talk about the time a special television program comes on. For example, 8 o'clock. Make a clock face on the paper plate and help your youngster draw in the hour hand pointing at number "8." Point out that the hour hand is shorter than the minute hand. Next have your child draw in the minute hand pointing at 12 o'clock. Take his or her finger and move it along the hour hand while you both say "hour hand." Then move that finger along the minute hand as you say "minute hand." Repeat this exercise until your youngster understands how to tell time.

PARENT TIP: **Purchase a "Time Mat"™ at your toy store or Parent-Teacher store. This mat has a clock with movable hour and minute hands. Pictures are shown to depict daily activities from 7 a.m. to 9 p.m. Have the youngster move the hands to match the times on the pictures.**

Graphs. As in preschool, you may use colored blocks to help your child build a graph on the kitchen table. By first grade, he/she will be ready to color in the squares on a pad of paper.

Decide what you wish to graph such as number of blue, red, yellow, white and black cars in your neighborhood.

On the pad of paper you could print "Colors of Cars on Flower Street." If there are five blue cars, help your youngster draw five squares and color in the squares to form a tower. Continue with the other cars. Ask, "How many blue cars? How many yellow cars? How many black cars did you see? Help me find out how many cars altogether." Post the graph on the wall in your child's room.

First-grade math has been largely a continuation of what your child learned in kindergarten except that a little more material has been covered. As your youngster moves on to the second grade, he or she will learn even more about numbers, counting, time and measurement, but the learning pace will be faster and the math concepts will be more complex.

Make Math Count Grades Two-Three

"Learning basic facts is essential for future success. Children are exposed to math daily, from a trip to the school store to dividing into teams at recess. Children who see math as part of their lives are not threatened by it.

You can create excitement and enthusiasm by making math real. One example is using things children can handle and manipulate such as dried beans or blocks to help them visualize basic math facts and make math come alive."

Cindy Howard, Third-Grade Teacher, Sara Collins Elementary, Greenville, South Carolina

Karen, one of my second graders, was a whiz at math. She loved numbers and calculations and enjoyed tutoring other students when they needed help. This didn't just happen; she had an excellent example. You see, Karen's mother came into my classroom each week to help. She encouraged Karen in school and was available to her at home. Her involvement with her child really paid off.

Second graders enjoy being in school, following directions and doing good work. Use this enthusiasm to encourage good work at home as well. Be there to help provide a quiet place to work; and praise, praise, praise your child.

NOTE: Changes are taking place in the way math is being taught. New textbooks feature more of the "investigative approach" to math. Children are asked to investigate how to find answers. They work to create more than one solution to a problem.

An example of one of the problem types would be: There are 17 Canadian Mounties and 42 horses. Question: Are there enough horses for each Mountie to ride? Can each Mountie have two horses?

Children must show how they reached an answer. One child might say, "I multiplied 2 x 17." Another might say, "I added 17 + 17." A third might say, "Yes, I took 42 and then subtracted 17 and got 25. Then I subtracted again and got 8 and I knew they had enough horses."

What your youngster is being asked to do is go from "math thinking" into "math-process writing." Children are asked to write out the process they used to reach a specific answer.

When you go to your Back-to-School night, ask the teacher to talk about how math will be taught. "Will the students use textbooks?" Or, "Will they use mostly hands-on materials?"

Basic facts. By second and third grade, your child needs to know the basic facts of addition, subtraction and multiplication. Here is where you particularly need to help, because children do not have the time in school to fully learn their facts.

Your child's teacher will probably send home a list of basic math facts for your child to learn, things like 3 + 9 = 12, 9 - 5 = 4 and 5 x 6 = 30. If your child does not receive the list, you can easily create one.

PARENT TIP: **There are times when you should place a Success Chart on the refrigerator or your child's wall. As your child memorizes the basic facts, a reward of a star or colorful sticker is encouraging. Also, discuss with your youngster the number of facts to learn each week, month or semester. When that goal is reached, take your child out for a special dinner or day at the zoo. The award should be something of interest for him/her.**

$$
\begin{array}{r} 14 \\ +\ 2 \\ \hline 16 \end{array}
\qquad
\begin{array}{r} 18 \\ -\ 3 \\ \hline 15 \end{array}
\qquad
\begin{array}{r} 25 \\ +\ 4 \\ \hline 29 \end{array}
$$

Counting. By second grade, your youngster should be able to count and write to 1,000. And by third grade he/she should be able to count and write numerals to 99,999.

Many students have problems writing numbers in order, but I've found that a Consecutive Number Folder is a great learning tool. This is a folder just for writing numbers.

Have your child write "My Number Folder" on the front of a manila folder, then decorate it with stickers or pictures having to do with numbers.

Fold seven pages of lined paper (8 1/2 by 11 inches) in half lengthwise, then crease again to create four vertical columns.

Staple all seven pages to the inside of the folder. Four staples should do. Staple only the tops of the pages.

Explain to your youngster that when there is free time, he/she can use the folder to write numbers from 0 to 1,000 (or more if in the third grade). Numbers should run from 0 to 25 in the first column, from 26 to 51 in the second and so on.

HINT: Prior to beginning this exercise, talk with your youngster about a prize for writing to 1,000 correctly. This might be a trip to a

fast-food place, a special book or an over-
night with a friend.

Also, tell your child that the work
must be done correctly. The page numbers of a big-city phone book can provide
the answer to "what comes next?"

CAUTION: Occasionally, check the
number folder. Don't allow your child
to sit and write numbers out of order.
This puts false information into the brain
and requires considerable time to remove
and be replaced with the correct
numbers.

HINT: Children also love to count backwards. When I show a
film, my students yell out, "ten, nine, eight..." at the beginning of each
film. Provide your youngster with opportunities to do this, as well.

Time. Children need to be able to tell time both on a conventional
and a digital clock. They also need to be able to figure out differences in
time. It's best to teach time when it relates to some part of your child's
day. A simple clock is easy to make.

• Use a nine-inch paper plate.
• Help your youngster make the hour numbers from 1 to 12
   around the clock face, spacing as evenly as possible.
• Show your child how to mark a large dot in the center of the plate.
• Help cut out an hour hand and a minute hand.
• Using a brad, help attach the hands to the plate so they can move.
• Help your child show the time he/she gets up in the morning
   and the time to go to bed.

Here are some clock exercises you can do with your child. Put
out six circles. Have your child draw the hands at the appropriate hours
using crayons of various colors.

Bus arrives at 7:30 a.m.   I arrive at school at 8:05 a.m.
How long does it take me to get to school?_____minutes
School lunch at 11:40 a.m.   School lunch ends at 12:15 p.m.
PE begins at 1:35 p.m.   PE ends at 2:05 p.m.

Make up four or five more time questions based upon school and home activities. Have your child draw clocks to illustrate the time each activity begins and ends.

Measurement. Help your child use a ruler to answer these questions.
My scissors are between _____ and _____ inches long.
My pen is between _____ and _____ inches long.
My paint brush is between _____ and _____ inches long.

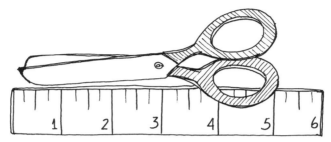

Calendar. Purchase or make a large wall calendar for your kitchen wall or your child's office. Go over the dates for family birthdays. Have your child color in each special date on the calendar. Have him/her tell you the month and day.

While your child looks at a calendar, you can ask questions like these.
- "I get paid on the third Friday of each month. Show me when I'll get my next paycheck."
- "We pay the rent on the last day of each month. Show me when we will pay our rent."
- "The dog gets her next shot at the vet's on the first Monday in December. Show me that date."

HINT: Be sure your child knows his/her birthday. This means month, day and year. I've had students even in fifth grade who had no idea as to when they were born.

Money. Buy a book about coins for your child. You can find inexpensive ones at coin shops and bookstores. In my classroom I use the *Handbook of United States Coins* by R. S. Yeoman.

Children love money and enjoy handling it, particularly <u>real</u> money as opposed to the cardboard and plastic money in the classroom.

I have an 1865 one-dollar gold coin found by my Great-aunt Mae in a vacant lot many, many years ago. I keep it in a safe-deposit box in the bank but take it out to share with my students when we study money.

The coin is very small, smaller than a dime, in fact. I point out the tiny "P" on the coin and explain to my students that it was minted in Philadelphia. I give my students the opportunity to look over the front and back of the coin and point out the year it was made.

For additional interest, I ask my students to bring an old coin from home. Not an old, old coin worth a great deal of money, but one suitable to bring to class.

PARENT TIP: **At home set aside a plastic jar for collecting. Tell your child to go through all the loose coins and pick out the old ones. Help him/her find the listing for them in the coin book. It will give the current prices being paid for those coins. Children are often surprised at the amount of money one coin can be worth.**

Frequently parents are reluctant to discuss money with their children. Instead, it should be part of the conversation in the home, the car and when shopping. Help your child to feel comfortable about knowing how to handle money. He/she is moving out into the larger world and needs to understand and take responsibility for finances. You could begin this training by having your child take care of his/her school money.

- Purchase a wallet or coin purse to carry lunch money to school. The youngster needs to keep the purse or wallet securely inside a backpack or a belt pack.
- Talk to your youngster about what to do with the money at school so it will be safe. Realize though, the teacher may have a definite preference about what is done. Possibilities might be to keep the coin purse in a desk, keep it in a pocket, leave it in the backpack or give the purse to the teacher for safekeeping.

NOTE: Some teachers refuse to hold money. A number of teachers will keep money; however, remember that the more responsibility we let adults have, the less youngsters will assume.

Prepare your child for a possible loss of money. Talk about the person your youngster should tell if the money is lost or stolen. Decide if you'll replace the money or if this will be a learning experience. Ahead of time, talk about what will happen if money needs to be replaced. Will it come from the child's allowance or will he/she have to earn it? Your child needs to know ahead what procedure you'll follow.

HINT: The first person your child should tell about missing money is the teacher. Since the money may have been lost on the playground at recess, the youngster needs to go to the office also to alert the staff. The school secretary will be on the lookout for money turned in which might belong to your child.

There are a number of other things you can do to help your child learn more about money.

- Encourage your child to begin putting money in parking meters when you shop or pay the attendant at parking lots.
- Give choices. Say, "You can use the money to purchase the toy you want or something to eat. It's your decision."
- Teach price comparison. Say, "How much did you pay for the ice cream bar from the truck compared with what you paid at the grocery store?"
- Contracts. Write out a pencil-and-paper contract with your child. For cleaning the _____ Taylor will earn_____ after Mom_____ checks to be sure it's a good job.
  Signed _____child
  Signed _____parent

As you provide more and more opportunities for your child to experience having money, earning it and deciding what to do with it, he or she will become much more confident about the world of finance.

Graphing. By second and third grades, children are doing more complex graphing than in kindergarten or first grade. Often, the teacher will send home a list of items for your student to bring to school for a graphing project. Also, the teacher may ask your child to bring in family information to be placed on a graph.

This might be the ages of family members. It also might include ages of grandparents and uncle and aunts. Have this available for your child. Another project might be to graph the heights of all family members. Again, be sure the information gets to school.

PARENT TIP: **Some newspapers have daily graphs. Look at the paper, as some feature a variety of graphs, from a pie graph to stacks of books or bar graphs inlaid in cars to illustrate numbers of people falling asleep at the wheel. Graphs are colorful, simple in design and eye-catching. Also, look in major magazines for colorful graphs which accompany feature stories.**

I ask my students to count all the windows and doors in their homes for a graph. They are usually amazed to find that the total number of windows and doors really adds up. Since children this age love large numbers, it's a great lesson to teach.

More and more when we teach math, we are relating arithmetic to the life of the children in the classroom. This way math is not some abstract idea which has nothing to do with the children's real world.

Problem solving. When helping your youngster with problem solving, ask the child to read the problem, think out loud and reread the problem. Also, say that when solving problems, there may be more than one right answer.

Here is one to think about. At a dog show, there are 22 dogs in the main ring. How many heads and paws are in the ring?

Fractions. Children enjoy doing fractions if they are provided with "hands-on" materials. For example, have your child fold a sheet of paper into fourths. Then say, "Color two of the squares and write down the fraction you've made."

When that is completed, tell your child "Take a sheet of paper and fold it into eight equal parts. Color three of the squares. Write down the fraction you've made." After that is done correctly, say "Take a sheet of paper and fold it into ten equal parts. Color seven of the squares and write down the fraction made."

Fractions with food. Children love pizza so use this food as a way of teaching fractions. Take three paper plates and have your child color each plate to resemble pizza. Talk about serving three, four or five children and how your youngster would write the fractions. Have your child divide one pizza into six slices, another into eight slices and the last into ten slices.

HINT: I have often found that when children do not know the vocabulary for fractions, they do not understand the operation. For example, they need to know *numerator, denominator, improper fraction* and *mixed number*. Also, *halves, quarters* and *three-quarters*.

Many children cannot remember the words numerator and denominator. Neither can they recall how they should be written as a fraction. One way to help your child remember that the numerator is on top and denominator at the bottom is to make a sign like the one here.

Teach fractions when cutting up apples, dividing berries from a basket or cutting a watermelon.

Look at the chapter on computers for good ideas about software for teaching fractions.

Place value. This is a difficult concept for many children. I find this place-value game helpful in the classroom. To play "Toss Out," make a game board by taking a sheet of paper and drawing three card-size spaces on top and one below. (Each player has an individual game board.) Write "Toss Out" in the bottom space. Write "Ones" above the Toss-Out area. To the left of the Ones write "Tens" and label the last one "Hundreds."

Remove all face cards and tens from a deck of playing cards. Shuffle the remaining cards. Explain to your child that you'll deal four cards which could be from Ace (which equals 1) to nine and will be face-down for each player. Nobody can look at the cards.

Explain that the object of the game is to get as close as they can to the highest possible score of 999. Then snap your fingers and each of you look at your top card and decide where to "permanently" place it on your game board. The best chance of winning comes from placing the highest cards in the hundreds space and putting numbers like one and two in the Toss-Out area since they won't count. Part of the fun and thinking practice comes from not knowing what numbers are on the cards below the one you're playing.

Afterward ask the players what number they made. Then ask, "How many 100s did you have? How many tens? How many ones? Who had the highest number?" Reshuffle cards and play again.

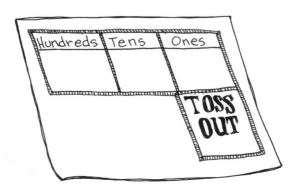

Geometry. For Christmas have your child use cardboard to make a set of colorful circles, triangles, rectangles and squares to hang on the tree. Provide yarn to hang the ornaments and glue and glitter to decorate them.

As your child puts them up ask, "How many sides does a square have? A triangle? A rectangle? A circle?"

When you're out walking or driving, look for the same kinds of shapes, as well as octagons. Have your child point these out to you so you can talk about their sizes, colors and often special meanings.

When you arrive home, have your child draw the shapes, color and label each one correctly and tell you how the signs are used.

HINT: In my classroom, I had my students draw shapes on old, clean pieces of sheets which we had cut into the size of placemats. Each design was then embroidered in a different color of thread. Even my boys had fun with this project, and their parents were thrilled to receive their placemats.

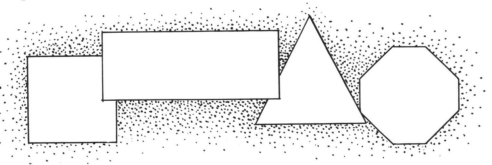

Mental math. Children at this age like mental problems. You can do these together at home or in the car.

Slowly say, "Four plus four, take away two, times six. What is the answer?"

Say, "One plus four, times three, divided by five equals what?"

Say, "One hundred times two, take away fifty, plus three. What is the answer?"

Parent-Teacher Bookstores and Teacher Bookstores offer a wealth of resources for you and your child in math. Stop by sometime and browse around. Don't hesitate to ask for suggestions. I've found most salespeople at Teacher Bookstores are extra helpful. Quite often they have classroom experience.

Your child is now leaving primary and moving on to the intermediate grades. You've provided many experiences in math, and your youngster should be able to move into fourth grade and be able to confidently handle the next rung on the mathematics ladder.

Make Math Count
Grades Four-Six

"Make math a 'real-life' part of your child's life. For example, comparing the estimated and actual cost of a trip leads to an understanding that math is a useful skill to have. Does your child want a raise in that weekly stipend? Have them make a chart graphing what they earn as well as how and where they spend the money. It provides help in collecting and organizing data and just may persuade you that they really do need an increase."

Esther Chlapowski, Fourth-Grade Teacher, Linford Elementary, Laramie, Wyoming.

Phong, a bright sixth grader, looks forward to math each day. Her grades are outstanding and she was chosen to represent my school at our district math contest. To prepare Phong for the contest, her father and uncle spent hours tutoring her each night in math. She did well; and all the extra family tutoring helped her achieve a high score.

Why math is important in the intermediate grades. During the primary years, your child should have been building a math foundation utilizing basic facts as well as informal experiences in measurement, geometry, money and problem solving. Having a firm foundation is essential for children moving into the intermediate grades.

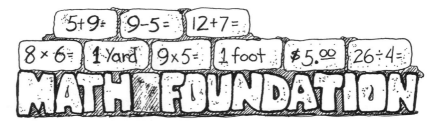

If your child lacks any of these math skills, it is essential that you take the time now to arrange a conference with the teacher. He or she may recommend that you work with your youngster yourself, or have the child tutored or send him/her to summer school. Reaching out for help in this most important subject is essential, since students who enter the intermediate grades lacking specific primary-grade skills often get farther behind. These students show signs of dropping out of school sometimes at junior high and even more often at the high-school level. Take charge now. Get help immediately if your child's grades and skills are below average.

In the intermediate grades, children begin to be involved with their friends. My fourth graders often prefer talking or writing notes to their friends rather than doing schoolwork. They are social, yet I've found they still respond to school rules and my classroom procedures.

Fifth graders love to play and have many outside interests. Right now they are eager to share their latest CD with classmates. (This can definitely interfere with schoolwork.) They also have a short attention span at this age for both textbook and pencil-and-paper math and would much rather do oral math (mental math games) than sit and do written work. They love to talk!

My fifth graders are an active group. The girls enjoy chatting with girlfriends while the boys spend time teasing them. I have found that at this age they can be critical of other classmates, which frequently leads to problems. (I settle these in daily class meetings.) However, in math they enjoy doing addition and subtraction and will work a few word problems, particularly if they can do these on the computer.

I have found my sixth graders like math and are willing to take time to think about a problem before writing it out. They enjoy doing graphs, math crossword puzzles and even division problems on the computer. A number of sixth graders tell me that math is their favorite subject. Use this natural enthusiasm to help your child make even more progress in the subject before going on to junior high.

There are a number of important math concepts for the intermediate grades. Casually see if your child understands them. If not, work on them from time to time.

NOTE: Many words used in math are so important and you must be sure your child knows and understands these italicized words.

Basic facts. Use *arrays* (a systematic arrangement of numbers) to help your child understand math. You could use washers, coins, tiles, buttons or beans.

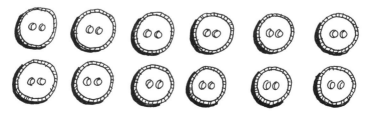

For example, sort twelve items into various combinations. As your child sees two rows of six buttons, you can point out that two times six equals twelve. Or twelve buttons divided into six sets of two also equals twelve. Doing this type of visual math will lead your youngster into multiplication and division.

If your child continues to stumble on the facts, provide flash cards for drill and practice or have him/her make practice cards.

NOTE: Your youngster <u>must</u> know the basic facts before being able to add, subtract, multiply or divide. Go to thrift stores and buy math games or make your own cards. Only after the cards and games can be done without hesitation, should you ever consider a calculator. These instruments have a place in math, but it's necessary to first know basic addition, subtraction and multiplication. If the child stumbles or hesitates, he/she does not know the facts. Write down missed facts and have them studied again.

Place value. It is vital that children understand the relative values of numbers. I have found that place value continues to be a big problem for many in the intermediate grades. They are beginning to work with big numbers and if they did not fully understand place value in the primary grades, they'll have even more trouble now.

On a long sheet of paper, have your child make a "Big Number Chart." Post the chart above his/her desk. It can look similar to this one and serve as a guide when your youngster is asked to write out large numbers.

Have your youngster read and pause at each comma. "Three billion, three hundred eighty-two million, seven hundred and seventy-one thousand."

Another way to teach place value is to use pennies, dimes and dollar bills. Children enjoy working with money, especially *real* money. I always go to the bank and purchase $30 worth of coins for my money units. Students like to handle these, count them and add a variety of different denominations. Do this at home.

HINT: You can go to novelty stores and purchase fake money which looks real or even "make" your own.

It's important when children write down sums of money that they understand there is a dollar sign and a decimal point to separate the dollars from the cents. Also, it is necessary that numbers be written in straight columns in order to get the correct total when adding or subtracting.

Ask your child to sit next to you as you pay bills and observe as you write checks, enter the amounts into the check register and bring up a balance.

Make several copies of a blank check and have your child write checks for fun. Youngsters need to know how to date a check, fill in the payee or company name and the amount to pay, as well as how to write the full sum on the correct line. They should also fill in the name, amount and reason for the check on the check register.

HINT: I have found that youngsters in the computer lab like to use software where they can practice writing a check on the computer. Look for such programs for your family.

I believe that any time parents can provide hands-on activities for their children they are helping build for the future. So much of my teaching is out of textbooks, I appreciate parents who provide the "extra-teaching moments" which there simply isn't time for in school.

Encourage older children to earn money outside the home. Traditional jobs for youngsters include a paper route, baby-sitting, mowing lawns, shoveling snow or caring for pets and yards when neighbors are gone. Help your child decide how much extra spending money is desirable and calculate how many hours at a set rate; or how many tasks at a set rate would earn that sum.

Help your child make a budget for back-to-school clothes. Ask him/her to make an inventory of existing usable clothes, discuss the needs for the coming school year and then compare prices in stores, newspaper ads or catalogs.

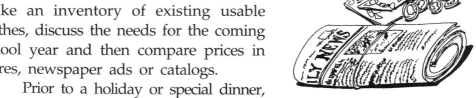

Prior to a holiday or special dinner, ask your child to use the food section of the newspaper to plan the menu and make out a grocery list. Allow a specific amount of money. At school prior to a holiday, I give everyone a "pretend" $40 check to use with the grocery ads to plan a menu within the budget. Your child will enjoy the challenge of this lesson while learning a great deal about addition, subtraction and some estimation.

Save as a family. At a family meeting discuss some special overall needs or wants. This might be a major expenditure like a car, a television, vacation or a special treat like a pizza party at the end of school. Make a money thermometer, which is actually a form of graph. As family members contribute to the bank savings account for your goal, color in the new figures so you can rejoice together.

Involve your youngster in planning your next vacation. Hold a family meeting and discuss your budget. Talk about miles-per-gallon and how many gallons of gas you'll need to reach your destination by car. Talk about the amount its tank holds and the distance your car can go on a tank of gasoline. How often will you need to stop? Later, together figure the miles-per-gallon you actually used on vacation.

Tell your child how much money you have budgeted for overnights. He/she can call and get prices on motels. Calculate your food budget and compare the cost of restaurant meals and some do-it-yourself picnics.

Your child should work on the basic facts of math by using every-day information in informal settings. You might say, "Here is $5.00 to look for the best buy at the store for different sizes of breakfast cereal." Or, "We're having ten people for dinner; decide how large a watermelon we'll need."

Sense of number. Children need to understand what numbers <u>mean.</u> We call this *number sense* and it needs to be developed. For example, does your youngster know what the fraction 7/8 stands for? Five hundred stands for what? There are many reasonable answers. One is that five hundred is one-half of what number? Or $500 is what part of $1,000? Your child also needs to feel comfortable with estimation. Say, "How far do you think it is from Los Angeles to Chicago?" Or, "How many pennies are in that jar?" Another term we use is *guesstimation.* This means "Come as close as you can by estimating."

If your child is asked to use pencil and paper to add the fractions 1/2 + 1/3, could he/she do this? What about 4 1/2 + 6 2/7? Or, 8,660 -:- by 7?

Compare numbers. Number comparison is another concept frequently used to help with our everyday math. Measure and write down the heights of your family members from the tallest to the shortest. Compare the distance from one planet to another. What does a given item cost in each of three different stores? Write out numbers from largest to the smallest. Example: 250, 249, 248...

PARENT TIP: **Many school districts are asking teachers to use fewer math textbooks and do more "hands-on" math and investigative activities. For this reason, you'll need to provide resources at home for your child. I found a simple folder at a drugstore that is a gold mine of charts such as a "Table of Measures" which includes both metric and our customary English systems. It also has a glossary of math terms like** *cylinder, factors, liter* **and** *vertex.* **See the measurement tables in the Resource section in the back of this book.**

Addition. Home activities can be used regularly to increase your child's skills in adding.

- Encourage your youngster to bring home one of the book-club order blanks received by most classroom teachers. Talk about the amount of money available and what might be purchased. He/she should fill out the order form, including the total cost of the books plus any shipping or tax, and write out the check. You need to fill in the signature line.
- Take your child to the grocery store. After you get home, have him/her check off each item on the receipt, add the prices to be sure the total is correct and then put away the groceries.

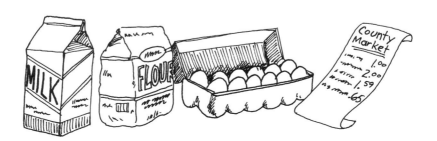

- Take your child to the bank, when you'll be depositing one or more checks. Have him or her make out the deposit slip, place all numbers in the correct columns and record the total amount of the deposit.

PARENT TIP: **Purchase math-fact place mats for your child to use at the table or to post on the wall in his or her office. These mats are available at toy stores or Parent-Teacher Bookstores and come separately for addition, subtraction, multiplication or division facts. They are "wipe-away" mats and can be written on with Fluid Markers™, crayons or non-toxic grease markers. By making these available, you'll provide an additional method for learning basic facts.**

Subtraction. When I was growing up and doing subtraction, we "borrowed" numbers from the column to the left if we didn't have enough value in the column we were working on. But over the years that we borrowed, we never returned those numbers. Finally, someone decided that borrowing without payback was not a good example to teach in school, so now we use the term "regrouping" instead. Both principles are the same.

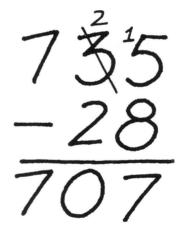

Some ideas to help your youngster understand subtraction are:

- Have your child observe as you subtract your transactions in your checkbook to reach your current balance. This is valuable practice not only for subtraction, but also to learn place values as mentioned earlier. It could even help show how and why budgeting can be important.
- Have your youngster subtract several transactions as you watch and can observe the process to be sure he/she fully understands subtraction.

- Provide a small allowance notebook and have your youngster use it as a daily checkbook for deducting purchased items and keeping a total of the balance.

- Encourage saving ten-to-twenty percent of all income such as birthday gifts and earnings. Take your youngster to the bank and help him/her open a savings account. This is a good time to start saving money.

- Go to a Parent-Teacher Bookstore and purchase booklets containing pages of subtraction crossword puzzles. Have these in the car when you travel and place a booklet on your child's desk.

- If you hold a garage or toy sale, encourage your youngster to take part, particularly in making change.

- Encourage your child to use the scores found in your newspaper's sports section to determine how many more runs, baskets, free throws, errors or goals one team scored than the other.

HINT: Many children have problems when subtracting zero. Have your youngster make these signs and post them over his/her desk "When zero is subtracted from a number, the difference is that number." Or a more-fun sign would be, "Zero is a Great Big Nothing!" Also, your child needs to understand that when a number is subtracted from itself, the difference is zero. (Use beans or pennies to help illustrate this concept.)

PARENT TIP: **Math skills can be enhanced by more than books and paper-and-pencil activities. I've used many games in my classroom to develop basic facts for my students. A few you could play at home are "cribbage," "bingo," "Chinese checkers," "dominoes," "Monopoly™," and "Go Fish™." Most of these games can be found at garage sales, flea markets, drugstores, game stores or Parent-Teacher Bookstores.**

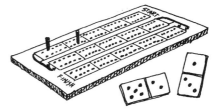

Multiplication trains. A multiplication train is an outstanding "hands-on" way to help your youngster understand and memorize the multiplication tables. Provide a paper cup filled with beans, and ask several multiplication facts. If there is hesitation on a particular one, write it down. Continue until there are three or four missed facts on your list.

If 7 x 4 = 28 was missed, begin with that one. Have your youngster arrange twenty-eight beans in a single row as shown.

o o o o o o o o o o o o o o o o o o o o o o o o o o o o

Talk with your youngster about what number could be divided into twenty-eight to give an even number of sets. The answer might be "two" and, if so, have him/her take a finger and count two and then make a space. Continue until finished.

Next ask if the beans could be divided into larger sets. When you hear "four," it's time to count four beans and then make a space. Continue this to the end of the beans when there will be twenty-eight beans in seven sets, as illustrated.

o o o o   o o o o   o o o o   o o o o   o o o o   o o o o   o o o o

Ask, "How many sets do we have? How many beans in each set? How many beans altogether?"

Do the first one together as an example; then let your youngster figure out how to do other trains. For children having problems with paper-and-pencil multiplication, it's essential that they move objects around so they can see the process taking place.

Students can use coins, buttons, washers, beans or even toy soldiers or peanuts-in-the-shell when making math trains. Use whatever interests your youngster. Remember it takes twenty-six times of seeing, saying or doing something for the fact to be imprinted in the mind and many more times to unlearn a mistake.

Each time a multiplication train is finished, have your student repeat the fact three or four times aloud to help him/her remember it.

HINT: Some numbers will not divide evenly. To illustrate, I ask my students to put 29 beans on top of their desks. I say, "Now put these into sets of two." Right away they yell, "We can't." I explain that the twenty-ninth bean is what we call a "remainder," but I like to call the division remainders, "little bits that are left over." They love this, and whenever they divide and have an extra number they add a tiny "LB" by it. However, when we divide large numbers having BIG remainders (over 25), I have my students write the traditional "R" for remainders.

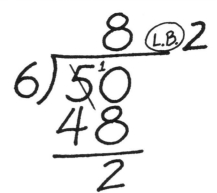

In the Resource section in the back of this book you'll find a chart of multiplication tables from the ones through twelves. Your youngster should spend ten minutes memorizing the facts each night and should be able to say them without hesitation. It is <u>essential</u> to know these facts in order to do math. By sixth grade, all children should know the multiplication tables from the ones through tens. In fact, some schools require that youngsters know them from the ones through twelves.

I have found that many youngsters in the intermediate grades have serious difficulties understanding how to do division. Over and over, I've found these children have one underlying problem in common; they don't know their multiplication tables. Be sure your youngster does and knows them without hesitation. This is an essential rung on the academic ladder that students cannot skip over.

One good way to help your child learn these facts is to use a cassette tape player. Record all the basic multiplication facts in random order. Do this in twelve-second intervals. Then have your youngster take a sheet of paper and number from 1 to 120, start the tape player and write down the facts and answers. The cassette player is not to be turned off at any time. Any missed items need to be reviewed.

Continue to use the tape test once or twice each night until your child has a nearly perfect score most of the time. Your youngster <u>must</u> know these in order to do word problems, play math games or do division and fractions.

Mental gymnastics. Intermediate students particularly enjoy doing oral math. This can be done at home, in the car or on vacation. By this age, youngsters like larger numbers and like to think about several at a time.

Say to your youngster, "Here's a math problem to work in your head and give me the answer." Slowly say, "Twenty-five plus twenty-

five, times two, plus forty-nine, take away three equals what number?"
Or, "Seventy plus seventy, times three, take away twenty, divided by
two equals what number?"

This can become a family game with all the children and parents
participating. At the same time, your children will be increasing their
knowledge of the basic facts of math, along with improving their mental
agility.

Fractions. Young people need to understand fractions in order to
cook, sew or become a construction or automobile worker. To do fractions,
they should think about the problem. Use glossary terms such as
numerator and *denominator* to understand the process. Then draw a
picture of the problem before they begin.

Use "hands-on" items around the house to help your child understand fractions. For example 2/8 + 4/8 can be better understood by
using eight sections of an egg carton. Use two red and four black checkers,
one in each section of the carton to represent the problem. It's much
easier for a youngster to understand how fractions work when demon-
strated this way.

Another illustration is to line up six apples on a table and put a
piece of yarn around each set of two apples. Ask your child, "How
many groups of apples?"

Say, "One group has how many members?" Now your child will
know that one-third of six is two.

Have your youngster use an egg carton, string with beans or other
counters to illustrate the fractions shown on the following page.

Tell your child to put down seven buttons and then pick out three.
Ask, "What fraction have you made? How would you write this fraction?"

Continue to make up fractions and have your child put down buttons (or acorns or colored paper clips) to illustrate each one. Children like to work with a variety of objects.

HINT: I keep washers and colored paper clips in small separate containers for students. Buttons, beans and macaroni shells also make good markers. Children seem more interested when they have a number of different items with which to work.

One way to help your child understand fractions is to have graph paper available. For example, to show 4/6 have your child cut out a piece of graph paper showing six squares. Then four of these should be colored. Make up other fractions and do these together.

Look in the chapter on computer software for additional ideas on using computers to teach fractions.

Some glossary terms your child should know are *numerator, denominator, common denominator, unlike denominators, common multiples, equivalent fractions, mixed numbers, whole numbers* and *reduce to lowest terms.*

PARENT TIP: **Two book suggestions for you or grandparents to purchase for a birthday or other gift are** *Running Press Cyclopedia* **and** *Measurements & Conversions.* **Both are published by Running Press and are inexpensive and small. Youngsters find them easy to hold in their hands. Inside you'll find a wealth of math information, graphs, multiplication charts, fractions and decimals.**

Problem solving. I see so many children displaying an "I-can't" attitude even before they begin math. As a parent, you can help change this way of thinking, particularly about problem solving. You need to constantly foster an "I-can" attitude. Some suggestions follow. Listen quietly as your child reads the problem. Let him/her explain it to you and discover how to solve it. If necessary, point out some facts, which combined, produce the answer.

HINT: In order for youngsters to do problem solving, they must first take the time to carefully read the problem.

Here are two sample problems for your child to read and think about.

- Michael played with his baseball cards for 20 minutes and spent 45 minutes doing homework. How long to do both things? Give the answer in hours and minutes.

- Four children are at the seashore collecting shells. A mother and two children join them. How many children are hunting for sea shells?

Remember that problem solving does not have to involve paper and pencil. We problem solve all day long. If I'm having twelve for dinner tonight, I must determine how large a roast to buy. If the depth of tread on my tires is thin, how many more miles can I safely drive?

Using the newspaper to understand math. Many newspapers have a wealth of math information on the weather page. Some Sunday newspapers also have a Kid's Math page. There are numerous questions you could ask your child to answer after looking at the weather section.

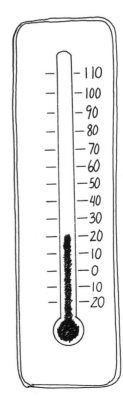

- What was the high temperature in Acapulco today? In Bangkok? Cairo?

- Use these temperatures and make a weather graph.

- How long will the sun be up today?

- What time do the sun and moon rise and set today?

If your local paper lists high and low tides, rainfall, air quality, pollen count, snow depth or other local figures, have your youngster keep a graph for a month.

Use sports interest for math practice. Youngsters, boys in particular, love to collect sports cards. If your child has none, consider a set as a special gift. They can provide a variety of math skills for children to practice.

- Compare individual averages of players.
- Sort the cards by same team or by the same position (pitcher, quarterback).
- Arrange in order of batting or free-throw averages from high to low.
- Sort by colors of teams in baseball, soccer or football.

Comparing numbers and making predictions. Have your youngster compare the number of stairs at your local City Hall with the number at the library. If there are ten steps to the first floor, how many steps are there to the tenth floor? Compare the number of flowers on one bush with those on another. Encourage your child to look all around to discover numbers in nature.

Measurement. We measure all our lives. We measure lines, fabric, drapes, floors and car parts. Sometimes these are in *standard form* and other times in *metric form*. We need to also understand *grams, liters, ounces, pounds, bushel baskets, tons* and talk about *area*.

Some additional glossary words your child will need to know and understand regarding measurement are *a.m., p.m., noon, diameter, gallon, gram, metric units of measurement, inch, foot, yard, perimeter, protractor, radius* and *unit*. Make sure your child knows what each term means and see how many you can apply together to your daily living.

When you're building a new garage, a dog house or putting on a porch, have your child help measure. Use the word *perimeter*. When you measure fabric for new drapes or bedspreads, again ask your youngster to help. Talk about *inches, feet* and *yards*.

HINT: *Area* means covering something. *Perimeter* means the distance around something like a fence or a baseball diamond.

Time. Through the years many of my students have come to school wearing watches but could not tell time. Today most students wear digital watches but can't tell time on a conventional clock. However, they still need to know, and there are a number of questions you could ask to help them become familiar with a regular clock.

- If you need to be at school at 7:30 and it takes twenty minutes to walk, what time must you leave?
- If I need to be at work at 8:45 and it takes me fifty minutes to drive, what time should I leave?

Your child must also know and understand the following terms and be able to apply the definitions to specified problems: *circumference, common factor, congruent figure, diameter, segments, rays, obtuse angle, quadrilaterals, equilateral triangle, radius, line of symmetry* and *right triangle.*

Geometry. To help your child understand geometric concepts involve him/her around the house. Here are some suggestions.

- Make a floor plan of your home. Measure each room to determine its *area.*
- Build a model airplane, skateboard or bookcase together as another way for your child to work with shapes.
- Look at the outline of traffic signs. A stop sign is an *octagon,* for instance, and a yield sign is a *triangle.*
- Make a kite.
- Use a camera to take pictures of interesting shapes.
- Go on a field trip to a city and look at all the shapes found, particularly on old buildings.
- Calculate the amount of fertilizer needed to fertilize a lawn or garden based on *square footage.*

Art idea. My students enjoy doing line designs each year. After the designs are finished, I post them on the classroom wall. Later the children take them home and some use them as gifts. You can help your child make a similar design from the following instructions, but for anything more complicated it is best to purchase a line-design book at your Parent-Teacher Bookstore or a craft shop. One book I've used is *Creating Line Designs* by Randy L. Womack.

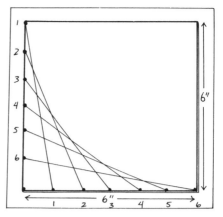

Use a colorful seven-inch-square piece of tagboard. Have your youngster draw a square six inches by six inches inside as shown. Make holes with your needle on the left and bottom lines you've drawn. Number the holes from one to six, one inch apart, starting at the upper-left-hand side of the tagboard and working down. At the bottom left-hand corner, indent one inch and number from one to six again toward the right. Using a needle and thread, connect the two dots that have the same number, starting with number one. Connect all the numbers. I have my students use a small piece of masking tape instead of a knot to hold the beginning and end of the thread in place. They use thread in many colors and a needle with a large eye.

Probability. This is the number of times something will probably occur over the range of possible occurrences which we express as a *ratio*. One way to help your youngster understand *probability* is to use money. Have your child toss a penny on the table. Ask these questions:

- How many possible outcomes are there?
  Only two. Heads or tails

- Is each outcome equally likely? Could it be either heads or tails?
  Yes

- What is the probability that you'll get heads?
  1/2 or one time out of two tosses

- What is the probability you'll get tails?
  1/2

- What if you tossed two pennies down on the desk? What is the probability that both will come up heads?
  1/4

Talk about the probability of rain. Ask your child, "What is the probability that it will rain this week?" Have your youngster listen to weather reports and give a guess.

More knowledge of math skills needed. I have not been able to cover every math skill your youngster needs to know in the intermediate grades. Some others which need to be known and understood are *decimals, ratio, percent* and *integers.*

HINT: If your child needs extra help in math and a book is not always available, call your school district warehouse. Some schools store old books at the warehouse and are willing to give them to parents.

If your youngster is behind in math, consider summer school or a tutor, or call the school district for help. Some districts have a list of available tutors, including retired teachers. Also, many colleges and universities have a list of students who will tutor your child. The cost is usually pretty reasonable.

Today we are looking for mathematically powerful kids, those who can use the basic facts of addition, subtraction, multiplication and division to solve problems. A strong grade-school foundation in math will be part of your youngster's success in the upper grades as well as in future employment.

Cultivate Science Learners Preschool-Kindergarten

"Encourage questions from your child, but don't be quick to give the answers. Instead, help your child learn ways to find out — either in a book, or by going out into the yard and looking, or by doing and discovering. The best answers to use are, 'I'm not exactly sure; let's look in this book and find out. What do you think? Let's try it out and see.'"

Karen Chong, Kindergarten/Grade-One Teacher, Albion Elementary School,
Maple Ridge, British Columbia

PRESCHOOL

One goal of introducing preschoolers to science is to help them observe (notice) their world and to be able to understand what they have seen.

Mrs. Connor's preschoolers discovered how force works one afternoon as they sat eating their snack. The classroom's outside brick wall had been defaced by vandals and a sandblasting crew arrived to clean up the graffiti.

Mrs. Connor explained to her students how the motor in the machine produced a strong force to blast the sand at the wall and wear away all the paint.

Incidental learning. After the graffiti removal, the students experimented with force of air by blowing through straws to move cotton balls across the table. We call this "incidental learning." There are many other happenings in everyday life that can help your child discover science. When walking or driving you might see a lady bug, a forklift, a jackhammer, leaves falling to the ground, a bird building a nest, a mother duck and babies crossing a road, a layer of fog on the ground, or a helicopter. These are all unexpected experiences which can be used as "teachable moments" for your child.

IDEAS FOR INTRODUCING YOUR CHILD TO SCIENCE

You can help your child in a number of ways to experience success in science while having fun. Hopefully, you will enjoy some of the following activities just as much.

Electric milk. Pour three cups of slightly warm whole milk into a clear bowl. Have your child add two drops of red, then green, blue and yellow food coloring in different places on top of the milk. Then add a few drops of liquid soap to the milk.

Your child will be thrilled to see the results of adding food coloring and soap to the milk to form a minor explosion of colors. When the soap hits the milk, it creates a ripple effect which pushes the colors out into a vibrant array of colors. One little boy seeing the action yelled, "We made electric milk!" Enjoy, but don't drink.

Collecting. As you walk around your neighborhood, start collecting things like leaves, rocks and perhaps shells. Of course, for the most benefit, you'll need a place to showcase your special "finds."

PARENT TIP: **Use either a child's small table or a sturdy cardboard or wooden box to make a "Science-Collection" table for your child to use. Place the table in the child's room or in the family room out of the way of traffic so things won't be knocked over. As you take your walks, collect rocks, seeds, leaves or feathers and place them on the table to talk about later.**

Rocks. Your child needs many opportunities to collect rocks from a variety of places. When you travel, find rocks in the mountains, at the seashore, along river banks or creeks.

Questions to ask: "How does this rock feel? What colors do you see on it? Is this rock large or small? Is it light or heavy? Where did we find it?" Words to use are rough, smooth, long, short and colors.

Seeds. Collect various seeds as you walk around your neighborhood and place them on the science table. Some others to place on the table are peas, beans, corn, watermelon, pumpkin and sunflower. An avocado pit is even a seed. At this age, the larger seeds are best so the youngster won't be tempted to put them in his/her mouth.

When talking with your child about seeds, use words like smooth, shiny, little, big, color or shape. Then ask, "Where did this seed come from? What color is it? Is this a seed we can eat? How does this feel?"

Help your child create a picture by gluing various kinds and sizes of seeds on a small wooden board or a piece of cardboard covered with

construction paper.   Hang the picture on the bulletin board for all
to enjoy.

Magnets. Children love to play with magnets, so use this enthusiasm to help your child learn more about how they work. Buy several
small magnets at a hardware store.

Have your child put a variety of items into a cardboard box. Use
things like cotton balls, paper clips, copper pennies, nails and plastic
buttons. Hand your child the magnet to see which items it will attract
and which ones won't stick. Help your child understand the differences
by asking questions like, "Why didn't the magnet pick up the cotton
ball? Why didn't it pick up the buttons and why did it pick up the
pennies, paper clips and nails?"

Another experiment is to place a penny on top of a light cardboard. Hold a magnet underneath and move it. Your child will enjoy
seeing the penny move across the top.

Explain that magnets can lift things because they have a magnetic
field which attracts objects with metal in them.

Animals. Since children like to observe animals, they can learn
about their eating, sleeping and waking habits as they watch them during
the day. This is a good home activity if you have pets. In addition, take
your child to visit a farm, zoo, park, pet store or aquarium to observe
other animals. There are also excellent nature programs on television.

Plants. Children should observe plants growing, living and dying.
This will help them later to understand the life cycle in the plant world.

An easy way to do this is to help your child plant a lima bean
seed in a paper cup filled with dirt. Poke a hole in the bottom of the
cup and place a plastic lid underneath to catch the extra water. Talk
about the need for water and sunshine for the plant. At the same time,

take a lima bean seed and wrap it in a small piece of wet paper towel and place the bean inside a plastic bag. It will sprout just like the bean planted in the dirt if you keep it on a counter in your warm kitchen. Every few days have your child peek inside to see if the bean has sprouted.

Take a sweet potato and halfway bury it, root side down, in a pan of dirt. Have your child water the potato and watch it sprout. (This makes an attractive vine.) By doing these things, your child will see that plants grow, but they need air, water and sunshine to continue growing.

Sink and float. Children will be interested to see that some things sink while others float. During the summer this activity can be done outside in a small plastic pool. In the winter, the experiment can take place in the bathtub. Be sure an adult is with the child. Play a game to see which of the following will float in the water: a sponge, plastic and metal spoons, a rubber duck, a ruler and a small block of wood.

Solid or liquid? Show your youngster the differences between things in the environment that are solid and those which are liquid. Pour milk into a glass while your child watches. Say, "The glass is solid but the milk is not. It is liquid." When you turn on the water faucet to give your child a drink, say, "The faucet is solid (tap it with your finger) but the water is liquid." Have your youngster put his/her hand under the water and feel the liquid flowing into the sink which is solid.

Weather. On a calendar with large squares, draw pictures to illustrate the weather each day. On windy days, draw a tree bending over. Draw a snowflake on snowy days. Add a large sun on sunny days and on rainy days, show a couple of big raindrops.

Look outside as you draw and talk with your child about the weather. Use words such as wind, snow, rain, sunshine, winter, summer, spring and fall. Explain to your child that we normally expect certain weather during each of the seasons of the year.

Make a book. Children particularly enjoy talking about plants and animals. Help your child make a book of each. On one cover print, *Scott's Animal Book* or *Scott's Plant Book*. Talk about either one animal or plant. Have your child dictate, with your help, a simple sentence to put on each page. Draw a picture together or cut one out from a magazine to describe each idea.

A mobile. Use a clothes hanger to make an animal and plant mobile to hang in your child's room. This could be especially helpful after you return from a mini-field trip around the neighborhood. If you saw leaves, draw or cut out pictures of leaves and glue to small cards. Attach the cards to the hanger using string of different lengths. Do the same for an animal mobile.

Modeling clay or dough. Children love to be creative with clay or dough. They like to roll it, push, pile it, flatten it and make snakes by rolling it between their palms. They also like to use tools such as a potato masher, an old rolling pin and cookie cutters. You can make your own modeling dough from this simple, inexpensive recipe provided by preschool teacher, Carolyn Bennett from Lincoln, California.

> Mix together in a pan: 1 cup flour
> 2 tsp. cream of tartar   1 cup salt
> Mix and add to pan:
> 1 cup water   6 drops food coloring
> 1 Tbs. oil

Stir constantly over medium heat for about five minutes or until dough pulls away from the sides of the pan.

Take out of pan and let cool. Knead the dough until it is smooth and similar to bread dough. You'll have about two cups of dough and

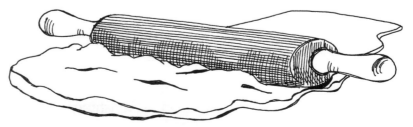

the recipe can easily be doubled for a larger quantity. Keep in a covered container and it should last from one to two months.

As you watch for opportunities to awaken your child's interest in the world around, you may even find yourself seeing things differently. Watch for relationships and differences, the "how" and the "what" and above all, the "why" of things.

Why? That single question, is a real key to learning, not only for preschoolers but for famous scientists, as well.

KINDERGARTEN

Science is the study of the world around us and its evidence is everywhere. As I write, a rain shower has ended and the insects are stirring. My cat, carefully carrying a beetle in her mouth for me, slipped inside through her cat door leading into my office. Later she brought in a Praying Mantis. I rescued the insects and carried them to the field across the yard. As they fluttered away, I wished them a long life and freedom from curious cats.

Children are just as curious as cats. They have an innate joy of learning coupled with endless imagination. Capitalize on these characteristics when working with your kindergartner.

The more children understand science now, the better prepared they will be to make wise decisions as adults. They will use science when cooking; when caring for their bodies; and in dealing with nature, medicine and technology.

New science books. Most schools adopt new science books about every seven years. Last year, however, instead of regular books, my school district bought science kits which are arranged by themes. More and more emphasis is being given to hands-on activities for youngsters in place of textbook teaching.

Science for kindergartners covers four major themes: The Human Body, Physical Science, Earth Science and Life Science. I'll talk about each separately and provide some ideas on how to help your child achieve a lifelong interest in science.

THE HUMAN BODY

The body is a wonderful machine with many parts which work together. Your youngster's body collects and uses energy to change and to grow, as I'm sure you've noticed.

Kindergartners start to understand how the body works and what it needs to stay alive, stay healthy and perform well. They're also learning how to care for their own bodies.

The Five Senses. Tell your child we each have five senses and each performs a special function.

Sight. With our eyes we see colors of the rainbow and the shapes of buildings, signs and trees.

Take your child on walks around your neighborhood and point out a blue bird, an orange cat or yellow flowers. Talk about the wonderful pair of eyes your youngster has and how useful they are to explore the world.

Sound. Our ears help us hear raindrops on the roof, popcorn popping and a dog barking.

Take your child on a "sound walk." Say, "What does that little stream sound like?" Or, "What is that sound coming from the train?" Talk about our ears and how well they work for us and why we need to take good care of them.

Smell. We'd miss the smell of baking bread and scents in a forest or a garden of flowers without our noses. We can also detect burning toast and the "stink" from some kinds of fertilizer being put on soil or lawns.

Before dinner ask, "What do you smell?" If there's something in the oven, ask, "What's baking? Can you recognize the odor?" Talk about the sense of smell and how it helps us to better appreciate our world of fragrant flowers and trees in blossom. This usually tells us that it is the spring season of the year.

Taste. Our tongue and taste buds help us to tell the difference between chocolate in a yummy brownie, the sourness of a pickle or the sweetness of candy.

Present your youngster with many different opportunities for tasting foods and talk about learning to enjoy all foods. Ask him/her to describe the taste of chocolate frosting, lemonade or the salt on popcorn.

Touch. Through our skin, usually that on our fingers, we can feel rough and smooth, cold and hot and tell the difference between cloth, metal and cotton balls. A child should feel the difference between cotton and velvet fabrics, between wood and plastic, between sandpaper and a cotton ball.

As you walk through fabric stores, have your child feel a variety of materials. Take your youngster when you visit the lumberyard. Encourage touching lumber, sandpaper and a metal pipe. Take your child to a petting zoo and let him or her feel the fur of a rabbit, the bristles of a pig and the hair of a goat. Talk about the various feelings experienced.

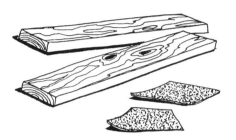

Have your youngster play a game of "Guess What?" In a cardboard box (like a shoe box) place a number of things from around the house such as a pencil, paper clip, a piece of string and a peanut in its shell. See how many items your youngster can name by touch alone.

Body parts. Talk about the parts of your child's body. Help him or her learn as you ask, "What part of your body do you use when you run? Sing? Swim? Eat? Read? Write? Throw a ball? Talk on the telephone?"

SUGGESTIONS: Help your child measure his or her hand, foot and thumb. Use popsicle sticks or large, colorful paperclips as your unit of measure. For example, say, "How many red paperclips long is your foot? How long is your thumb?"

Help your child draw the outline of his/her hand or foot. Do the drawing on colored paper and have your child decorate the drawing to become a card for Grandma on Mother's Day.

Measure. To demonstrate body growth, select a door frame as your yearly measuring post for your child's height. Each year on the youngster's birthday, place a mark showing how much he/she has grown.

After you measure, get out your child's baby pictures. Ask, "How have you changed since you were a baby?" Remember, bigger is not always better, and children grow at different rates.

Questions. When you walk by a store window ask your youngster, "What would that Teddy Bear feel like if you touched it?" Or, "Do you think that red flower smells sweet or bad?"

Staying healthy. Children need to know their bodies are like very special "machines" and they must learn how to care for them. This can be the basis for lots of discussion.

- Food is to the body as gasoline is to a car.
- Staying well requires eating good foods.
- To stay well, you must wash your body with soap and water.
- To have healthy teeth, you need to brush regularly.
- To stay healthy, you need to live in a clean environment.

HINT: Walk around your neighborhood and when you find a littered area, talk about how you could clean it up. This might be taking along a trash bag on your walk the next day. As you pick up litter together, your child will begin to understand the importance of helping to keep the environment clean.

Litter and garbage can create homes for rats and bugs and insects. Some of them may carry diseases. By keeping our surroundings clean, we are helping to ensure that our bodies will be protected from creatures which could hurt us.

LIFE SCIENCE — ANIMALS

Life science is the study of animals and plants, how they live and grow and the differences in how they reproduce. Do as many things as you can to help your child become more observant about animals around your home, neighborhood and community.

Read. Read books or stories to your child about animals. Many different kinds are available.

- *Endangered Baby Animals* by Ruth and Bill Morehead
    A delightful series of stories about harp seals, cheetahs, grizzly bears and more
- *More Endangered Baby Animals* by Ruth and Bill Morehead
    Stories and colorful drawings of otters, golden tamarin monkeys, African wild dogs and more
- *Spiders and Scorpions* by Jill Wolf
    Stories and photographs of a black widow spider, giant hairy desert scorpion, orange-kneed tarantula and others
- *Sharks* edited by Jill Wolf
    Details about a variety of sharks including the great white shark, the hammerhead, and the lemon shark

Trips. There are many places to see animals. Museums often have exhibits of pre-historic animals as well as today's animals. There are numerous commercial opportunities such as zoos and marine-life parks. Don't overlook community nature centers, your county or state fair or even a neighborhood pet store or aquarium.

Projects. Hands-on experience is also valuable. Go for a walk and look for a bird's nest. Pick up feathers as you walk, and talk about their size and color. Look for a bird which matches them.

If you have the time to care for a pet, consider getting one. It can be as simple as a couple goldfish in a bowl. Take your child shopping as you buy food for the pet so your youngster will understand the types of food the animal should eat. Ask, "What else does your kitten (fish or puppy) need to live?" Discuss why animals need both food and water for survival.

Differences. Talk about animals and how they move in similar or different ways. A dog's feet and body are different from a squirrel's and they don't move the same way. A cat's paws and build are different from an elephant's, and cats don't move like elephants.

Discuss the skins of animals and birds. Some have fur while others have feathers or hide. Questions to ask: "Can you match babies to their parents? What do babies need to survive? How do you think they get the things they need? Which animals run? Jump? Crawl? Scamper?"

Art.   Help your child draw a
picture of a favorite animal. Post it on
your bulletin board or the refrigerator.

Homes.   Animals come from
different places around the world. Some
live in very wet, warm places and some
live in very cold, dark places so they have
different homes.   Some live in nests, some in trees, some in the water
while others live in caves. Show your child pictures of animal homes in
books and magazines. Watch nature specials on television and talk about
them together.

Food. Go to a seed and feed store and discuss the various foods
for birds, cats, dogs, hamsters, rabbits, cows and horses. Encourage your
child to smell the bags of food.   Say, "See how each one has its own
smell."   By this time your child probably will be able to answer questions
like, "Where do eggs come from?   What foods come from cows?"

Water. Discuss the importance of water to animals. Explain how
the rain helps animals live, especially those out in the wild.

Visit a farm and look at the large tubs used for watering the horses
and cows. At a feed store, look at all the shapes and sizes of containers
for water used by animals. Some are small for birds while others are
large for big farm animals.

LIFE SCIENCE — PLANTS

By now your child should have taken many mini-field trips around
the neighborhood and be aware of trees, flowers and, perhaps, vegetable
gardens. Observations may include information about shape, color, size
of leaves and stems and special plant features such as flowers or fruits.

PARENT TIP: **Have your child stand near you as you cook. Talk about vegetables such as celery, string beans and peas. Talk about fruits such as apples, oranges and bananas. Point out that most fruits have seeds and vegetables do not.**

Seeds. In the spring, plant a small garden. Plant carrot and radish seeds. Talk about how seeds travel. Some travel by the wind, others are carried by birds and some are carried by animals.

Read the book *The Carrot Seed* by Rachel Krauss. As you read ask, "Why is the farmer whistling? Where do we plant carrot seeds? What must we do to make them grow? How long do you think it takes for a carrot to grow to be large enough to eat?"

Sing this little song about the carrot seed.

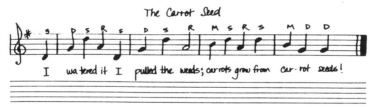

When the carrots you've planted are ready for eating, cut off the top inch of three carrots, and help your youngster "plant" them again. Insert toothpicks through the sides of a Styrofoam cup to hold the "carrots" (the inch which you've kept for planting). The toothpicks should be placed about an inch from the top of the cup. Fill the cup with water until the water touches the bottom of the carrot. Add water every few days and watch them sprout.

Talk about the "top" of the carrot and the bottom, the root system, and ask, "Where do carrots grow? Is it light or

dark in the soil? What do carrots need to live? What other things need water and sun to grow?"

HINT: If you don't have room for an outside garden, plant radishes in a dish garden. They grow quickly and you'll have fresh vegetables to eat.

Make a terrarium. Use a large jar with a wide-mouth opening and cover the bottom with charcoal chips, small rocks and potting soil and add some small plants. Water lightly and place in your child's room. Talk with your child about the importance of carefully watering the plants and placing the jar in just the right amount of sunlight for growth. Stress the importance of minimal handling to prevent jar breakage and/or disturbing the plant arrangement.

Trips. There are many places to take your child to <u>observe</u> plants. These can range from national forests to neighborhood nature areas. Many zoos also have interesting plants. Don't overlook a commercial nursery. Some cities or colleges have botanical gardens or even conservatories.

Water. Children need to be aware of the importance of water for both animals and plants. Talk with your youngster about how rain helps plants to grow and animals to thrive. Discuss how water is preserved for people, animals and for farmers so they can grow crops. Visit a pond, a lake or a reservoir. Talk about dams. Visit the source of water for your home. Is it a river, a well, or a water tank? How does the water get into the tank?

Living things. Children should learn that living things are made of cells which react to light, touch, heat and cold. Help make your child aware that living things have basic needs such as an energy source and water.

Nonliving things. Discuss things which are <u>not</u> alive. Many things, even toys, move but only because they have batteries or are pushed. Sit on the floor with your child and arrange living and nonliving things in a circle. Examples could be a teddy bear, a plant, a dish, a baby kitten, a fish in a fish bowl, a jump rope, a stuffed rabbit and an orange or apple.

PHYSICAL SCIENCE

In this section, your child will learn how the physical world is governed by special laws and will start mastering some of the tools we use in our modern world.

Your child needs this scientific foundation for two reasons:

1. To understand ideas
2. To solve problems

Matter is the name we give to all the "stuff" in our physical world. It can be animal, vegetable or mineral: stars, dirt, lions or strawberries.

Tools are things like microscopes, thermometers, rulers or clocks which help us observe and do experiments in our world.

It takes practical experience for your child to form concepts. These are fostered as you provide varied experiences to observe and explore his or her surrounding world.

Heavy or light. You can provide an experience at bedtime on comparing differences in weight. As your child brushes his/her teeth ask, "Which is heavier, the toothbrush or toothpaste? Which feels lighter, your comb or hairbrush?"

By making your child aware of differences in the weights of objects, you are establishing a foundation of knowledge about weights for future explorations.

In the classroom, I have my students weigh a banana and an apple and compare the difference. Then I slice the fruit for them to eat. You can do this at home.

Colors, shapes and sizes. So your child can begin to understand the differences in colors, shapes and sizes you need to compare objects.

Have your youngster play with a tennis ball and then a basketball. Ask, "What color is the tennis ball and what color is the basketball?" Talk about their shapes. How are they the same? How are they different?

Hot and cold. Children will learn that heating or cooling things can sometimes change them. One way you can help your child understand the process is to make applesauce. Begin with firm apples and prepare them for cooking. After you cook the applesauce, cool and serve it with one of your meals. Ask, "How is the applesauce different from the apples?" Show your child that apples are firm and hard and applesauce is soft. Talk about the different smells and tastes between apples and applesauce.

To illustrate the changes when things become cold, have your youngster help you make a gelatin dessert. Before you add the boiling water to the powder, have your child taste the powder. Ask, "How does it taste?" He/she might say "sweet" or "like candy."

Explain you'll now use hot water to dissolve the powder and make the dessert. Let your child do the stirring. Point out that a "liquid" has "no shape." Have your youngster walk with you to the refrigerator and help you place the gelatin on a shelf. Ask, "How does the refrigerator feel inside?"

When the gelatin is set, serve it and talk about the changes. "How does it look now? Can we pour it? Can we drink it? Is it soft or hard?" Finally ask, "What made it change?" Your child should say "the cold refrigerator."

Objects that float. You can help your child understand things that float and those that sink when he or she takes a bath. Some objects to put in the water are pennies, a plastic glass, a cake pan and a cork. Provide your child with the time to play with the objects. When talking, use terms such as "float" or "sink." As you talk about the ones that stayed up or went down, your child may decide that objects lighter than the water usually float and the objects heavier than water usually sink.

Push and pull. Get some clay and spend time making a variety of shapes with your child. Talk about how things can change when we push or pull them. Explain that another name for push and pull is <u>force.</u> As your child pushes down on the clay, ask what force was used. <u>Push.</u> Continue to play with the clay. Have the youngster pull on two sides of the clay. Ask, "What force did you use?" <u>A pull.</u>

Light and dark. Children need to be able to describe the various sources of light in their world. They also should be able to distinguish sources of light. Here are a few ways to help your youngster understand light and dark.

Sometimes when I'm reading poetry in the classroom, I'll close the drapes, turn off the lights and turn on a small flashlight to read aloud to my students. You can do this at home.

Ask your child, "Why do we need the flashlight on?" Or, "What color is this book in the dark?" Or, "What color is the cover in the light?"

As you drive along at night, look for the bright lights of trucks, gas stations and stores. Driving through a tunnel during the day, talk about why we need headlights.

As you walk around your neighborhood, ask your child how it looks now in daylight. Later take the same walk at night. Ask, "How does it look now with only the moon or only the street light?"

Movement. Children need to understand that objects can move or be moved. In time, your child will know why objects move in a certain direction.

Provide a Yo-Yo for your child to enjoy. Model how to make it go up and down. Then have your youngster try it.

When you see a big clock with a pendulum, talk about how the pendulum swings "this way and that way."

Go outside when the wind is blowing and watch the trees blow from one direction to the other. Talk about the force of the wind and how it moves trees, plants, flowers and sometimes even people.

Energy. Tell your child that energy is an important part in his/her life. For example, if someone wants a bowl of hot soup for lunch, the stove must be turned on (energy) and the soup heated.

Also, if your child wants ice cream, say, "We must keep the refrigerator-freezer plugged in so the freezer will keep our ice cream frozen."

Other energy sources to explore with your child are a windmill, batteries in a flashlight, gasoline in a car and water going over a dam.

EARTH SCIENCE

If children understand the land, water, sky and weather all around them, they will be good caretakers of their world.

Land and water. By reading stories, watching science programs on television and talking together, you can help your youngster better understand the world. Explain how we need the land for raising food and livestock as well as for play and recreation.

At a discount store, purchase an inexpensive globe. If possible, buy one with raised mountains. Talk about this being "our world." Let your child touch the globe. Talk about the water and have your child point to the continents. Help him/her identify different landforms on the surface of the earth such as mountains, valleys, oceans and deserts.

Point out where you live and have your child touch the spot. This will help convey that this is his/her world as well.

PARENT TIP: **Help your child draw a small picture of your house and tape the house on the spot on the globe where you live. Darken the room and hold a flashlight for the sun. Slowly turn the globe around. Ask as you turn, "Is it day or night at our house now?"**

Soil. Poke around in the dirt in your yard or a window box and play with sand in a sandbox or at the beach. Go to the mountains or a park and look for different types of soil.

NOTE: I grew up in an area where the soil had lots of iron which made it a brilliant red. I still think of the contrast of that soil with the dark brown soil around my home today.

Sky. Your child should be aware of the night-sky and the day-sky. Take time to go outside on a clear night and point to the stars, the moon and the darkness of the sky.

Go outside on a clear day and look for clouds and the sun. Talk about the air all around us which we need to breathe. While you are outside, talk about shadows. Say, "Can you make a shadow?" Have your youngster observe where the sun is in relation to one's body and one's shadow.

Help your child draw pictures of a day-sky and night-sky. Post them in your child's room.

Weather. Draw pictures for the seasons, Fall, Winter, Spring and Summer. Post on a bulletin board.

Ask questions like "What do we do on a rainy day?" Talk about raincoats, boots and umbrellas.

Ask, "What do you wear in the wintertime?" Help your child understand the need for coats, caps and gloves. Do the same for spring and summer. I've found that children have trouble comprehending the seasons. Spend extra time on this. Make a *Season Book.*

Water. Explain to your youngster that all too often we take water for granted. We should not. We should use only what is necessary, because we need plenty for animals and humans to drink. We need it for plants and crops, too.

Tell your child that water can be polluted and we should keep our environment clean so we will have plenty of good, pure water for everyone.

HINT: Put a large, clean can in your back yard and collect rain water. Help your child measure it with a ruler. You could also chart this on a rain graph for each month of the year. Discuss the amounts of rain, or lack of rain, each month with your youngster.

Talk about the amount of snow in the mountains and how important it is to the water supply. Visit a snowy area, melt snow and place the water in a cup to measure the amount. Normally it takes around ten inches of snow to make one inch of water.

Go camping. A family camping trip can provide your family with a variety of hands-on experiences. Use these times to talk to your youngster about the different colors of soil, point out the stars in the sky at night and walk along a mountain stream. Some of my most exciting adventures and times for acquiring knowledge have been on camping trips.

Watch for "teachable" moments each day, presenting them as exciting discoveries and explorations.

Always remember that being able to really <u>see</u> what they are learning is vital to kindergarten children. They need to be made aware of everything everywhere. Spend lots of time talking about things and remind your child to use all five senses often to observe the things around home and also when he or she goes somewhere.

Cultivate Science Learners Grades One-Six

"It's important for your child to be aware of things. You can encourage this awareness by being curious and aware yourself and sharing experiences with your child. Build a rain gauge. Buy an ant farm. Take a night walk and find the Big Dipper."

Diane Wilson, Owner/Director of A Child's Garden. The Learning Center for Children and Parents.
Carmichael, California

For children to fully understand their world, they need a generous exposure to science.

Much of this understanding comes from simple experimentation and observation. Water + dirt = mud. Yellow paint + blue paint = green paint.

The more opportunities you provide for a wide range of experimentation and observation, the better prepared your child will be for a more formal study of science in school.

What kind of experience is best? I really recommend a generous variety. By the time your child reaches first grade, you should have provided opportunities to:

- Observe plants, animals, sun and sky.
- Explore in the backyard or park, observe a bug, watch a bird or touch a flower.
- Handle things: pour milk, play with water and roll out clay or cookies.
- Compare things: heavy and light, rough and smooth, hot and cold.
- Organize things by size, color or shape.
- Children should be familiar with parts of the body: nose, mouth, ears, eyes, arms, and legs.

You may want to read the chapter on kindergarten science for suggested activities.

Science in the classroom. Science today has moved away from textbooks to a much more "hands-on" approach to learning. More attention is being paid to environmental issues. Schools are also helping students develop the abilities to read and write about science as well as understand the processes of this field and develop the skills to discover new knowledge.

In addition, many teachers are committed to encouraging girls and minority students to develop an interest in science.

PARENT TIP: **Across the country more and more museums are being developed as hands-on centers where children can interact with animals, sea life, engines and electricity. If you don't have such a museum nearby, arrange a time when you, your child's grandparents or other**  **relatives might schedule a vacation to such a place. Children enjoy the interaction with things they've heard about and studied in the classroom.**

A partial list of outstanding regional interactive museums is:
- Liberty Science Center, Jersey City, NJ (201) 200-1000
- Miami Museum of Science, Miami, FL (305) 854-4247
- Ann Arbor Hands-On Museum, Ann Arbor, MI (313) 995-5439
- Louisiana Nature Center, New Orleans, LA (504) 246-5672
- The Inventure Place, Home of the National Inventors Hall of Fame, Akron, OH (330) 762-4463
- Oregon Museum of Science and Industry, Portland, OR (503) 797-4000
- The Exploratorium, San Francisco, CA (415) 561-0360
- The Flandrau Science Center and Planetarium, Tucson, AZ (602) 621-4515

What does science include? Science from primary through intermediate grades encompasses many specific topics which vary from one part of the country to another.

I suggest you obtain the *Science Curriculum Guide* for your state. If your child's school doesn't have a copy, ask the Department of Education at your state capital to send you the guide. Sometimes it's free; seldom does it cost more than a few dollars.

By taking the time to look at the guide by grade levels, you'll see what your child will be studying in science each year. Use the science guide as a checklist to be sure your youngster is moving up the academic ladder in science one step at a time. In the *Science Curriculum Guide*, you'll also gather ideas to help your child decide upon a science project for the school Science Fair.

The science process. The study of science involves a process consisting of a number of steps.

- Observation. For example, over a period of weeks your child can observe the growth of a plant in a pot, or watch the development of a baby rabbit into an adult.
- Communication. This might be through photos, charts, writing stories or reports.
- Comparing. This includes measurement or showing how things are similar or different in other ways besides size.
- Organization. This involves discovering patterns and arranging things in methodical ways.
- Experimentation. What can we discover about a subject and its behavior?
- Curiosity. Always answer your child's questions or help find the answers.

PARENT TIP: **In order to succeed in science, your child must be able to read and do math and feel confident in both subjects. Much reading research will need to be done and math is often used when doing experiments.**

The three strands of science. Science is a very large subject and is broken down into three parts.
- Life Science includes life and human biology and is the study of living things, cells, genetics and ecosystems.
- Earth Science includes earth and environmental strands. Astronomy, geology and natural resources, oceanography and meteorology are part of Earth Science.
- Physical Science includes physical science and technology and covers matter, reactions and interactions, force and motion and the many sources of energy such as light and heat.

NOTE: Science is a large subject to cover. I've picked out just a few science projects which you and your child can do around the home. For additional ideas, check out science books at your local library. They have a large selection of books with science projects to serve as a resource to you and your child.

LIVING THINGS — PLANTS

Plants. Provide your youngster with many opportunities to plant things and watch them grow.

My second graders called our local Park Forest Ranger and asked for assistance planting trees. We followed her advice and ended up with a most successful project.

- We planted six tree seeds in large cans filled with potting soil.
- My students watered the plants and kept them in sunlight.
- The students measured the trees monthly and charted their growth.
- The class displayed the trees at the Science Fair. The trees were 18 inches tall and the class won a blue ribbon.
- The students returned the trees to the Forest Service to be planted along our local bike trail.

How to watch plants grow. Your child can choose from numerous planting ideas which can be done at home.

- Grow an avocado from the pit placed partly in water.
- Sprout a sweet potato plant in your kitchen window.
- Place the top end of a carrot on a layer of pebbles in a shallow dish. Fill dish with water just above the cut end of the carrot top.
- Plant radish seeds in a bowl.
- Plant flower seeds in a pot or in the yard.
- Plant grass seeds in a cup.

PARENT TIP: **As a birthday gift, take your youngster to a bookstore and together look for guidebooks on flowers, trees, animals, birds and fish. Help your child develop a love and understanding of the world all around. Most of these books are filled with exquisite drawings and** a paragraph providing details of the plant or animal. The books also include maps of the United States showing where the plants and animals can be found.

My neighborhood is filled with Valley Oak trees. You may have other varieties of oak trees near you, as they are scattered throughout the United States. Experiment with planting acorns. Maple trees grow easily from their "propeller" seeds, and many varieties of pine can be grown from seed.

Collecting. Begin by collecting leaves, seeds, pine cones or acorns from the trees near you. Then have your youngster recognize what kind of tree from an identification book.

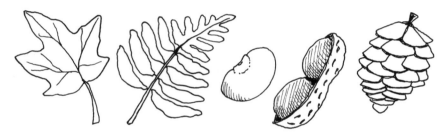

Planting a tree seed. In the autumn, the tip end of a healthy acorn will split and the taproot can be seen.

Wash out and dry a two-quart cardboard milk carton. Push the flaps upward to form a taller container.

Poke a couple of small drainage holes in the bottom of the carton so the acorn won't rot. Have your child place potting soil in the carton to within five inches of the top and then plant the acorn on its side, one and one-half inches below the surface of the soil.

HINT: Have several cartons available and plant several acorns since some may not grow.

What plants need to grow. A plant must have sun, water, air, nutrients and soil.

If you grow the seedling indoors, do not give the seedling direct sunlight where it might get too hot. Remind your youngster not to place the plant near an air conditioner or heating vent. The best temperature is between 65 and 75 degrees.

Caution your child to not give the seedling too much water. One way to check is to have your youngster place a finger in the soil. If the soil is dry, give it some water.

Photosynthesis. All plants need light for photosynthesis to take place. Photosynthesis is the process by which plants use light energy to make food.

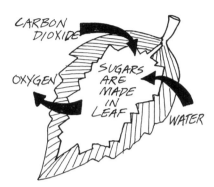

Have your child study this illustration and draw one to post on his or her own bulletin board.

Your youngster needs to understand that plants need light in order to carry out photosynthesis to convert light energy, carbon dioxide and water into oxygen and carbohydrates. Plants carry on this vital process which replaces oxygen for other living things.

Planting time. When your tree is large enough to plant outdoors, it's time for your youngster to answer several questions.

- Do I have enough space for this tree to grow? Do I know how large it will eventually be?
- Must my tree compete with other trees, shrubs or buildings for soil, nutrients, water and light?
- Am I planting the tree in an area with good drainage?
- Will it be in danger from deer or other animals who might eat the tree?

Planting. Have your youngster dig a hole twice the diameter of the container. Carefully remove the seedling from the box and place it in the hole. It is important to not injure the root system.

The tree should not be planted too low in the ground. When planted, it should be mounded up from one to two inches above the ground. This will keep water from drowning out the root system. Finally, the hole should be covered over with two inches of mulch. If animals are a problem, place a circle of wire or several stakes around the seedling.

On this special day, arrange to have your family gather around the area where the tree is to be planted. Your youngster should know that this is a special occasion. Make it a joyful time and talk about how the tree might look when grown and what it will do for your family.

Questions. Ask your child some questions to see how much he or she may understand about growing plants. "What does a seed need to grow? Tell me how you know a plant needs water. How much water should you give your seedling? How can you tell when your seed has too much water?

Sharing with others. If your child has one or two other healthy seedlings, talk about sharing these with someone else. Your child might call the park service to see if they would like an extra tree. What about older people, or grandparents, who might need a tree for shade?

Children, very early in life, need experiences where they can be taught to share things with others and this science experience could be a good opportunity. Help your child discover the joy in helping other people.

Finally, have your child make a *Tree Book* and tell the story from seed to full growth. This can be an ongoing record of success. Each year on the occasion of the planting, have your youngster go outside with a camera and take a picture of the newest tree to place in the book. If past years' trees are available, current pictures of them would be interesting also.

The environment. Explain to your child that by planting a tree, energy has been saved. Trees provide shade in the summer and cut down on the need for electricity for cooling houses. Trees also keep water in the ground and help prevent erosion and runoff from storms.

HINT: A good book for your child to read about trees and how they help other people is *Johnny Appleseed* by Steven Kellogg. Point out how much widespread influence one single person can have even if he isn't famous or doesn't have a lot of money.

Field trips to see plants. Get an inexpensive tree and plant guide, then visit a park, nature area or a nursery. In a city, you might visit a conservatory or florist. Some communities have an arboretum complete with labels on trees and plants. Take a walk through your neighborhood and look for unusual trees and plants. Take a nature walk with a naturalist. They like to answer questions. Walk along a stream and note the different plants which grow near water. Visit a farm and look for plants such as hay and alfalfa used for feeding animals.

Ask your child, "How are these plants different from the plants in a vegetable garden? How are they the same? What do they need to grow?"

Resources. Several books which will help your child understand growing things are:

> *Kids Gardening, A Kid's Guide to Messing Around in the Dirt*
> by Kevin and Kim Raftery
> *175 Amazing Nature Experiments* by Rosie Harlow and Gareth Morgan

LIVING THINGS — ANIMALS

Children enjoy being around animals. In my classroom we often have a small "zoo" including a caged bird, fish, hamster, snake or guinea pig.

Another teacher brings her pet rabbit to school. Children work hard to earn points so they can hold the rabbit during the day. The rabbit sleeps on their laps and allows them to feed and pet him. The teacher has discovered that some unruly students become relaxed and quiet when holding a big furry rabbit on their laps.

A small pet for the home. At home your child might ask for a hamster or rat for his/her room. Before you get a pet however, sit down with your child and ask a few questions.

- Do you have time to care for a pet?
- Will you be responsible to feed and water the pet and keep the cage clean?

Buying a pet. If you feel your child is old enough and mature enough to care for a pet, consider a small animal. This could be a hamster, guinea pig or rat.

A hamster is inexpensive to feed and maintain and it can be left alone for several days when you go away. Cages can be found at pet stores, garage sales, thrift stores and through the classified ads, so you don't need a large outlay of money. Also, an empty bird cage or fish aquarium can be used but be sure the doors and covers are secure. Hamsters are real escape artists.

Food, such as a packaged mixture designed for hamsters, is good. To add variety to the diet, add small amounts of fresh fruits and vegetables.

Before buying a pet, it would be helpful for your child to read a book or two about special pets and their care. Some good resources for children to look over are:

A Step-By-Step Book About Hamsters by Anmarie Barrie
Guinea Pigs: A Complete Pet Owner's Manual by Lucia Vriends-Parent
The New Rabbit Handbook by Lucia Vriends-Parent

NOTE: Each year I explain to my students that dogs and cats are wonderful pets but they should be neutered. I tell them that **each hour** in the United States 720 dogs and 660 cats are put to death because no one wants them. That means over 12 million unwanted animals die each year.

As I drive to my post office each week, I have great difficulty passing the building where the animals are kept in cages until put to death. All children should be taught to be responsible for feeding their animals and also to keep them from breeding again and again when there will be no home for their babies.

EARTH SCIENCE — WATER

Water is all around us. Have your child trace the outlines of the oceans on a globe. Afterward, discuss the concept with your youngster that water floats up in the sky as clouds and falls down to the earth as snow or rain. Also discuss the fact that water seeps into our soil and can pass into the cells of organisms.

Your child should understand that we have two types of water, the salty water of the ocean and the fresh water of rivers, streams and most lakes.

Who needs water? All animals and plants need water to live. When you plant a garden, the plants must have water to grow.

Also remind your child that humans and animals need water to stay alive. As humans we need it not only for drinking but for bathing, washing clothes, brushing teeth and cleaning our houses. Animals need water to drink, and some stand in water in hot weather to stay cool.

We also use water in the oceans to transport ships around the world with supplies to help us live better lives. We use water in lakes, canals and rivers for transportation as well as recreation.

Remind your child that water is so precious we dig wells to draw it up from under the ground, build dams to store it and also keep it in reservoirs and water tanks.

Make a wave-in-a-bottle. Your child can learn that mixing a variety of ingredients together can create different reactions. A simple way to do this is to make a wave-bottle which is really a tiny ocean.

You'll need a large, empty plastic soda bottle, vegetable oil (baby oil works well), water, food coloring and turpentine or paint thinner.

- Begin with a clean, clear plastic two-quart soda bottle.
- Fill 1/2 full with water and add six drops of blue food coloring.
- Fill 2/3 of the remaining space in the bottle with baby or vegetable oil.

- Add turpentine or paint thinner to fill the bottle entirely.
- Put the cap on and seal tightly, then set on its side to settle.
- Tip the bottle back and forth gently to make waves.

SCIENCE FAIRS

Most schools hold science fairs which provide students with the opportunity to work independently on displays or experiments. The following are some topics my students enjoyed turning into projects at our fairs.

- Earthquakes or volcanoes
- Weather, including demonstrations about rain, clouds, wind or air pressure
- Astronomy, focusing on stars, meteors or comets
- Physics projects such as electricity, gravity or energy

Science Fair Reports. The scientific method is reflected in the report used for the science fair. Your child's teacher may have a particular form to use. Many schools have printed outlines available and teachers go over these in their classes before the fair. In this case, your child should follow the rules set down by the Science Fair Committee at his/her school.

If there isn't a form, remember that the science fair report has two parts. They cover how your child set up the experiment and what was learned while doing the research for the project.

The report contains the following information:

- The hypothesis. This is the statement that is tested during the experiment to see if it is true.
- The experiment. This is the method used to check if the theory is correct.
    1. List the materials used.
    2. Note the numbered steps your youngster performed.
    3. Your child then shows the results.
- A conclusion
    Your child will explain what the experiment shows, including whether the original hypothesis was proved or disproved.

Your child may also want to include a bibliography of all books, magazines and perhaps CD-ROM encyclopedia resources. Help your child do this.

Displaying the project. For your display, you want something that is eye catching, easy-to-read and explains all the important aspects of your project.

- Check with the instructor in charge of the Science Fair for dimensions of the display.
- Start with sturdy, brightly colored cardboard or tagboard sheets fastened together so they will stand up.
- Help your child select a "grabbing" title so people will stop and look.
- Use pictures, bright colors and large letters on the display.
- Tell the story of the project on the cardboard panels in a well-organized manner.

HINT: If your child is doing a demonstration which needs electricity, remind him or her to alert the person in charge of the fair of the need to be near an electrical outlet with an extension cord provided.

Encourage your child. As you encourage your youngster in science, you may find your own interest whetted. One father got so involved in

an elementary book on sun and rain, he bought himself a comprehensive weather book to study.

And a mother, helping plant some radish seeds, ended up with a windowsill herb garden and a new cookbook.

Both of these parents show their children that science is much more than book learning.

I would suggest that you begin early in your child's life to provide experiences where the youngster can observe the world both at your doorstep and also well away from home. Visit national forests, zoos, planetariums, fish farms, a dam or a flower garden in the park.

After observing, when your child asks questions, answer them the best you can. If you don't know the answer, say, "Let's go to the library and see what we can find." Ongoing encouragement will help your child continue to delve into the world of science.

IDEA: Television offers many outstanding programs on science. Consider programs on the Discovery Channel, Learning Channel or The Public Broadcasting Service. Refer to my chapter on computers for outstanding science software for your child to explore.

Here are some outstanding science books for your child's home library.

What Makes It Rain? by Susan Mayes

Where Does Electricity Come From? by Susan Mayes

What Makes A Car Go? by Sophy Tahta

Introduction To Physics by Amanda Kent and Alan Ward

Discovery: Inventors, Scientists, Explorers by Struan Reid and Patricia Fara

Writing Is Essential Preschool-Kindergarten

"First and foremost, unless children — <u>especially</u> children with disabilities — learn to read, write, spell, keyboard, and communicate from the earliest and most precious formative years, their fullest potential will be lost. Parents should begin this teaching process in their own home."

Carol Lee Berger, Communication Disorders Specialist, National Autism and Communication Research Institute, Walterville, Oregon

Some people claim that television, cellular phones and other modern technologies will make the written word obsolete. On the contrary, competent writing ability is a skill which is the passport to learning and eventually to rewarding employment.

Writing skills are essential. We often jot down notes or thoughts regarding things to do, people to see and items to buy. We write letters to friends, create reports at work and fill in applications for credit, employment or a driver's license.

Studies indicate that by the time today's children enter the workforce, at least half of them will use computers on their jobs. Being able to write is absolutely necessary to operate a computer.

The Information Age has arrived and your youngster must be ready to navigate the information highway. This includes knowledge of sending e-mail messages, writing out reports and memos and accessing databases and resource material on the Internet.

Recently, for example, the Library of Congress developed THOMAS (named for Thomas Jefferson), an on-line service providing information on Congressional activities. People with computers and modems can view Congressional Reports, study bills and obtain a directory of all members of Congress.

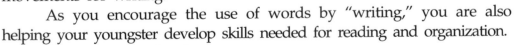

The ability to write lets children share their knowledge, experiences and feelings. Very young children like to make marks with pencils and crayons. They also enjoy what we term "scribble-writing."

Guide your child with his or her scribble-writing from left to right and putting words in a column. This gives your youngster experience in the correct movements for writing.

As you encourage the use of words by "writing," you are also helping your youngster develop skills needed for reading and organization.

Children write for three reasons:

- To communicate
- To entertain themselves
- To try something new

They learn a lot about language from their writing. They often start by identifying the letters in their own name. Later they will identify single words, then phrases and finally a sentence. Provide your child with many opportunities to build a strong foundation of words.

Writing supplies. An important way to encourage your child to write is to provide plenty of writing materials. Start as early as ages three and four to encourage your child to keep supplies together.

All of my students have a special box with writing supplies inside their desks. When they write, this box is placed on the desktop so they have everything they need at their fingertips.

Your child's "office" should have a desk with plenty of writing paper, pencils and pens in the drawer. If the desk doesn't have a drawer, place a basket or box on a shelf and keep it filled.

Materials should include pencils (both lead and colored), crayons, erasers, scissors (rounded ends for young children; left-handed if needed), colored pens, ruler, stapler, transparent tape and glue. Of course, the amount or number and kinds of materials placed in the basket will depend upon the needs, ability and age of the child.

PARENT TIP: **Remind your youngster that pencils, pens and other objects don't belong in the mouth.**

Writing experiences. At the preschool-kindergarten age, it is vital to provide your youngster with many writing experiences to develop eye-hand coordination, fine motor coordination and to train large muscles. You should encourage writing in all possible situations.
- Model writing for your child from an early age.
- Have your child sit with you when you address Christmas cards, make a grocery list or write thank-you notes.
- Set an example of writing thank-you notes <u>before</u> you use the gift.
- Have your child dictate notes and messages to relatives or friends.

Scribble-writing. When you sit and write your grocery list, have extra paper and pencils available. As you say "soap" and "bread," have your child scribble-write on a piece of paper while you write on your list. Always remind the youngster to write from left to right and in columns.

Writing booklet. To encourage your preschooler or kindergartner to write often, make a writing journal by stapling about fifteen four-by-eight-inch pages together. Make a construction paper cover and put the child's name on it. Make several of these at a time and always have one in your child's writing basket.

Your child should scribble-write in the writing booklets. He or she may use a crayon and make only marks, circles or scribbles but this is the beginning of letters. Encourage this.

Painting easel. If you do not have an easel, look for one at garage sales or flea markets. Using an easel to make big circles and long lines promotes large muscle development for your child.

Purchase pads of large paper for your child to use with paints or large felt pens. Some pens are scented, so these could be used as a special treat. (Be sure you don't get permanent markers by mistake!)

IDEA: Have your child wear an old shirt turned backwards as a painter's smock. This will keep clothes clean and be easy to wash for the next painting session.

In the kitchen. Have paper and pencils available for your child to use while you work. Children enjoy copying words and pictures from cereal and other boxes, for example.

Field trips. Anything children see can be an experience to write about. That is why a variety of experiences will enhance your child's writing. Take your child to the zoo, your place of employment, a bowling alley, an airport, a candy factory or an auto mall. If you do not have the time, ask grandparents or friends to take your child when they visit interesting places in your community. These experiences can then be transferred to paper, either in pictures or scribble-writing.

Seasonal writing. A good angle for writing and drawing pictures is to use the themes from holidays such as Valentine's Day, Arbor Day, Easter, Mother's Day, Father's Day, Fourth of July, Harvest Festival Days, Halloween, Thanksgiving, Christmas, Hanukkah and Kwanza.

Let's take Valentine's Day as an example. Making Valentine cards is an old tradition.

- Brainstorm with your child and ask questions. "Why do we give cards to people we love? Why do we celebrate Valentine's Day? What do you want to write and draw on your card to Grandma and Grandpa?"
- Together decide on the size of the card and then cut one out using construction paper.
- Allow time for your child to either cut out colorful hearts or color a picture on the card.
- He or she can dictate a message for you to write. Then ask to have an additional message "scribble-written."
- You can also write the child's message using dots and let the youngster connect the dots.

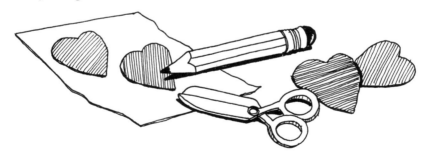

Writing while in the car. When I take my students on field trips, I prepare them ahead for writing and drawing.

You can keep a writing booklet, pencils and erasers stored in a plastic bag or box ready for writing. Use the box lid, a lap-sized clipboard or an art pad as a writing desk.

At toy and teacher bookstores, you can find Stowaway Plastic™ boxes with Dry-Wipe™ boards fitted into the top. Add Dry-Erase Markers™ which come in a variety of bright colors.

Writing dictation. Since preschoolers and kindergartners enjoy dictating stories to adults, this is a good way to expand your child's vocabulary.

After an exciting event, whether happy, sad or even frightening, have your child describe what happened. Write this on a large sheet of writing paper, leaving space to illustrate the story.

Ask, "Where did we go? What did you see? What happened next?" Continue eliciting information from the experience. Afterward, read the story to your child and encourage artwork.

Post the pages on the refrigerator or on your child's bulletin board for all to see and admire. After a while, mail the story to a relative who is likely to write back. Positive feedback will increase your child's interest in writing.

Writing Is Essential Grades One-Six

"Read good literature to your child to help make the connection between reading and writing. As you provide these experiences with published works, your youngster will be able to get a glimpse of the ideas and experiences that can inspire a written work.

"Also be sure to expose your child to a variety of literature, from brochures, to road maps to flyers for a play. Children are interested in things that make a difference in their everyday lives."

Christina Cheng, Fourth-Grade Teacher, Pelham Road Elementary School,
Greenville, South Carolina

PRIMARY GRADES

When children can string words into sentences, it's time to develop the "art of writing." One way is to make it an important part of your family communications. Enclose an affectionate note in your child's lunch box. In a written note, invite your child to go to the video store.

Post a message requiring a written reply on your family bulletin board. Mail a postcard to your child, even if you're both at home.

Write a note of appreciation and leave it on your child's pillow at night. All these brief written messages will make writing useful and real to your child.

An important aspect of writing is the use of correct grammar. I'll discuss interesting ways you can help your child develop good grammar and then provide you with information on how your child can develop into a successful writer.

Grammar games. Few people really enjoy grammar and most of us stumble occasionally. (Should I say, "Joe and me" or "Joe and I"?) But there are some fun ways to teach grammar and parts of speech.

When children first begin to write sentences, they need to understand the difference between a "noun" (naming part), a "verb" (action word) and an "adjective" (describing word).

Talk about "nouns": words that name a person, place or thing. Nouns tell us who or what we are talking about.

Write out nouns and scramble the letters as you write the words on small pieces of paper. Use words such as cat, house, store, nose and foot. Set the timer and see how quickly your child can unscramble the words.

Next use "verbs": words that show action such as walk, clap, climb, skipped, blew and swam. Have your youngster pantomime words by blowing, clapping or skipping in place.

Finally, introduce your child to "adjectives": words that describe, such as big, old, four, long, yellow and sweet. Talk about the importance of describing words in our world. Explain that these words put color and numbers into our writing and make sentences more accurate and interesting.

Once your child understands parts of speech, you can play a game. Write a sentence with each word on a separate slip of paper, with a period after the last word.

Use crayons to make one blue line under the noun, three red lines under the verb and one green squiggle line under any adjectives.

Then "shuffle" the words and see how quickly your youngster can form the sentence correctly again.

PARENT TIP: **If you would like a language book to use at home, ask the school principal if any will be given away at the end of the year. Or ask if you can go to the district warehouse and pick up a discarded book. Also, Parent-Teacher Bookstores have excellent books and grammar workbooks to help your child improve language and writing skills.**

Ask, "Does this sentence make sense?" Or, "Where is your noun, your verb or adjective?" Do not allow your child to make the same mistakes over and over because it is difficult to break a pattern.

During the primary grades, children begin to write sentences, then move on to paragraphs and short letters. Continue to check the work each step of the way.

Indenting, capital letters and periods. I've had a problem getting my students to take the time to punctuate their writing correctly. Many of them want to rush through an assignment rather than follow the rules.

Your child must take the time to make a capital letter to begin each sentence, use a period at the end and leave space between sentences. You may need to remind your youngster to form a habit of punctuating correctly <u>all</u> the time. By working on this at home, the pattern will carry over to school and he/she will become a much more successful writer.

Discuss why certain sentences require a period and others an exclamation point or question mark at the end. Ask your child to read sentences aloud so you can decide together the type of punctuation needed.

HINT: Remind your child to start a new paragraph each time a thought changes. In the primary grades, I insist that my students place two fingers next to the margin when they begin a new paragraph. This helps them remember to indent.

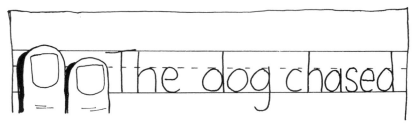

PARENT TIP: **Children do not like to proofread their work but they must practice catching their own errors. If you do not have time to check your child's work, ask an older sibling to proofread with the youngster. By doing this, you'll cut down on the amount of homework which must be done over. Praise your youngster each time the work is done neatly and correctly.**

A proofreading checklist. Here are some questions to ask your child as you look over writing assignments.
- Is the paper written neatly?
- Is the title on the top line and in the center of the page?
- Did you draw straight margins?
- Do all sentences begin with a capital letter?
- Did you use the right punctuation at the end of each sentence?
- Is the spelling correct?
- Did you proofread your work?
- Did you use your best handwriting?

PARENT TIP: **Teachers seldom give writing assignments without first passing out an information sheet, placing an outline on the chalkboard for the child to copy or explaining what is expected in detail. Be sure** your child comes home with some type of paper describing the writing assignment. If your youngster says, "I forgot," have him or her call a friend for the information. Some children "forget" assignments on purpose. Much later the parent receives a warning notice from the teacher. Don't let this happen to you.

Sample of a friendly letter. Friendly letters have a heading, salutation, body, closing and signature. It's fun to include a postscript (or even two), as primary students *love* writing postscripts. Here is the letter one of my children wrote to her parents from camp. This is the model for a friendly letter.

> Trout Creek Camp
> Troutdale, Oregon
> July 6

Dear Mom and Dad,

I went swimming today but the water was cold. My teeth chattered. I swam from the dock to the boat ramp and it was fun.

We had pizza for dinner last night and I ate it all but the olives. You know how I hate olives.

Can you come up early on Sunday so you can see what I made in crafts? I made something special for you.

Love,

Taylor

PS. We toasted marshmallows at a campfire last night.

A business letter. I ask students to write several reports during the year. Depending upon the information needed, they can write for material on their subject to a Chamber of Commerce, Department of Fish and Game or perhaps a Visitors' Bureau.

Business letters include a heading, inside address, salutation, body, closing and signature.

Your youngster will write a business letter when asking for information, inviting a guest speaker to class, making a complaint, offering suggestions or writing to public officials.

This is a sample business letter a student might write to an entomologist (insect specialist) soliciting help for an assignment.

106 Blackhawk Drive
Hometown, CA 95422
October 12, 19__

Mr. Al Villegas
106 Main Street
Bugtown, CA 95424

Dear Mr. Villegas,

We are doing a science unit on bugs this semester and I want to write about the Goliath beetle of West Africa. My friend told me you have information and pictures on this large beetle. Could you send me a picture and some information about the beetle? I need it by next Wednesday so please hurry.

Yours truly,

Rocky Marshall

Thank-you letters and notes. I frequently invite guest speakers to come to my classroom. After the visit, I have my students write thank-you letters. I ask them to illustrate their letters with a picture about the subject discussed.

The parts of a thank-you letter or note are the date, salutation, body, closing and signature.

Your child may also write a thank-you note for a gift or to someone who helped on a project.

One of my students wrote this letter after we had a guest speaker from the Department of Fish and Game.

Nov. 5, 19__

Dear Mr. Thomas,

    Thank you so much for coming to our classroom and telling us about the fish in the Sacramento River. I loved the part about when the fish were swimming up the special pools called a fish ladder.

    Thank you for bringing the slides for us to see. I could not believe how big some of the fish were.

    What you said will help me write my report on salmon.

Thank you,

Michael Y.

The envelope. Your youngster also needs to know how to address an envelope correctly. It is important that the address not be in pencil but that ink or a typewriter be used. Also, the handwriting must be legible. It should look like the following:

```
 _____
| David Lu                        [stamp] |
| 554 Apple Ct.                           |
| Histown, NE                             |
|     68501                               |
|                                         |
|            Susan Long                   |
|            3312  Ridge Drive            |
|            Hertown, OR   97208          |
|_____|
```

Other forms of writing. Many children who dislike writing letters will write rhymes, poems, jokes or puns for others to enjoy.

    HINT: Help your child make a *My Friends* booklet. Primary girls, in particular, enjoy having their friends write little thoughts in this book. Rather than buying one, help your youngster make one out of lined paper (about four-by-six inches) and cover the booklet with construction paper. The child can either draw a picture or use stickers to decorate the cover.

Many primary children also enjoy writing with extra-tall pencils (with different objects hanging from the top) and clever erasers. These are writing items your child might enjoy receiving for a birthday or Christmas gift.

Many teachers encourage youngsters to write a story for the Book Fair each year. Children write and illustrate the story and design and make the book cover. The books are displayed and prizes given; often the children are honored at an awards assembly. Check to see if your child's school offers such a program.

Writing supplies. Children quickly lose interest in writing if they must hunt for a pencil and paper. Be sure to keep a ready supply in the "home office." Besides paper, pencils, felt pens and scissors, older children will enjoy a stapler, paper clips and a ruler, colored felt pens, ball point pens, paper, tape and scissors.

Some students enjoy writing much more when they can design their own stationery. Buy a tablet of colored writing paper. Encourage your youngster to use a felt pen to draw pictures or make wavy borders around the edges of the paper. Colorful stickers may also be used.

Primary girls, in particular, enjoy developing their own unique writing style. This often means drawing a heart instead of a dot over the letter "i" or beginning each sentence with a flowery capital letter. As long as it is readable, I accept this type of writing in the primary grades.

Writing experiences. A great deal of your child's writing at this age will come under the direction of the teacher as class assignments.

However, you should still provide your child with a number of experiences to stimulate writing ideas.

A family bulletin board. Your child will spend many hours working on letters, a journal and reports. This activity needs to be recognized. Set aside a space in your home where you can display writing accomplishments. Buy blue ribbon and make your own First-Place ribbon award for writing in your home. This tells your child, "You are special and a budding writer."

IDEA: Some supermarkets and stationery stores now stock ready-made award ribbons in a variety of colors.

Using a computer. Writing by hand is a chore for many youngsters, but they love writing on a computer. If the teacher agrees, have your youngster write letters and reports on the computer.

PARENT TIP: **I am *very* much against letting children do the "hunt-and-peck" method of typing on the keyboard. Start by using a program that teaches correct finger placement for typing. As your child moves into the workplace, this will become even more important in job competition. For information on keyboard-learning software, see the chapter on computers.**

INTERMEDIATE GRADES

"The writing process is not a recipe to follow, but a journey to explore."
Pam Lloyd, Fourth/Fifth Grade Teacher, Klatt Elementary School, Anchorage, Alaska

In the intermediate grades youngsters will learn more about the parts of speech as writing becomes more sophisticated and complex. Besides the nouns, verbs, and adjectives I've already discussed, it's necessary that children know and understand the proper usage of "pronouns," "conjunctions," "adverbs," "prepositions," and "interjections" in order to write well.

"Prepositions" are words such as in, on, under and before. They tell us how things connect one to the other. For example, a sentence which I had my students write follows:

A beautiful black cat lives <u>under</u> our classroom.   (This was true until we adopted the cat and brought it inside to live.)

"Adverbs" are words which provide us with information about the verb.   A sentence using an adverb is, *The boy walked <u>slowly</u> down the street.*   The adverb tells us how the boy walked.

Children enjoy using interjections.   When writing, they can toss in a word or two to indicate strong feelings.   The following is an example.

Good Grief! He missed the ball.

Continue to note errors in your child's writings in the intermediate grades and set aside a few minutes each night to drill him/her on the proper usage of grammar.

In grades four, five and six, your youngster will begin to write more often and will be asked to write longer reports about a science project or social studies.   Book reports will be longer and more detailed, as well.

Writing a report.   Your child should follow a checklist for each writing assignment.

- Choose a topic if the teacher hasn't assigned one.
- Develop the ideas for the report.   Be sure it has a beginning, middle and end.   Do interviews, take notes, use resources.
- Write an outline.
- Write a draft.   Your child should read the draft, and have someone else read it, too.   Does the report or story flow logically and make sense?
- Write the introduction with the main topic sentence.
- Write the body of the report.

- Write a conclusion. Repeat the main idea and sum up what needs to be said about the subject.
- Proofread and edit the report.
- Write the final draft. Is it neat and readable? (Did someone help proofread it?)

NOTE: Some reports require a Bibliography. If so, a sample entry using one of my books is included here.

Williamson, Bonnie. *101 Ways To Put Pizazz Into Your Teaching*. Sacramento, CA: Dynamic Teaching, 1991.

Writing a book review. Your child's teacher may have a preferred form to use for fiction, non-fiction, essays and reports. If not, here is a suitable book-report format.

Also, your child should know whether this is to be both a written and an oral report. If an oral report is required, your youngster should practice in front of family members several times before giving the book report in class.

- Write the student's name and date at the top left side of the page.
- Center the title of the book on the top line of the page and underline the book title.
- In small letters write "by" centered under the title with the book author's name centered under "by."
- Indent and begin the paragraph. Begin with the name of the book (underlined) followed by a theme statement. This is the main idea of the book. Make that first paragraph interesting so other students will want to hear more.
- Give the summary of the story. What was the plot? (This part of the report should have a beginning, middle and end. Readers should know the names and something about the characters in the story.)

- Finally, critique the story. (Your child is no longer in the primary grades and "This was a good book" isn't enough any more. Ideas to explore: What conflicts were resolved by the characters? What did they learn? Describe how they dressed in the story.)

PARENT TIP: **Some teachers give extra credit when students include either a hand-drawn illustration of the story or pictures cut out of magazines. Youngsters who are nervous standing in front of peers often feel more comfortable when they can show something while giving a book review.**

Some children enjoy writing and drawing comic strips to share with friends. Encourage your child to be creative when writing. Ideas will flow and your youngster will enjoy the process.

Using a computer. Many children prefer writing on a computer. If you have one available, see that your youngster learns how to do word processing, using appropriate function keys or the mouse. Again, remember that correct fingering on the keyboard is very important.

SUGGESTION: KidDesk™, a software program for children ages three to ten, can be accessed through America Online. The Edmark Education Company has developed this outstanding program which allows America Online to connect your child with a Pen Pal.

The program provides an opportunity for your child to develop a friendship across the miles; and it requires writing. There are education newsgroups on Internet with similar programs.

Produce clean copy. When children use a computer, always have them print out the first draft. Sit down together and proofread the work. Often, mistakes are overlooked on the screen. By using a red pencil on the draft, you can help your child develop what editors call "clean copy." Have your child then go back to the computer and make corrections on the screen. (Some teachers will want to see draft copies as well as final copies.)

Writing for fun. The things your child might write are limited only by his or her imagination. Create greeting cards. Some children are now writing wedding invitations for their mothers and fathers if they marry for a second time. Your youngster can use the computer to publish flyers for a garage sale, an invitation to a party or family reunion.

Some classes even write entire books, often in connection with the annual Book Fair. This is the time to encourage your child to use the computer. The work is neat, clean and easy to read. Also, your youngster can use a variety of fonts to make the report interesting to the viewers.

Becoming a graphic artist. A number of my students who have problems writing reports are budding artists. If your child shows an interest in drawing, encourage it.

One young student draws constantly with his parents' encouragement. When they go out to eat, he immediately takes the folded paper napkin and brings out his drawing pens. He entertains family members with his clever drawings while waiting to be served.

Not every student will become a writer but some might become illustrators. The field of design pays well, and your child, if interested, should be given all the encouragement needed to pursue such a career.

Other reports. I have provided you with only a few of the reports your child will be expected to write in the intermediate grades. Check with your child's teacher for classroom writing forms to follow.

While all aspects of learning are important, a person's ability to express himself or herself accurately, logically and legibly in writing is crucial.

Computer-Wise Kids
Preschool-Sixth Grade

"I've found that children get motivated when using the computer. Whether a student is in the primary or intermediate grades, speaks fluent or limited English, or even dislikes schoolwork, using a computer can greatly increase his or her interest in reading and math.

Children can also write short stories, illustrate them and read them to their families. I've found that many boys and girls having difficulty with writing become budding authors when encouraged to write their stories by using a computer's word processing."

Mark Larson, Fifth-Grade Teacher, Mt. View School, Shelton, Washington

Kids and computers go together. My students walk into the computer lab with big smiles. They enjoy the bright colors, the lessons which move across the screen and the ease of writing their reports.

Half of today's children will use computers when they move into the workforce. Your youngster must begin to master these new technologies now.

In this chapter I'll give information to help you select a computer for your child, talk about where to purchase one, talk about building your own and provide information about computer software, magazines and books.

Understandably, some of you will be more "computer-literate" than others so I'll define major computer terms I use in a short Glossary just before the Software Review at the end of this chapter. Also, I'll cover only some of the more important aspects of computers as they relate to your child and school. For those who want more information, dozens of computer books are available.

Read this entire chapter before you make a computer decision. Some accessories, CD-ROMs and other software may be of particular interest and are discussed just before the preview of software programs at the end of this chapter.

Take-home computers. Many school districts provide the opportunity to borrow a computer for a while. Prior to checkout an instructor may teach parent and child how to use and care for the computer and how to operate the software. The child gets software lessons corresponding with his/her level of subjects at school. Check to see if your district has such a program.

Choosing a computer. Parents often tell me, "I want to buy a computer for my child. Should I buy an IBM or a Macintosh?" Both have many advocates. IBM PCs and compatible PCs have good power, price and speed. They have more available software from which to choose. Also, they're more widely used in the business world.

The "Mac" is usually easier to use and master. But IBMs and Macs are becoming more and more similar and children have very few problems moving from a Mac to an IBM.

When choosing a home computer some suggestions might help.

- Pick one you are familiar with at work or elsewhere.
- Ask what kind of computers your child uses at school.
- Be an informed customer.
- Look at computer ads in the newspaper. Study words such as RAM, modem, Windows©, sound card, HD, monitor, video card and CD-ROM. Find out what they mean if you don't know.

NOTE: If you're just thinking about buying a computer, consider the following statement.

"When a student turns in a clean, typewritten paper, teachers have a tendency to grade that paper as much as a full grade point higher because of readability and presentation," says a school resource teacher. Research also shows that when students use word processors, they tend to show an increase in both the quality and quantity of what they write.

If you've ever written or typed an item the conventional way, you know how discouraging it is to discover something important left out or some incorrect information and have to redo the whole thing.

It's even more disappointing for a child to have to rewrite a whole assignment. A computer can easily make the necessary corrections while the rest of the material remains intact. After the changes, your child can push a couple of keys and reprint the material which then becomes an acceptable, perfect-looking report.

Since writing is more pleasant this way, your child will often find it's something he/she <u>wants</u> to do, rather than <u>has</u> to do. Also, his/her competence and interest in reading, language, spelling, math and science can all be considerably increased through computer use.

No matter what major item I purchase, I always check the *Consumer's Guide* and similar resources at the library. Ask the reference librarian to help you find the latest information on home computers.

Take notes or photocopy helpful information and charts which indicate product quality, durability and service availability.

Look for books which tell how to purchase a computer. Find a glossary of pertinent terminology. Review the resources at this chapter's end and consider buying some computer magazines and books. When you enter a new land, you must understand the language.

Besides reading, if possible, this is the time to set aside a few additional hours to help prepare for buying a computer. Enroll in a class to learn about computers in general, the vocabulary and hardware. You might find such help in an evening extension class at a community college or high school, a learning-exchange program, an alternate learning program or a class through a computer users' group.

You will learn that children's software and CD-ROMs require a great deal of computer memory (RAM), especially for graphics. If possible, buy enough right away rather than upgrade later on. You'll often hear the term "bundle" used in stores. This means the store sells the computer system, monitor, keyboard, printer and software all together. They often include a modem and CD-ROM drive. In some cases the price is right. But be sure the computer has enough power and the printer is the type you'll need. You should consider these things and your needs before you go out and actually buy a computer.

SUGGESTIONS: If you plan to buy a computer, be aware that hardware requirements can change drastically in six months in this field. Also, remember that children's educational software and games need heavy-duty hardware. For any kind of flexibility in the programs you will want to run, you'll need to purchase a multimedia CD-ROM which is used for encyclopedia and similar programs and many games.

Before you buy a computer, spend several hours looking at software, preferably with your child. Take along a clipboard and pencil to copy the system requirements listed on each package of interest. You'll see whether you need an IBM PC or a Macintosh. You should also see how much RAM you need, if you must use Windows©, whether

CD-ROM is required, what type of monitor, and whether a special kind of printer is needed. After your research, you should see an emerging pattern for the amount and kinds of hardware you'll need for the types of programs you will want.

If you have a computer-wise friend, sit down together and go over the notes you've made and the knowledge you've gained. Include your child here and in your research if he or she is old enough and has any computer knowledge and/or interest. List the good points of each computer and your various options. Decide also how much computer and what accessories you will need now and in the reasonable future. Can you justify and afford the "desirable" package (or better)? If not, buy as much as you can afford.

Good word processing and help with basic school skills are your biggest necessity and are not expensive in themselves. Rather than do without a computer altogether, postpone the "nice-to-haves" like lots of speed and power, the latest games, modems, etc. and concentrate on having good-writing and basic-skills capability available for your family.

You can always upgrade later, and by then you will have even more choices. Also, your young "computer whiz" may have a number of additional good ideas to add toward what your family actually needs (and wants) in a computer. For now, your next decision will be which store(s) to visit. If feasible, take your youngster along to help make your all-important purchase.

Where should you buy your computer? Again, this is where you need to do your homework first. If you live in a city, you'll find a number of stores and types of stores selling computers. Don't get confused. Take your time to listen and learn.

- Independent computer dealers usually have smaller stores where they build, package or sell only computers and computer-related merchandise. You can even have a computer built to your specifications there. I had this done and am very happy with mine. When I have a problem, I pick up the phone and get prompt help.
- Other stores are called computer superstores or warehouses. At these stores, you'll find aisles and aisles of computers and software. Their prices are often cheaper than other stores,

and their sales help may or may not be as knowledgeable as at the independent dealers.

- Electronic department stores and discount houses sell televisions, washers, stereos and computers these days. They often have a limited selection to choose from and their salespeople may not be familiar with computers. These are usually not a good choice unless you know exactly what you want beforehand and you know their prices. If you can get what you want for less money than elsewhere, then it may be a good idea.

- Mail order is another option. Look in computer magazines for listings. Ask your computer-wise friend to help you select a known, reputable dealer. I purchased my VGA monitor from a mail-order store with good results. Their prices are usually good, but make sure service problems can be handled locally.

CAUTION: There are a number of questions to ask and things to think about when you shop.

- "Where did you (the salesperson) get your computer training, and do you own a computer?"

- "How much service can I expect from this store if a problem develops? Must I bring the computer in to you? Can someone come to my home and repair it? If so, how much extra does it cost? Must I send it to the manufacturer?"

- "What kind of support will you give me? Can I call you on the telephone and get help? For how long?"

- "What kind of warranty do you give? One year? Two?" (Try for two years.)

Your special needs to remember when buying a computer are well-trained salespeople, an adequate and dependable computer and accessories, and good service and support after buying the product.

Printers. When you buy your computer, you'll need a printer. Base this purchase on the age and needs of your child. How many reports is the child asked to write? Could the youngster get by with a dot-matrix or should you invest in an ink-jet or laser printer? Keep in mind that ink-jet and laser-printer prices have come down. This might be a wise investment for now and the future.

If you can, consider a color printer. One outstanding product is the HP (Hewlett-Packard) Color Ink-Jet printer. If you're buying an ink-jet or laser printer, be sure there's enough RAM on the printer to permit your child to print graphics. Some good color printers now cost under $300. Try to purchase a well-known brand.

If you're on a tight budget, buy a 24-pin dot-matrix printer. Again, buy a name brand. These don't print the sharp, crisp copy that ink-jet or laser printers do, but some are considered "near-letter-quality." They're acceptable for most needs.

Purchase a surge suppressor. With all the money spent on a computer and printer, it's vital that you have a surge suppressor that is more than a plug strip. In case of a sudden surge of electricity, the suppressor will protect against an overvoltage which might burn out your equipment.

Buy back-up disks. It's also important that you periodically back up your files. That way if any should ever be "lost" or inadvertently erased you'll still have the backup.

HINT: If you're working with vital information which you can't afford to lose, store one set of back-up files away from your home. While writing this book, I've stored updated disks in my bank safe-deposit box. If a fire or burglars should ever hit my office, I'll always have a backup.

Computer desks. I often feel sorry for my young computer-lab students who can be uncomfortable when they sit at tables in large chairs where their feet can't touch the floor.

A California man, Eric Ayzenberg, has solved the problem if the computer will be set up for child use only. He designs and builds brightly painted, adjustable computer desks and chairs for youngsters aged three to twelve. For more information call (818) 584-4070.

Build your own computer. While writing this chapter, I took a class called "Building Your Own Computer." I was fascinated by the information and pleased that I was able to understand a great many of the technical terms used.

To summarize, it appeared to me that a computer is a metal box in which you place a lot of components which reminded me of Lego™ parts. You hook up "A" to "A" and "B" to "B." You put a certain function board in this slot and another in that slot. I'm making this sound very simple, which it isn't, but watching the process of building the computer reminded me of hooking toys together.

While most people would probably be better off to buy their first computer outright, some might like the challenge and satisfaction of building their own. If you belong to the latter group and wish to consider building a computer, take a class on how to do it. You'll learn the parts such as the motherboard, power supply, hard and floppy drives, monitors, controllers and keyboards. You'll also watch an instructor take a computer apart and you'll learn how to put it together again.

Several of my friends have taken a similar class and built their own computers, one with the help of his child. His son built a keyboard out of old keyboards. However, I need to warn you that this

is risky business if you attempt to do it "on-the-cheap." Unless you are a "computer whiz" and really know your way around computer swap meets or salvage stores, don't do it! One young man in my class went to a swap meet and purchased thirteen computer components. When he brought them home, not one of them worked and he couldn't return them.

Rather, if you wish to build a computer, take the class but purchase your components from a reliable dealer as did one man I met. He bought all parts from a nearby dealer who was available to answer questions as he worked. The original cost for building the computer was less than one he had planned to buy, but like so many people, he decided to add numerous "bells and whistles" which escalated the price.

I certainly recommend you take a computer-building class. Even if you never build one, think of the knowledge you'll gain and how you can share the information with your youngster. It will make you more knowledgeable and more comfortable with your system. Your computer will have lost its mystery, and you'll know how you can upgrade it in the future. You also should be able to make any necessary repairs, or at least recognize where problems are.

An outstanding reference book for this area is *Upgrading and Repairing PCs* by Scott Mueller.

Spend time with your child on the computer. After you've bought or built your computer, you will want your child to become familiar with it as soon as possible. Experts say that children under the age of three should be playing with blocks and fun toys instead of computers. But from age three onward, children can begin to do computer lessons.

At first, you'll need to mostly stay with them at the computer since children this age need supervision and guidance. Teach your youngster to use the mouse, to click on the screen and to use the keys on the keyboard.

Be there to help the child do the lessons. Your youngster will have many questions, so sit alongside and enjoy watching him/her work.

Children can improve a number of skills through computer use.

• Computer software use increases competence in reading, language, math and science.

- The computer can help your child develop positive attitudes toward problem solving. Software will allow your youngster to obtain Thesaurus help, check spelling, edit on the screen and sometimes even check grammar.
- The computer can help your child draw a picture to illustrate a story or design a map for social studies.
- Your child can write invitations to birthday parties or family gatherings.

From third grade onward, let your child work alone on the computer but be ready to answer questions. This is the time to encourage your youngster to learn to do word processing, math, art and other school-work such as book reports, in-depth reports on one or more of our states and science research.

SUGGESTION: I urge you to get your youngster into a keyboarding program by fourth grade. To be proficient in today's fast-paced world, he/she must be able to type fast, clean copy. See the end of this chapter for suggested programs.

Should you log onto the Internet? The newest and fastest growing use of computers is the so-called information highway, accessed through a variety of online services. All it takes is a modem and some communications software which often comes bundled with the modem. Internet costs vary from free to very expensive, depending on what's offered and the time used. Free online services are usually local, limited and rare. Some commercial services are America Online, Prodigy, CompuServe and the Microsoft Network. They offer a variety of information like encyclopedias, stock quotes, AP news and e-mail (electronic mail).

Online providers such as America Online and CompuServe offer a variety of educational support benefits. Homework help is one that may be helpful to you and your child. Check with your customer service about this and ask about specific charges.

One large computer networking company now serving hundreds of schools nationwide is considering going on the Internet. If it does, your child may be able to receive individual tutoring in such areas as reading, math, language and science. There will be a charge but think of the expert individual help your child would receive.

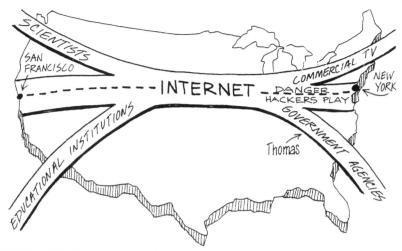

WARNING: Be aware of the problems your child might encounter when using online or commercial services. Unfortunately, some "chat" and writing on the Internet are not suitable for children.

When going online with a commercial service, ask about a "lock-out-to-kids" access. That prevents your youngster from going into adult areas without your permission. Also, warn your child of the potential dangers in giving out personal information online (no last name, no address and no phone number without your permission).

Resources for your child's home computer. Software is continually being updated and improved. Children's software has moved very quickly from 3.5- and 5.25-inch floppy disks to CD-ROM.

Definition: CD-ROM means "Compact Disc Read-Only Memory." A CD-ROM disc requires a CD-ROM player connected to the computer. One disc can hold as much information as several *hundred* floppy disks. A single CD can hold an entire encyclopedia including full picture images or video clips and high-quality sounds from a symphony or a bird song. The CD allows the user to access numerous multimedia programs that have special effects to enhance the program.

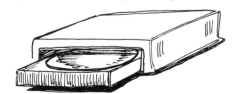

When my students do research on our school CD-ROM encyclopedia, they can print out the pages they need so they can continue to work at home.

If you can possibly afford it, I feel it is important that your intermediate child have access to a CD-ROM encyclopedia. Think of the hours you'll save driving your youngster to the library at night. This resource will reduce the amount of time your youngster needs to search for information.

NOTE: Read the system requirements on software before you buy. Newer programs specify minimum amounts and/or levels of RAM, hard disk, Windows©, DOS, etc. needed for operation.

Purchase CDs and other software only from reputable dealers. You could run into bootlegged disks from unscrupulous sources who ignore copyrights. The quality will not be as good as an original CD and you could pick up a virus.

You may find another virus source if you swap software. If this should happen, you can usually purchase an antivirus program to clean up your disk, but you may lose your data in the process.

NOTE: Bootlegging cannot be done by average people as it takes expensive equipment to copy a CD.

When purchasing children's software, look for the words "interactive" or "editor" on the package. This allows you to manage your child's access to the various disk programs. As the parent, you can decide what you want your child to do. This might be working on the alphabet or doing math facts from 1 to 5. In other words, the program can be customized for your child's needs.

HINT: Can you share your CD-ROM with another family in your neighborhood? How about forming a network of CD-ROM users? Consider a school or neighborhood swap, since a disc can cost $35 or more, and your youngster will outgrow the need for certain lessons.

Consider how long the program will be used by your child. One man I know purchased a CD disc for $55 for his son who used it three times and moved on to something else. When you are through with your CD, you might donate it to a neighborhood school, if it is appropriate, and write it off your income tax.

PARENT TIP: **Learn to operate the computer with your child. Be a model for your youngster of what learning is all about. Show that**

knowledge is gained through patience, the ability to read and the ability to problem solve. Ask your PTA to sponsor a Computer Awareness Night. Hire or recruit a knowledgeable person who can provide the necessary information and terms to help you, as parents, build a good understanding of computers, a working vocabulary and some ideas for good, current software for your children.

HINT: Computer software for children is fast-changing. However, some software programs are now "classics." These include **Children's Writing and Publishing, The Oregon Trail, Carmen Sandiego** and **KidPix.**

More than 1,000 software education titles are available today for your child. Over half are on CD-ROMs, with the number increasing every year. Consider a CD-ROM as a Christmas or birthday gift for your child. Then ask grandparents, uncles and aunts to select appropriate software for your child each birthday. Remember, you'll need to buy CD-ROMs and other software compatible with your system. For instance, Macintosh software won't work with an IBM compatible and vice versa.

For information, after the Mini Glossary, I'm listing a variety of available software, grouped by age. At the beginning, you'll see two programs for teaching keyboarding skills for children and adults. At the end of the section, you'll find a listing of CD-ROM encyclopedias and several other helpful resources including computer books and magazines.

NOTE: Don't feel the need to update your hardware or software every time a new edition comes out. Evaluate your child and family needs and how your current system is being used. You don't have to be first on the block with the largest hard drive or latest piece of software.

Maybe you can tell I'm really sold on computers. I've loved teaching in the computer lab at my school, and I see solid computer knowledge as a crucial rung on your child's educational ladder.

MINI GLOSSARY

Back-up disks Duplicate information stored for safekeeping away from files on computers.

Bundle When a dealer sells the computer system, monitor, keyboard, printer and software all together.

Caching Holding memory.

CD-ROM Compact Disc Read-Only Memory, a disc containing data that can be read by a computer and not modified.

DOS Disk Operating System which controls a PC's functions.

Dot-matrix printer A type of printer that creates characters by striking a series of dots against the ribbon. The dots create the character.

Floppy disk Portable 3.5" or 5.25" disk which stores information.

Hardware The physical components of computing, such as the computer, monitor, keyboard and printer.

HD Hard disk or hard drive. A high-speed, high-capacity, long-term storage device inside a computer.

Keyboard A device upon which one types messages to a computer.

MB Megabyte which equals one million bytes. The amount of hard drive storage capacity is normally measured in megabytes.

Microprocessor A computer's control or "brain."

Modem A device that transmits data from one computer to another over telephone lines.

Monitor The essential output device of the computer. The monitor displays what you type.

Motherboard The main circuitry board inside a computer.

MS-DOS The Microsoft version of DOS.

PC Personal computer.

Printer A device which attaches to a computer and prints information.

RAM Random access memory. Temporary memory storage which is erased when a PC is turned off.

Serial port A plug on the computer that enables you to hook up devices, such as the printer and the modem.

Software The programs or instructions which tell a computer what to do.

Sound card An electronic board added to a computer to provide it with sound capabilities.

Surge suppressor A special electrical device which protects a computer against an electrical overvoltage which could burn it out.

Video card Hardware inside the PC that stores the images displayed on the monitor. It receives and assimilates these signals from other parts of the computer.

Virus A software program to modify a computer's files or system configuration and to copy itself onto other disks or computers.

Windows A Microsoft software program; also areas on the screen where special text appears.

Word processor A program which makes computer-assisted writing feasible.

SOFTWARE REVIEW

Keyboarding Activities for Ages 8 to Adult

Microtype: The Wonderful Word of Paws. Students complete beginning typing drills as a cat prompts and reinforces messages. IBM and Macintosh. Order (800) 624-2926

Mavis Beacon Teaches Typing. Never the same lesson twice. Focus on word/letter combinations and progress charts. Program features a 10-key teaching mode and more! IBM and Macintosh. Order (800) 624-2926

Computer Software for Children Ages 3 to 5

Fisher-Price A-B-Cs. Ages 3 to 5. Children can learn their ABCs by doing a sing-along. While playing the ABC games, children learn the alphabet, letter recognition, beginning sounds, reading readiness, words and spelling. CD-ROM, Windows

McGee Series. Ages 2 to 6. **McGee** is a little boy and this is a problem-solving program teaching object/shape recognition and spatial relationships in thirty fun and familiar activities. **McGee at the Fun Fair** reinforces early learning skills like eye-hand coordination, cause and effect and storytelling. IBM and Macintosh

Interactive Reading Journey. Ages 4 to 7. This is a comprehensive reading program with several storybooks and more than 100 skill-building lessons. The lessons are set within an interactive playworld with a combination of activities and simple phonics drills. CD-ROM, Windows, Macintosh

Math Rabbit. Ages 4 to 7. This program builds math and thinking skills involving counting, number patterns, adding, subtracting, matching numbers to sets of objects and more. CD-ROM, DOS, Windows and Macintosh

JumpStart Kindergarten. Ages 4 to 6. A program to introduce and reinforce lessons found in kindergarten curricula nationwide with animated characters acting as guides. CD-ROM for IBM

Sammy's Science House. Ages 3 to 6. This is an introduction to science which will help your child acquire knowledge about plants, animals, seasons and weather. CD-ROM for Windows, CD-ROM and Disk for Macintosh

Bailey's Book House. Ages 2 to 5. Explore a world alive with language, experiment with letters and letter sounds, play Mother Goose rhymes, learn new words, make cards and create stories. CD-ROM, Windows, Macintosh

Millie's Math House. Ages 2 to 5. This program will teach your child fundamental math skills. Children develop a love for learning as they experiment and play with numbers, sizes, shapes and patterns. CD-ROM for Windows, CD-ROM for Macintosh

Animal Safari. Ages 3 to 8. This program helps kids develop the thinking skills they'll need to meet the challenges of the future with confidence. Six thought-provoking activities develop problem solving, creativity, critical thinking and memory skills. CD-ROM, Windows, and CD-ROM for Macintosh

Other outstanding software programs for children ages 3 to 5. Putt-Putt Joins the Parade, Kidsworks, Reader Rabbit, Kid Pix 2, and Playroom. Also, look for books on CD-ROM. Several companies have developed interactive books on CDs which read stories to children and encourage them to interact with the story.

Computer Software for Children Ages 6 to 9

Imagination Express. Ages 6 to 12. This storytelling program helps children create everything from simple picture books to multimedia productions. It's based on two themes: "Destination: Neighborhood" and "Destination: Castle." Each features a unique art style, animation, video clips, music, sound effects, story ideas and educational tips. CD-ROM, Windows

Math Blaster: Episode 1. Four action-packed learning games to boost your child's math and problem-solving skills. Over 50,000 different problems are possible in addition, subtraction, multiplication, division, fractions, decimals, percents, number patterns and estimation. CD-ROM, Windows and Macintosh

Fraction Action. Ages 8 and up. Add, subtract, multiply or divide fractions in an arcade game format. Incorrect answers are explained. IBM or Macintosh

CarmenSandiego, Junior Edition. Ages 5' to 8. Children become junior detectives as they learn world geography while having fun. CD-ROM, Windows

Spell It. Ages 6 to adult. 3,600 words divided into six levels of difficulty for spellers of all ages. Personalize the program by adding your own word lists. It also talks. CD-ROM

Alien Tales. Ages 6 to 12. This is a galactic game show where kids discover the joy of reading great literature. Read passages from award-winning books, answer questions, solve puzzles and match wits with celebrity panelists. CD-ROM, Macintosh

Undersea Adventure. Ages 5 to 12. This program brings the undersea world to life, with point-and-click exploration through hundreds of videos, articles and photos about mammals, fish and sharks. A special sea lab lets your youngster explore the insides of a lobster, shark and other sea creatures. CD-ROM for PC, PC 3.5" Disk, CD-ROM, Macintosh

My First World Atlas. Ages 6 to 9. This atlas teaches children about capital cities, time zones, religions, government, languages, currency, animals and famous people.

It also teaches children about their own country and the world around them. The program has live animation, sounds and real-life photos. CD-ROM, Windows and Macintosh

Thinkin' Things # 2. On CD-ROM, this program provides a set of tools and toys that help kids ages 6 to 12 become problem solvers, flexible thinkers and enthusiastic learners. The program also includes an interactive video for parents with a veteran teacher to answer your questions and help you understand the importance of strengthening your child's thinking skills. CD-ROM, Windows and CD-ROM, Macintosh

Other outstanding software programs for ages 6 to 9. Reader Rabbit 2 and 3, Math Blaster, Oregon Trail, Storybook Weaver, KidDesk, Children's Writing and Publishing, Kidswork, Word Muncher, Number Muncher, Print Shop Deluxe and Creative Writer.

A software club for your child to join. Club KidSoft is a software shopping club for children ages 4 to 12. Members get a quarterly magazine and a CD-ROM or periodic CD-ROMs with demonstrations of educational software. This will allow your child to try out the programs before you buy. To join, call (800) 354-6150.

Software for Children Ages 9 to 12

Sharks. Ages 9 to 12. This Discovery Channel software brings your child face-to-face with the great white shark while diving with underwater photographers on a deep-sea adventure. The program has 200 photographs, scientific experts speaking and glossary of words. CD-ROM, Windows

The Way Things Work. Ages 8 to adult. This CD is based on David Macaulay's outstanding book of the same name. Hundreds of fact-packed animations, from telescopes to telephones, lasers to light bulbs. "The Great Woolly Mammoth" acts as a guide to the CD-ROM. CD-ROM, Windows and MS-DOS 3.1 or later

Project USA. Ages 8 to 12. An interactive United States Atlas program complete with a geography learning package. Your youngster will learn amazing facts and important information about all fifty states. CD-ROM, Windows and MS-DOS

Stationery Store. Ages 10 to adult. With this program your youngster can design and create customized stationery, business letterhead, invitations, announcements, flyers, postcards and greeting cards. The program has three separate components: word processor, a database of templates and a card file for storing commonly used names and addresses. CD-ROM, Windows

Math Workshop. Ages 6 to 12. This unique software program has included a CD-ROM informational twelve-minute disc for parents showing them how to help their child learn and enjoy math. The child's program teaches basic skills of math, patterns and logic, fractions, computation and estimation. CD-ROM, Windows and Macintosh

Other outstanding software for children ages 9 to 12. Creative **Writing, Simm City, Ant Life, 2000, Carmen Sandiego Series and Super Solvers.**

CD-ROM Encyclopedias

My First Encyclopedia. Ages 3 to 6
CD-ROM, Windows
Explorapedia-The World of Nature. Ages 6 to 10
CD-ROM, Windows
Compton's Interactive Encyclopedia. Ages 6 to adult
CD-ROM, Windows and CD-ROM, Macintosh
The Random House Kids' Encyclopedia. Ages 7 to 12
CD-ROM, Windows
Grolier Multimedia Encyclopedia. Ages 8 to adult
CD-ROM, Windows
Microsoft Encarta Encyclopedia. Ages 8 to adult
CD-ROM, Windows

RESOURCE MATERIALS

Books
Kids and Computers: A Parent's Handbook by Judy Salpeter
Your First Computer — Second Edition by Alan Simpson
PCs for Dummies — Second Edition by Alan Simpson
10-Minute Guide To Buying A Computer by Shelley O'Hara
The Way Multimedia Works by Simon Collin

Magazines
Newsweek Computers And The Family, Family Computing, Home PC, Byte, Compute, Mac Magazine, Mac PC and Mac User

Dictionaries
Macmillan Dictionary for Children Ages 6 to 12
CD-ROM, Windows and Macintosh
My First Incredible Amazing Dictionary Ages 5 to 12
CD-ROM, Windows and MS-DOS 3.1 or later

Telephone numbers of outstanding educational software companies you should keep on hand
Davidson (800) 545-7677
Edmark (800) 691-2985
The Learning Company (800) 227-5609
Knowledge Adventure (800) 469-3466
KidSoft (800) 354-6150
Broderbund Software (800) 521-6263
Educational Resources (800) 624-2926

Software for the home
Microsoft Works Integrated software package
Claris Works Integrated software package
Modem Software Software to run a modem
Quicken A software program to keep track of home expenses, bills and a payment schedule

CHAPTER

18

Parent Conferences
Kindergarten-Sixth Grade

"Parents can make such a difference in their child's education. One key is by attending parent conferences. Reach out to your child's teacher, communicate with each other and work 'together' on goals for your child."

Shirley Rowan, teacher of a one-room "school-within-a-school" for Hearing-Handicapped Children ages four to twelve. Hagood Elementary School, Pickens, South Carolina

A parent conference is the same as a 30,000-mile checkup on your car. This is a time to stop and see how your child is doing academically, socially and behaviorwise at school.

It is a meeting between a teacher and a parent or parents of an individual child who share the common goal to improve the education of that child. Most teachers usually hold regular conferences each fall and spring semester. If there are problems, the teacher may suggest an extra conference and the parents may request an extra conference, too.

Three main reasons for calling a special conference are:

- The child's grades have drastically dropped.
- A family problem has developed which interferes with the child's academic success.
- A major health problem has developed which requires the teacher to arrange for special makeup homework for the child.

Before the conference, you should receive a form or note from the teacher to alert you that your child is having difficulties in a subject, behavior or work habits. You should not be confronted for the first time with a report about any of the following:

- Your child is failing this grade.
- Your child is doing below "C" in any subject.
- Your child's behavior is unacceptable.
- Your child may not be promoted to the next grade.

SUGGESTION: For more detailed information see my chapter on report cards.

PARENT TIP: **If at all possible, arrange a time to visit in the classroom prior to the conference. This isn't a time for discussion; rather it's a time to meet the teacher and quietly observe the classroom. Plan to stay a full class period and this will give you a broad overview of the room. Send a note to the teacher ahead of time so you will be expected. Most school districts require that you first check in with the school office. Ask whether you need to do this.**

HINT: Most teachers are happy to have parents come into their classroom to observe.

Child attendance at conferences. Some school districts and some teachers ask that the child attend the conference with the parents. I feel this is helpful, but some teachers don't. Check with your child's teacher to find out if your child should attend.

Most conferences allow thirty minutes or less, so you need to be prepared ahead of time. Often, during emotionally charged meetings, it's easy to forget vital things. Because of this I usually prepare a memo for the parent. You might also want to take your written comments plus a small notebook and pencil to jot down notes.

PARENT TIP: **If your spouse cannot attend the conference, ask the teacher if you might tape record the conference. This will allow the absent parent to feel a part of the child's educational program. It will also help you recall vital information which you might have overlooked during the conference.**

Here are some guidelines which I feel will help you have the most successful parent conference.

Be there. By attending the conference, you demonstrate to your child that you believe school is important.

I remember all too well the year I had 32 children and had arranged for parent conferences. A total of twelve parents came. Not surprisingly, the parents who came had children who were doing well in my class, and the parents I desperately needed to see didn't show up.

Keep the teacher informed. If you know of physical, emotional or social problems your child is having, you should have alerted the teacher the first week of school. If you did not, or if new problems have arisen, be sure to explain this at the conference. Teachers and parents need to work together for the good of the child.

NOTE: Whatever is going on at home comes to school. If I'm alerted to a child's problem, I can begin to seek out help such as a

counselor, a reading tutor or a talk with the nurse. I've always appreciated parents who fill me in on problems going on in the home.

A few years ago, for example, I had a most disruptive student in
my fourth-grade classroom. His mother came to me the first week of
school and let me know that the whole family was in counseling. Since
I knew the family was going for help and problems were being
addressed, I was able to be supportive at my end.

Typical problems are a death, separation or a divorce in the family.
Or the child might be dealing with an illness or even a vision or hearing
problem. Any of these can interfere with ongoing academic success.

Keep in mind that with cutbacks in funds, many school districts
have little money for nurses, speech therapists or psychologists. Check
with your school to find out what services are available there.

Prepare ahead. Some school districts provide a special checklist to
help parents prepare for the conference. Some teachers ask parents to
write out a list of the strengths, weaknesses and goals for their child each
year. You also need to jot down any concerns you might have.

**A Parent-Conference Question Sheet to photocopy and take
with you.**

You might wish to ask questions from this sample list at your next
parent conference.

- Do you have a list of outside tutors who could help my child
  in reading or math?
- Does the school have a homework hotline so I can check
  on what my child should be
  doing each evening?
- How can I help my child at
  home with reading, language,
  math and science, etc.?
- How can I help my youngster complete homework at home?
- How does my child get along with others at recess and lunch
  break?
- Does my child obey classroom and school rules?
- Does the school have a computer lab? How often does my
  child go? What lessons does my youngster do in the lab?

- What other resources do you have at school? A nurse?
  A speech teacher? A librarian? A resource specialist?
- Is my child doing grade-level work in reading, language and math?

For parents of bilingual students. You should ask the teacher some additional questions if your child is bilingual.

- Is my child getting help with English language development?
- Is my child receiving any primary language instruction?
- Does the program include self-esteem and cross-cultural activities?

NOTE: Parents of Bilingual students will need to alert the classroom teacher ahead of time if a translator will be needed at the conference. Be sure and do this at least two weeks ahead of time.

In the resource section in the back of this book, you'll find a grade-by-grade outline of what your child needs to be doing in the basic subjects. Place a copy of the appropriate grade level on your refrigerator or bulletin board and check off the skills your youngster has accomplished.

I've found that once a child falls behind in major subjects, it takes the cooperation of the parent, teacher, child and sometimes a counselor to get the youngster back on track. Plan ahead and don't let your child get behind. Frustration will build and your youngster might give up. Work with the teacher to help your student. See my chapter on "As The Twig Is Bent..." for ideas on how to make positive changes in your child's life.

Be on time. Sometimes in the past thirty years, I've had up to forty students at a time. Like me, most teachers can only allocate twenty-to-thirty minutes per child for a conference. It's important that you be prompt and, in fact, arrive a few minutes early.

Do not walk directly into the classroom. A conference might be going on and needs to be kept private. The teacher will probably provide chairs for you to wait in the hallway. Sit down and relax.

Look over your questions one more time. By being a few minutes early, you and your child can walk into the conference prepared and relaxed.

HINT: If at all possible, don't ask to reschedule the conference. Because teachers deal with so many parents in one week, it's often difficult to make changes.

Leave other children at home. If the teacher agrees, bring your conference youngster with you. However, siblings or other children, especially toddlers, should be left at home. Some schools now provide baby-sitting during parent conferences so call ahead and check on this if you need such service. If not, you should make other arrangements to have your younger children cared for while you go to the conference. Maybe you could exchange baby-sitting services with a neighbor who has a conference at another time.

You'll need to devote all of your time to the child attending the conference in order to make the time together much more successful. This includes taking notes during your meeting for later reference at home and indicates to your child the importance of the meeting.

Be positive. If your child attends the conference, be aware of what you say. Negative words expressed in front of your child can be very hurtful, and can increase the anxiety level in a child already anxious about the meeting.

Keep in mind that the family structure is a strong unit and when predictions, whether positive or negative, are made, some children feel subconsciously they should be carried out. From my observations, I know a child's loyalty to the family's expectations is very strong.

It seems simplistic, but it's so very true. A child who is called clumsy or stupid tends to be awkward and slow. A child who is called smart and competent tends to be a good student.

Shared information. Just as you've told the teacher about any changes in the family, be prepared for the teacher to share information with you such as, "We may need to talk about possible retention if Matt continues to slide in reading and math." Or, "Lily has not turned in any homework in a month. We need to talk about when she will turn in this makeup work."

Academic problems. Some teachers will ask a child having serious academic problems to sign a contract for the remainder of the year. Contracts can vary depending upon the teacher.

The contract should contain these main items.

- Child's name and date
- A listing of the areas which need improvement such as reading, math, work habits or homework
- A statement written by the teacher and agreed upon by the parent and child as to a deadline
- A recommendation of resources which will be helpful to the child such as a home office or specific study area equipped with a dictionary and encyclopedia. Or a statement, "Must work at library on reports and use resources there if nothing is available at home."
- A place where the parent, child and teacher can sign an agreement to the stipulations in the contract

A copy should be given to the parent, to the child and to the teacher who will keep one in the child's personal school folder.

Whatever commitment you make to help your child improve, I urge you to stay with the challenge for the long haul.

Over and over teachers have parents promise that changes will be made at home: homework will be completed, behavior will change and books will be brought to school. All too often this change doesn't last. Let your child know that you will check weekly on progress until the desired goal is reached. This will keep him/her from slipping back into bad habits.

If you keep a daily journal or appointment book, note your child's important deadlines. Also, have your child mark these dates in his/her own notebook. As a parent, you should not be expected to "carry the load," but you can be a facilitator to be sure your child meets the conditions of the contract.

I have found that contracts work very well with children. This is especially true if parents are behind the effort. Changes can be made and grades improved. At the same time, this is a powerful way of impressing upon children how important school is and how they can and must improve.

Stay on the subject. Since you'll have limited time for the parent conference, it's imperative that you discuss ways to help your child improve in school. You should not dwell on family problems unrelated to the child's school work. Most teachers are not trained counselors and are not equipped to help you solve a teenager's problems, a marital disagreement or a neighborhood dispute. Most schools, however, have a list of community resources along with telephone numbers. Ask for this list and if the teacher does not have one, ask in the office.

Taking appropriate action to deal with behavior problems. Often I've had to inform parents that their child's behavior in the classroom is hindering the child's own academic success and sometimes that of other students in the room.

When a child enters school, certain behaviors are necessary in order for the child to learn. A teacher and parent should be able to expect the following behavior from a youngster in the classroom:

- To come to school prepared to learn
- To come to school with homework finished — no excuses

- To be able to get along with other children in the room and on the playground
- To come to school with a set of manners and to use them throughout the day

- To come to school daily and on time if at all possible
- To come to school prepared with textbooks, homework and a positive attitude

A contract can be used to change behavior problems as well as academic shortcomings. Consider talking this over with the teacher if you feel it's needed.

Keep in touch. With thousands of young people dropping out of school (over 2,000 each day nationwide), parents <u>must</u> stay in touch with the teacher and the school.

This means you need to attend all parent conferences, Back-to-School programs and PTA meetings. This interest needs to begin in preschool and continue through high school.

Our world today is complicated and it sometimes takes more than the teacher or school to educate a child. I've seen cases where it takes even more than the home and school; it takes the community to provide a youngster with the best education possible but the results are worthwhile.

Here are a number of books, booklets and pamphlets on a variety of subjects on raising successful children.

Books

Bringing Up Kids Without Tearing Them Down by Kevin Leman
Straight Answers to the Questions That Rattle Moms and Dads by Kevin Leman
In Their Own Way by Thomas Armstrong
The Working Parents' Help Book by Susan Cristes Price and Tom Price
Positive Parenting From A to Z by Karen Renshaw Joslin
Mom's House, Dad's House by Isolina Ricci, Ph.D.
How to Develop Your Child's Gifts and Talents by RaeLynne P. Rein, Ph.D. and Rachel Rein

Human Brain, Human Learning by Leslie Hart
Six-Point Plan For Raising Happy, Healthy Children by John Rosemond
Endangered Minds by Jane Healy
Healing Environment by Carol Venolia
Please Understand Me by David Keirsey and Marilyn Bates
Positive Discipline by Jane Nelsen
Life in the Family Zoo by John M. Platt

Booklets and Pamphlets

Delattre, Edwin J. and Alice B., *Helping Your Child Learn Responsible Behavior*, Washington, D.C., U.S. Department of Education, 1993.

Rich, Dorothy, *Helping Your Child Succeed in School*, Washington, D.C., U.S. Department of Education, 1992.

About Parenting, South Deerfield (Massachusetts), Channing L. Bete, Co., Inc., 1983.

Parents and Children Together, Bloomington (Indiana), Family Literacy Center, Indiana University, 1991.

You, Your Child and School Readiness, South Deerfield (Massachusetts), Channing L. Bete Co., Inc., 1994.

Your Child Entering School, South Deerfield (Massachusetts), Channing L. Bete Co., Inc., 1980.

Your Parent-Teacher Conference, South Deerfield (Massachusetts), Channing L. Bete, Co., Inc., 1991.

Report Cards, Deficiency Notices and Retention

> *"Some parents put too much emphasis on report-card grades and not enough on the student's learning. Numbers don't indicate whether our students are able to communicate, problem solve, reason or connect to their real world experiences."*
>
> Cynthia Hillman-Forbush, Eighth Grade, Houlton High School, Houlton, Maine

REPORT CARDS

In most schools report cards are issued four times a year. Kids can't wait; parents hope for the best and teachers are happy when the cards are finished and passed out.

My school is one where this occurs four times a year. Each time it takes me about one week of evenings and a weekend, depending upon the grade level and the size of my class.

Days before I actually fill out the cards, I begin to think about what I'll write for comments because I've always considered report cards an important part of a youngster's life. I arrange folders filled with my students' work near me so I have access to their most recent work. I use a calculator, my grade book and notes I've taken about each youngster during the semester.

See sample report card for Grades 1 through 6 on page 226.

Different school districts use different formats. A legend is generally found at the bottom of the report card as a key to show what each check or letter means.

Some districts grade primary students with either an "S" for Successful or Satisfactory in a subject or an "I" for Improvement Needed.

At the same time, a district might ask teachers to evaluate students in grades four, five and six by using grades.

Kindergarten students usually receive a checklist which indicates their accomplishments. An example might be, "Counts forward to 31." Or, "Holds book right-side-up and turns pages from beginning to end." If the child can do these things, a check is made in the appropriate column.

Go over the report card with your child. Your child's report card should be a learning experience for you and your youngster. Use the information to help your child improve, if improvement is indicated.

Grade-Level Progress. If this is indicated on the form, spend time talking with your child about the marks in reading, language and math. Does your child understand what it means when he/she is doing below-grade-level work?

Be particularly aware if your child is doing below-grade level in any subject. This is a red flag and you'll need to talk to the teacher and work together to determine how improvement can be made.

Conduct Grade. Somewhere on the report card you should see an area titled "Conduct Grade" or "Social Skills." Under this caption, you might see phrases like "does not follow rules," "talkative," "disrespectful," or "inappropriate language."   Or, you might see phrases like "respects rights/property of others," "demonstrates self-control," or "observes class and school rules."

This is the area that tells about your child's behavior in the classroom and on the playground.   Indication of lack of respect toward others, use of bad language and disrupting the classroom should be addressed before they grow into serious problems.   By the time your youngster reaches the intermediate grades, these misbehaviors can lead to serious consequences.

If you see a check in any of these areas for more than one year, it's time to go for help.   A pattern is being established which can become difficult to change.

Many teachers are working in classrooms with thirty or more students each day.   Even one unruly child can cut down on the learning time for the other students.   I've had years when I had to spend far too much time getting several disruptive students settled down at the expense of teaching the others.

We see more and more serious problems in classrooms today and parents need to reach out for help.   If your child is having serious problems, you have several options.

- Ask the teacher to arrange for your child to see the school psychologist.
- Ask the teacher for the name and phone number of a private counselor.
- Ask for information regarding parenting classes.
- Ask if a buddy system is available whereby older students modeling good behavior and work habits spend time working with younger problem students.

Work Habits.   This describes the way your child treats the job of "going to school."   Remind him or her that successful students are likely to become successful adults.   Your youngster must take responsibility for doing the best possible job each day in school.

Look at each behavior noted on the report card.   Talk with your child about how changes can be made, and if needed, ask for help from the teacher.   I've found when parents and teachers work together, great progress can be made in a child's behavior and academic progress.

PARENT TIP: **If failure to do homework is a problem, consider using your dining-room table as the "Homework Center" for your family. Some children do not work well alone. Establish an hour when all children gather to do their work. At least one parent should sit with the children to answer questions. (Remember, you don't do the work.) To avoid seeming like a warden, you could read the newspaper or catch up on letter writing while the children do their own work. The social aspect of doing homework as a family project can be a powerful and positive influence upon your child's work habits.**

Attendance. Poor attendance is another red flag which needs to be addressed quickly. I've become increasingly concerned in the past ten years about the number of students who don't come to school every day.

Children who achieve, make good grades and progress in school are the ones who attend every day. Those who do not, are often barely hanging on from one grade to another as the rest of the class move on.

By allowing your child to stay at home without a specific medical reason, you are telling him/her, "School is only somewhat important," and you're teaching your child by your actions to not be responsible.

Comments. On the report card you'll see the comments teachers make. Pay particular attention to these. Your child's teacher sees your youngster six hours a day for about 185 days each year. If the comments are good, praise your child. If not, take these comments seriously, even if you don't agree with them.

If you question their accuracy, call and meet with the teacher. Most teachers spend a great deal of time thinking about what they write on report cards. Use their wisdom to help guide your child into a more productive school year.

The "C" grade. More and more parents come to me and say, "I don't want my child to get a "C." Today being average is no longer acceptable. As an example, I've had parents demand that their child receive an "A" in math even when they are aware the child did only average work and earned the "C" (which is <u>not</u> a bad grade). To insist that a teacher change such a grade is to model for your youngster that it's OK to receive a higher mark without earning it.

NOTE: Children need to learn that if they fool around and don't do their work, they will earn a poor mark. By allowing your child to expect high, unearned grades, you are setting up a pattern which will carry over into higher education and work later in life.

As my students dash out the classroom door with report card in hand, I hear them yell, "Look what she <u>gave</u> me in reading." I explain to them the next day, "You <u>earned</u> every grade received on your report card. I use my calculator to figure out your grades and I use my hand to write out that grade on your card, but I don't <u>give</u> any grade to anyone." Children must be taught to take responsibility for their own actions. Home and school are where this learning should take place.

PARENT TIP: **If you find yourself defending your child at each parent conference or when receiving a report card, stop and take a hard look at what is going on behind your child's poor behavior, low grades or bad work habits. Go for professional help, if needed.**

DEFICIENCY NOTICES

A deficiency note to parents of students with grades below "C" or problems with work habits or behavior, goes home three to four weeks before report cards and parent conferences. This note alerts parents or care givers that steps need to be taken immediately so grades in these areas may improve.

I've never enjoyed writing deficiency notices but follow my district's guidelines which require me to do this. I realize it's only fair that before receiving a report card, parents should know their child is not doing acceptable passing work.

I'm aware that many school districts are moving away from grades on report cards. Rather, they are marking a "Satisfactory" or "Unsatisfactory" grade. Still, many parents come to me and say, "What does this mean? I want you to tell me how my child is doing. I want to see a grade."

As a parent, you have the right to be informed about your child's progress in school. You should never walk into a parent conference without being told of a problem ahead of time. This is why most districts require their teachers to hand out deficiency notices several weeks before parent conferences are held or report cards are issued.

This sample form is used by one school district to notify parents of potential problems in their child's academic progress, work habits or behavior.

See sample Deficiency Note for Grades 1 through 6 on page 227.

Sit down with your child and go over each check mark on the deficiency form received in the mail. This is not the time to blame or criticize but rather to say, "We have a problem here and I want us to work on it together." Children are much more apt to reach out for help when a parent uses a non-critical approach.

Ask questions. These are some samples you might ask about reading. Use the same type of question for other subjects.

- What can you tell me about your problem in reading? Do you have any idea why the teacher marked this as being a problem?
- What can you tell me about missing homework?
- Tell me how you get along with your teacher.
  Is he/she willing to help you?
- If you don't understand something in class, what do you do?
  If you don't feel comfortable asking in class, can you stay after school and get extra help?
- How well do you see the chalkboard?
- Can you hear everything the teacher says?
- How is your notebook working for keeping track of homework assignments?

- Are other kids in the classroom keeping you from doing your work?
- Why is it important to learn to read?

HINT: I've had many children come into my classroom with no idea why reading, math or language is important today or in their future. I find spending a few minutes each week discussing why it is vital to students now and in their future helps keep them motivated.

I tell them, "You need to be able to read well in order to do word problems in math, write out a science experiment or work on a computer. As you grow up, you'll need to be able to read in order to understand a driver's manual so you can take the test to drive a car.

"You'll need to be able to read in order to understand how to do research and write reports and fill out your income tax. Reading well also provides you with the opportunity to read books which will entertain you and provide you with information for the rest of your life."

Getting straight answers. If for any reason you sense your child is not giving straight answers to your questions, call and ask to meet with the teacher. Don't wait for the parent conference. <u>Now</u> is the time to sort out the problem. School problems have a way of escalating.

PARENT TIP: **In the past, I sent notes about a problem home with my students. But I discovered that bad news is slow to travel home. I found notes to parents in the wastebasket after my students left for the day. For that reason, I prefer to mail all "bad-news" letters home. Suggest that your child's teacher do this for you, and provide the teacher with several stamps as a friendly gesture. A number of teachers also send home "happy notes" during the year and they appreciate postage stamps, as well.**

RETENTION

As a parent, it's upsetting to be notified that you need to consider having your child repeat a grade.

However, when a student continues to get behind in school, the teacher will often talk about retention. This is neither a subject that teachers enjoy addressing nor one parents enjoy hearing.

Kindergarten or first-grade retention. Over the years, I've had a hard time recommending retention. It is never an easy decision. A number of parents felt their children should go on, but I was often unsure. I'm particularly concerned with children having serious problems with reading, showing poor social skills or not being able to work on their own. To be an independent learner, to be able to get along with others and to be able to read are so vital as a youngster moves up the learning ladder. When one or more of these rungs is missed, we <u>all</u> need to rethink what would be best for the child.

I've had a number of parents call me with concerns about their children's readiness to enter kindergarten. The majority of these students are boys. After hearing parents' concerns, I generally suggest waiting one more year to allow the youngster to mature a bit. I've been pleased to learn that when these children entered kindergarten, they were nearly always at or near the top of their class. For most children, the extra year at home or preschool, with time spent preparing the child for regular school, certainly pays off in kindergarten as well as all the future school years.

What research shows about retention. Dr. David Berliner, a professor at Arizona State University, spent ten years studying students retained in elementary school. He says, "The students being considered for retention, have a lower self-concept than other students." In his studies he noted that ten years later there was little difference in the achievement between low-achieving students who were retained and those promoted.

NOTE: If a child is retained, I would suggest that the child return to the same teacher the following year, if possible. The teacher knows the child, knows the skills needed and with input from the parents, can develop a year-long lesson plan to improve the academics needed by the child.

At the same time, parents need to encourage their child, provide the youngster with opportunities to experience success and give much praise.

From my own personal experience, I feel the best place to retain a student is either in kindergarten or first grade. However, it is also my experience that many parents will fight a teacher who suggests this be done. I tell them, "Repeating a year now might make the remaining school years much, much easier for your child."

However, if a child <u>chooses</u> to fool around, not do schoolwork and bothers other people, the teacher and parent might need to consider retention after the K-1 grades. At times, repeating a grade for a year is the best way to encourage and to motivate a child.

A summer contract. I designed a "Parent, Student and Teacher Summer Contract" which I use as a way to offset a possible retention. A sample copy of the contract is shown on page 228.

During the school year, I talk with the parent and the child about a lack of interest or other problem in keeping up with classmates. I work all year to help the child but if this fails, I ask both the parent and the child to sign the summer contract.

This gives the family time to work together to help the child improve. You'll note that I list very specifically the subjects and skills needing improvement.

It is up to the family to get the child into a summer-school program or have the youngster tutored. He/she can make great gains over the summer if the desire and family support are present.

Two weeks before school begins, the child must bring in the signed contract so I can test him or her. If I see significant improvement, the child will move on with the class, but if not, retention is the result.

Except in very unusual circumstances, I believe it's vital that retention be done <u>before</u> school opens. A child who has to drop back a level after classes begin may be subjected to ridicule and name-calling by other children. Have your child placed in the proper grade from the beginning.

Keep in mind that parents who choose to protect their child from failure deprive that youngster from learning an important life lesson, that sometimes we fail even when we try. That does not make you a bad parent or your child a bad child. It is simply part of learning. By giving your child another chance at the same level, you often pave the way for much greater future success.

"Consider how quiet the forest would be if only the best birds sang."
Sherry Bartholomew, Substitute teacher, Central Square Central Schools, New York

Sample report card for Grades 1 through 6.

ORIGINAL - TEACHER'S COPY

GRADES 1-6

Name _____ Rm. ___ Grade ___ School _____

Quarter Dates _____ 1st | 2nd | 3rd | 4th   Assignment for 19 ___ Grade ___

PROGRESS IN SCHOOL ADJUSTMENT

WORK HABITS (Quarters 1 2 3 4)
Makes good use of time: Works independently;
Completes assignments promptly and neatly;
Tries to do his/her best

CITIZENSHIP (Quarters 1 2 3 4)
Accepts responsibility. Respects authority;
Respects rights and property of others

COMMENTS
Quarter 1 _____ Teacher Signature
Quarter 2 _____ Teacher Signature
Quarter 3 _____ Teacher Signature
Quarter 4 _____ Teacher Signature

PROGRESS IN KNOWLEDGE AND SKILLS

GRADE LEVEL PROGRESS* (First Quarter / Second Quarter / Third Quarter / Fourth Quarter — Above, On, Below)

Rdg / Math / Lang

Quarters 1 2 3 4

READING
MATHEMATICS
LANGUAGE — Spoken Language, Written Language
HANDWRITING
SPELLING
SOCIAL STUDIES
HEALTH/SAFETY
PHYSICAL EDUCATION
SCIENCE
ART
VOCAL MUSIC
INSTRUMENTAL MUSIC** — Band, Orchestra
LIBRARY**

*Based on SCUSD achievement standards, as outlined in the Elementary Report Card Marking Manual.
**Not graded at some levels

RECORD OF ATTENDANCE (Quarter 1 2 3 4)
Days present
Days absent
Times tardy

EXPLANATION OF MARKS
A - Outstanding Achievement   B - Very Good Achievement
C - Satisfactory Achievement   D - Limited Achievement
F - Unsatisfactory Achievement

Sample deficiency notice for Grades 1 through 6.

Deficiency Notice Grades 1-6

_____
School

Dear Parent or Guardian:

This notice is to inform you that, as of _____, _____
                                            Date   Student's Name
may receive a D or F grade this quarter in the subject(s) or area(s) indicated below:

SUBJECT AREAS

_____ Reading   _____ Spelling   _____ Art
_____ Mathematics   _____ Social Studies   _____ Vocal Music
_____ English, spoken   _____ Health/Safety   _____ Instrumental Music
_____ English, written   _____ Physical Education _____ Library
_____ Handwriting   _____ Science

SCHOOL ADJUSTMENT

_____ Work Habits   _____ Citizenship

PROBABLE CAUSES

_____ Frequent absences   _____ Wastes time
_____ Frequent tardiness   _____ Comes to class without materials
_____ Failure to make up work   _____ Shows lack of respect toward teacher
_____ Lack of regular home study _____ Shows lack of respect toward other
_____ Incomplete assignments   students
_____ Failure to seek extra help _____ Uses offensive language in class
_____ Inattentiveness in class   _____ Does not accept authority
_____ Lack of class participation _____ Talks excessively
_____ Poor study habits   _____ (Other) _____
_____ Lack of effort   _____

I would suggest:

_____ An immediate conference.
_____ This matter can be discussed during the regular conference period.
_____ Your giving extra help at home in addition to help given and work done at
        school.

In order to request a conference or to discuss questions related to this notice,
please telephone _____ and leave a message.

_____   _____
         Teacher   Date

I have read and discussed this form with my teacher. (Optional, grades 1-3; required,
grades 4-6.)

_____   _____
         Student   Date Given to Student

_____   _____
     Principal's Signature   Date

Please sign and return copy to your child's teacher not later than _____
to verify that you have received and reviewed this notice.   Date

I have read and reviewed this form with my child.

_____   _____
       Parent/Guardian   Date

Distribution: White - Teacher retains for CRC file; Canary - Parent/guardian signs
               and returns; Pink - Parent/guardian retains.

Form # 40-05495

Sample contract.

George Washington Elementary School

PARENT, STUDENT AND TEACHER SUMMER CONTRACT
June _____

In lieu of retention, I will seek educational help during the summer for my child,

_____
Name of Student

Check one   Summer School _____   Tutoring _____

Teacher to complete the following:

Grade level _____
Circle area(s) of needed improvement: Reading, Language, Math or _____.

1. Subject _____

   Skills needed: _____
   _____
   _____

2. Subject _____

   Skills needed: _____
   _____
   _____

Parent completes the following:

I, _____ , will enroll my child in (circle one) summer school/tutoring program in
       Name of Parent/Guardian
the areas noted by the teacher. I fully understand that my child must attend summer school, or be tutored, in order
to go on to the next grade in school. I also understand that my child must pass a test two weeks before school opens
to move to the next grade. I will submit a copy of this form to the summer school/tutor and will return the form at
the bottom of this page to George Washington School in the Fall.

_____   _____
      Parent Signature   Student Signature

_____   _____
      Teacher Signature   Date

TO BE RETURNED TO GEORGE WASHINGTON SCHOOL IN SEPTEMBER

- -

_____ attended summer school, or was tutored, at _____
          Student's name   Name of school
from _____ to _____. He/she missed _____ days during the program. I feel this child is
        Date   Date
ready/not ready to move on to the next grade.

_____   _____
      Name of Teacher/Tutor   Telephone Number

Enrich Your Child's Summer Vacation

"Summer is a unique opportunity for learning. The world is a stage, and puppets, live plays or some other presentations — complete with costuming, planning, set-up, clean-up and writing scripts, invitations and programs — can involve the whole family and be a great learning experience as well."

Diana Long, Fifth-Grade Teacher, Santiam Christian School, Corvallis, Oregon

At the end of the year, my students grab their report cards, yell "Good-bye" and head home. Two days later, while I'm cleaning the classroom, some students drift by saying, "I'm bored, can I help?"

Whether your youngster has vacation during the summer months or on a year-round schedule, there are a number of ways to have fun while reinforcing and increasing his or her academic skills.

Reading. During vacation, your youngster will have more time to do fun reading. Arrange for the child to go to the library at least once a week. Most libraries have summer-reading programs or special presentations for children. If you cannot take the youngster, have a grandparent or family member substitute for you at the library.

Encourage your child to volunteer to read to younger children in the neighborhood. This will help your youngster practice selecting interesting books to read for different ages. The children's librarian can also help pick out good books.

While school is in session, many of my students go to other rooms to read to younger children. The little ones look up to my students, and mine love the attention. They also like to show others what good readers they are.

The New York Times' Parent's Guide To The Best Books For Children by Eden Ross Lipson, *Best Books for Children Preschool Through Grade Six* by John T. Gillespie and Corinne J. Naden and *Choosing Books For Children* by Joanne Oppenheim, Barbara Brenner and Betty D. Boegehold are three outstanding books that can help you and your child pick out good children's reading.

Measurement. Vacation is a good time to encourage your child to do some building such as a bird feeder or a dog house. You might also plan for a garden. Help your youngster pick out a plot which gets plenty of sun and has good soil. Measure for the garden space, not less than a three-foot-square plot.

Kids Gardening, A Kids' Guide to Messing Around in the Dirt by Kevin and Kim Raftery is an excellent book and guide for your youngster to plan a garden, plant seeds and grow vegetables.

IDEA: Garden shops have children's small greenhouses in the shape and size of an old-fashioned black lunchpail. The dome-shaped houses are made of plastic and inside have six small pots filled with soil and seeds for raising seedlings for the outdoor garden.

Gaining the experience of raising even a small garden can turn into a lifelong hobby for your child. This also teaches the responsibility of caring for the garden by watering, digging weeds and the joy of sharing the fruits and vegetables with others.

When I was growing up, each summer my dad planted a large garden, but we had far too much corn and too many tomatoes and beans for our family. My dad built a small wooden stand in front of our house for my sister and me to sell vegetables and fruit during the summer vacation. We gained experience not only meeting the public but also making change for customers.

HINT: You might need to check with your local city offices to see if you need a license to operate a stand. Also, have an adult nearby in case any problems might arise.

If garden space is not available, help your child build a window box or use pots on a window sill for planting an herb garden.

Whether having your child measure for a garden spot, an area rug or to help build a porch, suggest measuring in different ways. Say, "How many tiny steps is it across this floor?" Or, "How many giant steps is it?" Children often have trouble measuring with rulers, paper and pencil but they can understand the size of their feet or hands. Provide them with these experiences.

But children also need practice using a ruler or measuring tape. I'm constantly surprised at how many of my students have trouble in this area. Have your youngster measure a variety of things around the house in order to become proficient in this skill.

Map reading. I'm amazed at the number of children and even teenagers who cannot give clear and concise directions. Now is the time to help your child become an avid map reader.

Start with a simple map of your neighborhood, no more than a few houses, mobile homes, or apartment buildings. Once your child understands how maps represent things, move on to a map of your community. Point out the streets you know. Talk about the friends who live on these streets. Move on to the major highways. Ask, "What direction do they run? East? West? North? or South?"

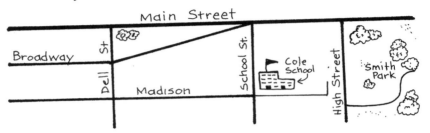

Talk about distances. Say, "Can you estimate how many miles it is from our house to the post office?" Then together check the mileage the next time you go.

No matter whether you're driving, flying or taking the train when you travel, your child needs to take a vital part in the on-going planning. Take this opportunity to teach how to read a map, to understand directions (North, South, East and West) and understand the legend on a map.

Later, when planning a summer vacation, purchase the maps you'll need and have your youngster help you plan the trip.

HINT: A number of automobile clubs provide free maps for their members. Go to your local office or mail a request for the ones you'll need. If you fly to your destination, your travel agent may have the necessary maps, or there may be small inserts in some of the travel information they provide.

Your child will need to know how many days you'll be driving, the destination and how many miles a day you wish to drive. Then let him or her plan where you might stop, stay and eat each day.

IDEA: I have found the Weather Channel on cable television to be very helpful when planning a trip. You and your child can check the channel several days before leaving and get a forecast of the weather you might encounter on your trip. This provides you with options for leaving on days when the weather cooperates with travelers.

Summer jobs. During the summer months when my husband and I take a vacation, we hire youngsters from our neighborhood to feed our cat, water the plants and take in the newspaper while we are away.

I have found it wise to observe the child at play on our street to see if he/she acts in a responsible manner. I then go to the parents and talk to them about the summer job I'd like their child to do. Often the parents will say, "He is almost eleven and wants to earn extra money and I think he can do these chores for you." I also ask the parent to check from time to time while we are gone to be sure the job is being done. In most cases it is done in a responsible manner, I am pleased and the child is happy to earn the additional income.

We have an occasional failure. In those cases, I point out to the child what has been left undone and how this is not acceptable. Naturally, we don't ask that youngster to work for us again unless we see examples of more responsibility.

If you feel your youngster who wants to earn extra money is responsible around the house, have him/her make a simple flyer stating that he/she is available to care for lawns, animals and plants of neighbors going on vacation. The child might also include taking in the newspaper and mail and checking to be sure security lights are on at night, but off in the daytime.

Have your child purchase a small notebook and set aside specific pages for keeping track of the jobs at each house. The youngster should note phone numbers in case of problems. Responsible children as young as eleven or twelve can also work as mother's helpers, not with full baby-sitting responsibility, but entertaining younger children for part of a day, perhaps.

Writing. When you begin planning your vacation, your child should be included at family planning sessions, because it's a good time to practice writing. Have your youngster take notes and volunteer to write for information about state parks, places to visit and places to stay.

Your youngster can also write the Chamber of Commerce or similar groups in the towns you'll visit, asking for maps and places to see, stay and eat. I usually send a check for $3.00 as a way of paying for postage and thanking the group for their help

Family or neighborhood newspaper. Suggest that your youngster use his/her computer skills to write a family newsletter or a neighborhood "newspaper."

Provide a summer notebook for taking notes on your family vacation. Your child can take notes about historical places, cities visited and interesting people met along the way. Upon arriving home, he/she could outline the material and give it a title such as "Summer Scenes from the Jones Family." The letter could be sent immediately or saved to share with family members during the Christmas holidays.

If your youngster has access to a graphics program, the letter could be illustrated. Better yet, have all family members draw a picture of one important place or person they saw on the trip. This will make the newsletter even more personalized.

With only a little adult guidance, a neighborhood newspaper could be a joint venture with the kids next door, down the street and around the corner. The children could elect an editor, reporter, illustrator and publisher. What a wonderful way to introduce your children to the world of publishing! The children could write about soccer events, a special kid's book at the library and talk about upcoming events in the community.

HINT: Another possibility is to make a trip scrapbook. Add pictures and specialized information from brochures of places you went. (The family letter could be incorporated.) When picking up brochures, take two of each whenever possible. Otherwise, you may have to choose material from only one side of a page when you really want to use both.

Begin a hobby. Vacation time is ideal for developing a new hobby. Hobbies established as a child frequently carry over into adult life. Collecting things is a very popular hobby whether coins, stamps or baseball cards.

To heighten interest in a hobby, take your youngster to a county fair, space museum, zoo, a state or federal park or automobile museum. Take a family trip to a ball game or ice show.

As a clue to your child's budding interest in a hobby, check to see what he/she is reading. This will give you a hint as to the direction of your youngster's curiosity or attention. Someone interested in coins will enjoy the *Handbook of United States Coins* by R. S. Yeoman. If your child shows an interest in visiting ponds, rivers or watching birds, a good book for his/her library is *The Young Naturalist* by Andrew Mitchell. An outstanding book for a child interested in the planets, space movement and travel is *Astronomy for Every Kid* by Janice Van Cleave.

Computer Skills for Summer. By the turn of the century, fully fifty percent of all young people entering the job market must be computer literate. Help your child this summer to prepare.

I've had much success while teaching summer school in my school district helping children as young as five become acquainted with the computer. They come each day eager to learn and explore and are intent upon following directions.

The older ones in the computer lab have more time to write letters, poems and jokes and to illustrate their creations.

Vacation time is also an opportunity when your older children can be increasing their skills doing word processing. I believe every intermediate student should be able to write and edit reports on the computer. To do this efficiently, they should be able to keyboard correctly. By this I mean, they can use their fingers correctly on a keyboard without looking at it. Your child should have and use keyboarding software such as *Microtype: The Wonderful Word of Paws*. Students complete beginning typing drills as a cat prompts and reinforces messages. This is available for IBM and MAC. Order (800) 624-2926.

NOTE: See my section on "Camping" in this chapter for additional information on providing your youngster with computer skills.

Encourage cooking. Children love to cook when given the chance. At the same time, they can learn to read a recipe, to measure, set a timer and read an oven thermometer. With some early supervision, children as young as eight or nine can be responsible for planning and preparing a meal once a week. (That's the night you do the dishes instead of the kids.)

Use the joy of cooking as a way for your child to develop his/her culinary talents. Buy one of the many cookbooks available for children of all ages. Two especially good ones are *Dinner's Ready, Mom* by Helen Gustafason and *Kids in the Kitchen* by Elaine Gazzolo.

If you are unable to supervise in the kitchen, ask a grandparent or older teen to help the child get started. Above all be positive. Not every casserole will be perfect but look only for the good and praise, praise, praise.

Your child can create simple main courses such as chicken stew, meatloaf, macaroni and cheese or stuffed eggplant. Your youngster could make a fresh salad using lettuce, radishes and tomatoes from the garden he or she planted. For dessert consider homemade gingerbread or chocolate pudding.

Plan a picnic. A variation of cooking is a picnic in the back yard, the back "forty" or at a park. Encourage your child to plan a family picnic. Talk about the amount of money to spend, a list of groceries needed and the number of people attending.

This will help your youngster develop organizational skills and the ability to take a large amount of information and distill it into a workable amount to use. This is also a chance to learn about prices, how to budget and how to provide your family with a warm and happy experience.

Promote exercise. I'm very concerned about today's children spending hours in front of the television or playing games on the computer. More and more, I'm reading reports about the amounts of fat buildup in children who do not get enough exercise.

Help your child plan large amounts of time for enjoyable physical activity during the summer. This might be inline skating or bike riding with a friend, bowling, swimming or playing baseball. Look into summer programs or day camps at your local school, park district or YMCA. Your local community college may have baseball or soccer camps.

Set a good example yourself and reserve times during the week to exercise as a family. Play ball, hike, walk or bicycle together.

Give your child a small notebook and ask for the pages to be dated and listed with the actual times the child will exercise. Ask what activities are scheduled each day. Have the child write down the friends who will be involved, where they will go and the amount of money needed (if any).

Summer enrichment activities. *Summer Bridge Activities*™ are books produced by Rainbow Publishing, (800) 598-1441, and written by two outstanding teachers to help your child retain information from one grade to the next.

For example, the first-to-second grade book has over 240 summer activities for your child to do from working on rhyming words, place value in math to problem solving and basic facts. The educators also list outstanding books for your child's summer reading. The summer activity books span from Preschool to Kindergarten, first grade to second, second to third and third to fourth. Each book contains incentive contracts for you to use with your child.

Another excellent book is *Playing Smart* by Susan K. Perry for children ages four to fourteen. Perry, a mother and award-winning independent journalist in Los Angeles, has created a treasure chest of activities which sharpen the senses, hone skills and encourage creativity. To order call (800) 735-7323.

Vacation camping. Some of my happiest vacations have been camping with my five nieces and nephews during their school vacations.

We tent camped and I had them help me plan menus, pick out the field trips we would take, clean up the tent and campsite and wash dishes.

I've also served as a camp counselor for youngsters in Alaska, Oregon and California summer camps. How wonderful it is for adults to share in the outdoor learning experience for boys and girls! Imagine what your children are learning while having fun. They learn directions, the interesting creatures that can be found in a pond and how to catch crawdads and cook them for dinner.

They also learn to pitch a tent, decide how much gasoline is needed to get to town and how many groceries and treats can be purchased for $18.00.

The Guide to Accredited Campgrounds is a booklet of campgrounds with planned activities for children and can be ordered by calling (800) 428-CAMP. Listed in the guide are 2,000 camps with a variety of features for all ages and interests. Call for a guide to campgrounds where your child might enjoy going.

Some of the topics covered at a variety of these campgrounds are computers, field trips, tennis, backpacking, cooking, art, campfires and nature-awareness. While having fun at the camp, your child will learn a variety of skills and meet new and interesting children. Most of these planned camps are businesses and come with a corresponding fee, so be aware of this when you call.

On the other hand, I camped with my nieces and nephews at state parks where we paid a minimal fee. We bought the food at discount stores, the kids swam and fished in the lake and at night I read an outstanding book to them (and any other interested campers) while they sat wide-eyed on logs surrounding our campfire. All of these adventures cost little money but brought lifelong learning and enjoyment to the kids and me.

Grandparents. Some parents find it difficult to get away for a week or two with the family while their children are on vacation. Instead, consider having the grandparents take the youngsters on a trip.

More and more seniors are living longer; they're healthy and eager to share time with grandchildren.

A number of companies now arrange or operate vacation trips for grandparents and grandchildren together. A few are:

- American Wilderness Experience (800) 444-0099
- Grandtravel (800) 247-7651
- Insider's Italy (718) 855-3878
- Rascals in Paradise (415) 978-9800

Some tours take children and grandparents to Wyoming where they explore Wyoming's Grand Tetons, and some go to the back country by wagon train and go rafting. Others go to Europe and take educational tours with a teacher-escort to provide the children with enrichment activities.

Elderhostel, a long-standing educational and recreational program for older adults, now offers intergenerational sessions where seniors may invite young people, often their grandchildren.

Children, along with grandparents, experience legends of "Little House on the Prairie" by visiting buffalo, cattle and sheep ranches; they feed calves and horses and learn why pioneers moved here and how they traveled by covered wagon.

Other programs range from cave exploration in Kansas, to studying pottery-making and prehistoric Native Americans in Arizona, to hiking and studying natural history near California's Lake Tahoe. Intergenerational programs are offered season-to-season throughout the United States and Canada. Children's ages vary, depending on the program. For more information call (617) 426-7788.

Grandparents wishing to stay closer to home can take children to the library, a fish hatchery, a children's museum, a local park or a candy factory.

Grandparents also have the opportunity to share a hobby with their grandchildren. This might be helping the youngster develop an interest in building model airplanes or a kite or starting a stamp collection. These are inexpensive things to share with children, but they can produce a lifelong interest in a hobby.

HINT: Over the vacation, grandparents might help their grandchildren write and publish a family history. Boys and girls love to see pictures of their parents as children and hear stories of their activities. Imagine the tales the elders can tell and what vital information the children can write. The book with a colorful cover would make a perfect and priceless surprise gift for family members on birthdays or holidays.

Grandma's Little Activity Book by Margolyn Woods is an outstanding book filled with ideas for grandparents to share with their grandchildren.

Music. Music is truly the universal language and certainly spans the generations. I had the most pleasant experience today standing under an ageless oak tree listening to a group of twenty people playing musical instruments. Each month these musicians, mostly seniors, join together to play their fiddles, guitars, mandolins, banjos and harmonicas.

We all joined together in toe-tapping to the beat of the music and singing along. Parents and grandparents should consider giving the gift of music appreciation to their child or grandchild. Check in your community for a jam session where your youngster can be inspired, perhaps, to take up a musical instrument. What a life-long gift to give a child!

Enjoy the summer vacation. At school we have recess twice a day and children look forward to the break from classroom activities.

Children who are <u>always</u> doing something don't have a chance to just think, dream and exercise their imaginations. Take the time during vacation to arrange for a "recess" now and then. Some suggestions are:

- Go outside with your child, lie on your backs and watch the clouds go by. See if any resemble familiar objects.
- Spend time simply walking through a park and talking about the flowers. Touch them, smell them and enjoy the beauty of our world while sitting on a park bench eating an ice cream cone.
- Set aside a day to fish in a quiet stream and listen to the sounds of birds, water rippling over rocks and leaves falling to the ground.

These are the golden memories your child will be storing, not only for today but for many tomorrows to come.

Meet The Needs Of Bilingual Students – Preschool-Sixth Grade

"Parents need to give children choices in everything they do — especially in learning. Say, 'Would you rather have me read a story or play a game with you?'

"Listen to your child's stories. Even if you have eight children, go somewhere with <u>one</u> child at a time and talk and listen. This makes each child feel special."

Sister Cora, Resource Teacher, Elementary-Community College, Member of Sisters of Mercy of Auburn Community in California

241

Tonya, a nine-year-old recent immigrant from Russia, gives up her recess each morning to help first graders in my computer lab with their lessons.

Tonya learned a great deal of English while doing lessons on the computer and enjoys working on it so much that she wants to share her knowledge with others.

During the past four years, I've worked with many immigrant children. Their cultures include Hispanic, Hmong, Mien, Vietnamese, Russian, Iranian, Pakistani and Chinese. I've learned that in order for these youngsters to succeed in American schools, we must reach out to them and their families with a variety of services. In this chapter, I'll tell you how you can help your children succeed in school and also provide you with a number of available resources.

I encourage you to read this chapter even if English is your child's first language. If you speak another language, you may be able to help some other family in your child's school.

These days, being bilingual can give young people a real edge in the job market and you can give your own child valuable exposure to another language.

Learning English. If you don't know English, I suggest you take classes now to learn it. A number of churches and schools offer the classes, often at several locations in a community. You'll find your transition into the American culture much easier when you can speak English. Also, its knowledge will be helpful as you take part in your child's education.

SUGGESTION: If you have a preschool child, you'll need to prepare that child to enter school. Provide him or her with a set of alphabet letters. As you sew or cook, point out colors and shapes.

I have worked with many young bilingual children entering school for the first time. Very few of them come prepared and it often takes several years for them to catch up. If you cannot tutor your child, have an older sibling do this. It will make the transition into school much easier for the youngster. See my chapter called "Prepare Your Child For Preschool."

What is bilingual education? This is a special program where bilingual children learn school curriculum content in specially developed classes in English which are often called "Sheltered English Classes." The teachers are trained to teach children by using charades and pantomime. They teach by saying, "Touch your nose, your ears, your mouth." In language arts, reading, math and social studies they are taught by listening, speaking, reading and writing.

In math, they learn to add by using colored sticks and blocks. They learn fractions by dividing paper plates into sections.

Prepare your child for school. It's important that you enroll your child in school as soon as you arrive. Let him or her know that it's important to have an education. Read my chapter on Homework, as this details how to help your child do well in school.

Getting it all together. Keep a box by the door with your child's name on it. All schoolwork, papers and books going back to school should be placed in the box before your youngster goes to bed at night.

Your child also needs a backpack to carry everything to school and bring home graded papers, books and class assignments. If you cannot afford one, check with the school PTA, a local clothes closet in your community or a church.

Study time. You must set aside a time each day when your child does homework, prepares for class projects or reads a book. Follow my directions in the Homework chapter and check to be sure your youngster is spending time each day keeping up with school work.

PARENT TIP: **You should try to provide a dictionary and encyclopedias to help your youngster do homework. See my chapter on Homework for suggestions on where you can purchase these items inexpensively.**

Set limits. Your child needs to become self-disciplined. To help with this in the beginning, you'll want to set a time for play, homework, chores, eating and sleeping. As your child grows older he/she can gradually start taking the responsibilities for using time wisely.

After-school activities. When your child comes home from school, check all graded papers. Be sure to look at the report card which usually comes out about four times a year. Always attend school conferences and try to go to Fall's Back-to-School Night and Spring's Open House.

If you don't understand some of the schoolwork coming home, ask your child to explain it to you. Your child may become a teacher to you but should <u>always</u> show you respect. Again, spend time listening to your child. If you see an unhappy face, say, "You don't look happy today. What happened?"

Read with your child each day. Reading is vital to a good education, and in order to become a good reader your child must read daily. Your kindergarten children should memorize nursery rhymes and songs and sing with motions. This will help them with reading.

HINT: Some school districts supply bilingual families with "dual bilingual books" which means, if you're Vietnamese, the top half of the reader will be in English and the bottom in Vietnamese. That way your child can read aloud to you in English while you read along in your own language.

After you've read a page, stop and ask your child questions such as, "Where did Maria live? Why did she go and visit her grandmother? What did they do after they left the hospital?"

Ask at your child's school if dual bilingual books are available in your primary language. As you share reading experiences with your child, the youngster will see how important it is to be a good reader.

HINT: Many books are written in Vietnamese, Spanish, Korean, Cambodian and Chinese. For more information on these books, call Children's Book Press in San Francisco, California at (415) 995-2200.

Older brothers and sisters can also help. Kao Saelee, a young Mien man from Laos, is a senior at one of our large universities in California. He is very busy with his own studies but takes time each week to read with his younger brothers, sisters, nieces and nephews.

Some evenings he gathers the children around him and reads fairy tales aloud. He models for them what good reading sounds like. He then asks them questions about what he has read. He also encourages them after they read or when they say their numbers. Afterward, he goes over the ABCs, counting numbers and months of the year and looks at their written reports.

You can ask an older son or daughter to do the same with your younger children. This will help them all become better readers.

HINT: Provide writing opportunities for your child. This might be writing to friends and relatives back home. Even if he or she writes in the primary language, needed skills are used to put words together to form sentences.

Storytelling. You've come to this country with many stories from your homeland. Share these with your child. Set aside a time each week when you tell stories of your culture and history to your youngsters.

One example is that Hmong and Mien families came to this country without a written language. As skilled seamstresses they design tapestries of stories into fabrics to make clothes. Using these designs for storytelling helps the children build a bridge into becoming successful readers.

If you have children's books in your own language, read those, too. Be sure your child understands and treasures your own culture.

Other ways to help your child with school work. Take your youngster to the grocery store. Have him/her read the labels on the cans as you select groceries. Ask, "What does it mean when it says 'three cans for a dollar'"?

Take your children to the library. Sit with them as they use the computer to look up books they wish to check out. Ask them to read the titles of the books to you.

Field trips. In order for children to be successful in school, they need many experiences in their community. If you do not drive, find out how to ride a bus to the zoo or a museum. Join your child on a school field trip. Some students go to historical places in the dress of the era depicted. You could help your child sew a dress or shirt to wear.

After the trip, children are asked to write a story about it. Have your youngster read the journal to you.

Gardening. Many immigrants come to this country with outstanding skills in raising fruits and vegetables. Use this talent as a way to help your school child. Have your youngster help you select a plot of ground for the garden, measure the space, purchase the seeds and plant them. Later your child can help you pick the vegetables, cook them and enjoy them at a family meal.

Sewing. Many women are excellent seamstresses. If you sew, have your youngster help estimate how much yardage you'll need to make a dress, coat or jacket. Later, ask the child to measure how much fabric you bought.

If you sell your sewing creations at fairs or schools, have your child sit with you to make change and tell you how much money you made. You'll be passing on many skills in sewing and running a business to your youngster.

Through a local church, I purchased a lovely vest made by a lady in Guatemala. I enjoy wearing this brightly-colored garment with my skirts and pants. At the same time, I know I've helped a person with a home business.

Cultural differences. Many families coming to this new land have different rituals and customs than we have here. Some of these customs are new to Americans and you need to inform your child's teacher about these so your child will not be frightened by the mix in cultures. None of us wants to offend you or your child by mistake. For example, in some cultures, children keep strings tied around their wrists and ankles. You or your child need to explain any special customs to the teacher.

Building self-esteem. Use kind words when talking with your child. Say things like, "You did a good job writing your history report." Or, "I was proud of the talk you gave at school today." Children are eager to please and want you to be proud of what they do. Show them you care.

When your child comes home from school, take time to ask about his/her day. Say, "What did you do in math today?" Or, "Did you recite the poem you memorized last night for reading?" Then sit quietly and listen. Children grow in confidence when given respect, love and your interest in what they are doing at school.

Community and school resources. Across the country, resource centers have been established either in the community or through school districts for new families coming to their areas. See what you might find where your live.

Even-Start Program. One outstanding resource program functioning in my area is the Even-Start Program. This is run by a world-wide religious community which works alongside local agencies to build low-income housing for needy families. Members of the Sisters of Mercy of the Americas provide support services such as health care and education for both parents and children.

In my own community, the Sisters have, with the help of the city, built a series of affordable apartments on a downtown city block. In addition, the Sisters provide preschool for children and parent-education classes for adults. Check in your community for such facilities.

Other groups providing help to the bilingual community are resource centers, Refugee Educators' Network, churches and school districts. These centers provide a good variety of services and resources.

- Catalogues for checking out books, magazines, films and videos. The subjects include health care, folk tales and stories written in English.
- Information on educational fairs
- Bilingual workers to help with job training
- English classes for parents
- Help for doing income taxes
- Information on getting a job

- Workshops on how to write checks, keep money in banks and use a safe-deposit box
- Help for high-school students taking SAT tests to enter college
- Help with school registration for your child
- Provision of translators when needed

Churches also provide a variety of services.

- Lutheran Social Services usually offer a clothes closet and can provide you with an interpreter. In some communities they provide parent education classes for Vietnamese, Chinese, Hmong, Lao, Mien and Cambodian parents.
- Many churches provide help with homework for your children, including tutoring. Some will even come to your home and provide lessons in English for adults.

Educational services. More and more schools are offering after-school programs to help both children and parents become established in this country. One sample program is the Twilight School. This program is springing up around the country and classes are usually held from 4 p.m. to 7 p.m. several days a week. The program addresses the needs of the entire family.

Preschoolers come and listen to stories and do an art project while parents attend English classes where they sing, are taught the English language and can attend workshops such as "Nutrition and You," "Parent Involvement," or "Strategies for Reading."

Children in grades one to six work in small groups with associates (tutors) in reading, math and English. Also, homework is supervised by volunteers.

Small-group meetings. In many schools, small groups of bilingual parents and their children are invited to attend weekly classes. Often the art-and-craft skills of the participants are used to create paper flowers or needlework projects to share with others.

Mothers and daughters work together, giving daughters the opportunity to talk to their mothers in English.

Men and women also attend classes on how to use a computer so they can get a job. Classes are also available in learning computer keyboarding as part of the weekly lesson.

Some school districts conduct monthly classes for parents. A few of the topics include "Parents As Partners in Reading," "Summertime Activities," and "Put Some Money in Your Pocket." A month-long course is given following the text of the outstanding book, *MegaSkills* by Dr. Dorothy Rich. In the class, you'll learn how to build confidence in your child, teach responsibility and keep him or her motivated.

Celebrations. Celebrations are held at many schools during Chinese New Year, Cinco de Mayo, and other ethnic holidays. Parents are often invited to the festivities. Children make puppets and face masks and dress in their native costumes. Then they parade around the school so all the parents and children can enjoy their musical and artistic talents.

During the school year food festivals are held when parents and children are invited to bring in special foods from their homelands to share with other parents, faculty and staff.

I enjoy going to these celebrations, and my students are always eager to have me taste their special foods. I look forward to these occasions with my boys and girls, as well as having their parents come into my classroom and share their artwork, sewing and pictures with all my students. You have many talents. Be willing to share them with others.

Here is a list of books which will be helpful in your home. If you are unable to purchase them or check them out of your library, ask your Resource Center to make them available to you.

Books for adults

Parent Involvement in School by Huynh Dinh Te, Ph.D.
Bridge to Literacy by Grace Massey Holt and Susan Gaer
Crossroads by Irene Frankel and Cliff Meyers
Parenting Curriculum for Language Minority Parents by Grace D. Holt
Grammar and Survival English by Oxford University Press

Books for children

Grover's Orange Book by Jane Zion Brauer is a book for children K-6, primarily for beginning students with a limited English proficiency. It develops oral language and good listening skills by using songs, chants and poems.

Chiquita's Diary by Bettina R. Flores is a book for intermediates to adults. This is the story of a young Hispanic girl's inspiring and heroic quest for a better life.

Dictionary

The New Oxford Picture Dictionary by E.C. Parnwell

Catalogs

Sundance K-8 Multicultural Connections, Littleton, MA

Bilingual Educational Services, Inc., Bilingual Educational Services, Inc., Los Angeles, CA

Consumer Information Catalog, United States Government Printing Office, Pueblo, CO

NOTE: The government printing office has outstanding publications which are either free or usually cost fifty cents or a dollar. These are most helpful booklets on subjects such as *Helping Your Child Learn Math* or *Science* or *How to Read*. Send for a catalog and order booklets which would be helpful in your home and community. When you finish a booklet, pass it on to a friend. The material is really informational.

Manage Home Schooling

"We're all 'teachers' at our school. Really, we're all 'learners' rather than 'teachers' because we help each other learn. My children's education isn't limited by my knowledge. They use computers, video programs, books and texts. Once children know how to learn independently, they'll be ready to apply their learning skills to get better educated at any level."

Lori Loranger, Washougal, Washington, who has always home schooled
her daughters aged eleven and seven

More and more parents are teaching their youngsters at home rather than sending them to public or private schools. In the mid-1990s, the number of children being home schooled is estimated to be between 300,000 and 1,000,000.

Parents give a variety of reasons for undertaking this major commitment. Their most frequently mentioned reasons are that they want to:

- Teach their children their own values
- Provide a place where their children's self-esteem can be nurtured
- Create more time for their children to develop special talents such as sports or music
- Educate their children while providing work experience, particularly if parents are engaged in a cottage industry
- Give children a safe place to learn and grow
- Permit individualized instruction for a child with a learning disability

NOTE: The information for this chapter came out of a number of interviews I did with home-school parents, both women and men. I also researched the subject extensively and talked with some home-schooled children.

Keep in mind that seventy-five percent of home-schooled students enter (or re-enter) the public or private school system at some point. Some parents choose to home school for a short period of time while others consider it a way of life.

Advantages of home schooling. A caring parent can select the learning style which works best with each youngster and focus on that. The child might be an auditory (hearing) learner, or a visual (seeing) learner and some are kinesthetic (touching) learners.

Also, homeschooling provides flexibility and time for an especially talented youngster with a particular passion. An example is sixteen-year-old Shawna from my area, who practices her violin three hours a day and will probably attend a prestigious music school in a year or two.

Home schoolers are less interested in "wearing the right clothes," or needing money to buy a certain brand of shoes. They tend to be less materialistic and less likely to be influenced by peer pressure. In many cases, they learn to relate earlier and better to both older people and younger children.

How to establish a home school. Each state has its own requirements. In my state of California, for instance, parents commonly choose from four alternatives.

- The parents file an affidavit with the local county establishing the home as a private school.
- The parents enroll the child in a private independent-study program.
- The parents enroll the youngster in a public school independent-study program.
- The parents belong to an umbrella group such as a church-school.

The classroom.   Ideally, you should have a room set aside for schooling. If this isn't possible, the children sit around either the kitchen or dining-room table or in a family room. Locate bookshelves nearby for materials to use throughout the year.

NOTE: Sometimes older students (ages 13 to 18) will gather up needed materials and retreat to their bedrooms for solitude to do their assignments, document their progress, and call upon a parent for help as needed.

A number of home schoolers network with others and this includes team teaching. In this case, it is important that the classroom be a large room such as a family room so that other parents and children can assemble for specific lessons. For example, one home-school mother specialized in economics in college. She teaches classes in her home on math, money and economics to twenty home schoolers.

Materials. Home-school conferences for parents are held in many cities during the year. Workshops are presented and vendors share the latest in home-school materials. You can often get publishers' catalogs at these conferences. A large number of publishers feature materials aimed at home schoolers with a religious emphasis.

Use your public library, go to garage sales and look for discarded books at local school districts and libraries. Sometimes you can find grade-level books at discount stores.

You may also send for books and supplies by mail order. Often the price is less than what can be found locally. Look at the end of this chapter for a list of resources.

PARENT TIP: **One parent who home schools purchases "Scope and Sequence" booklets for each subject from her state's Department of Education and uses the sequence list of skills as a checklist during the year. That way she knows she is covering every required skill in each subject she is teaching her children.**

The schedule. The home-school schedule varies, depending upon the needs of the individual family. Many experienced home schoolers teach the most difficult subjects early in the day and reserve hands-on learning for the afternoon hours.

Your state probably requires a specific number of days and hours of instruction. Check with your local county office of education for accurate information. Since home-school laws vary greatly from state to state, and home-schooling families consider their homes private schools, the actual hours and days taught are usually related to state laws governing private-school attendance.

NOTE: The public-school calendar is changing with the advent of more year-round schools. For instance, my school will go year-round this coming September. Many meetings are being held now to prepare the faculty, parents and children for the changes that are coming.

Some home schoolers prefer to adjust their teaching schedule so the family can take vacations which become field trips for the youngsters. It's great to be able to travel after the busy summer vacation season when there are fewer crowds.

The parents I interviewed usually begin school at 9 a.m. and take a lunch break at noon. When their child is working on a large project, the youngster continues to work for an hour or two in the afternoon.

Parents also take their children to the local library to use resource materials there for completing writing projects. In addition, some parents also arrange for their older children to volunteer to work at the local library to gain on-the-job training.

Networking. In my interviews, I've found a recurring thread in home schooling and that is <u>networking</u>.

A number of home schoolers indicate that education-at-home can lead to isolation from other people. By networking with other home-schooling families, however, parents provide their children with a time to socialize with other children while playing sports, attending group music lessons or being invited to a home for a special lesson. At the same time, parents can share joys and problems, exchange ideas and have social interaction with other adults. It becomes a time of encouragement.

Meetings. Every good-sized community has small-to-medium-sized local homeschool groups. These are good to join for continual encouragement and field trips.

Each state also has a state Homeschool organization for legal and community purposes. They hold conventions yearly. Example: California's organization is called California Home Education Association (CHEA).

Field trips. Many families join together to go on field trips after completing a unit of study. One group, after doing a newspaper unit, visited a large city newspaper. Their special tour took the children and parents through all departments of the newspaper operation with a guide to answer questions.

Contact the community relations person of the organization you wish to visit. Advance arrangements often translate to a group school rate and a guide for your field trip.

Be sure to have your students write suitable thank-you letters after your tour.

Other families go to zoos, parks and science museums. By having smaller groups than public-school classes, home schoolers can often have a more private or extensive tour of facilities. You may also attend musical concerts and plays.

Media resources. As computers become more a part of the home, many home schoolers rely on them as resources during the teaching day. More and more computer software is becoming available to enhance children's education. See my chapter on computers for age-specific recommendations.

Parents may also arrange for their children to have pen pals via various computer networks. Letters are written on the computer and then sent by modem to a contact across the country or even across the world.

A modem-equipped computer also opens a wide area of networking with other home schoolers on local electronic "bulletin boards" (BBSes). A quick look at a free, local Home School BBS showed a "library" of numerous educational software programs available to download as well as "discussion areas" on several topics. Commercial services such as CompuServe or America Online have easily accessible "areas" with many home-schooling resources.

CONCERN: Some home schoolers have become quite adept at roaming on the Internet. You must always be aware of what your youngsters are doing and saying there. They should never give out their names, addresses or telephone numbers. See my chapter on computers, particularly on the Internet, for additional cautions.

Many parents use the Public Broadcasting Service (PBS) on television as a teaching resource for their children. You can obtain teacher's guides from your local station.

Other outstanding programs can be found on the Learning and Discovery Channels on cable television. The Discovery Channel also publishes a magazine and a number of pieces of science software for the computer. See my computer chapter for more ideas.

Teaching physical education. In California, home-school parents are asked to set aside twenty minutes a day for teaching physical education. Check at your State Department of Education to get the required amount of time for physical education in your state.

One parent told me she jogs with her children each morning before the teaching day begins. Many parents use physical education to network with other parents. They use local parks for teaching and playing baseball, soccer and basketball. Teams are formed and skills taught to all the children.

Public Independent-Study Programs. More and more counties and school districts are urging parents to consider linking with the public schools when starting a home school.

This arrangement may work well for the public school as well as the parent. Although individual programs vary, all are governed by state independent-study laws and guidelines. Contact your local school district or county to determine what services are provided. In addition, it is wise to ask what the home-schooling requirements are.

Under one county's operations, the parent-teacher arranges an initial meeting with the coordinator of the county program to learn what the school district will do for the family. Once the home-schooling family makes a firm commitment to the program, some counties provide a number of services.

- The coordinator tests each child beginning in the program.
- Based on test results, the coordinator places each child in appropriate reading, language, math, science and social-studies books.
- The parent is given a teacher's guidebook for each subject.
- A well-trained paraprofessional makes monthly visits to each home school to answer questions and assist the parent.
- The home-school families come into the Community Service office each week and use the media center. Families are provided with laser disks, CD-ROMs, videos and encyclopedias.
- During the school year, youngsters are periodically tested and

provided with additional books as they progress.

District and county independent programs generate the same

amount of revenue from the state that would be collected if the child were attending a traditional school.

Record-keeping and paperwork. It is very important that records of daily home-school activities be kept in a specific place. Good record-keeping will lend credibility to your home school. States often like to see records organized by school subject, and when you are teaching several children, it helps you know what has been covered with each child. You should keep all the following:

- All legal and procedural papers
- Your statement of intent
- All evaluation documents
- Lesson plans, logs and curriculum guides
- Report cards and progress-assessment forms
- Schedules and calendars
- Attendance registers
- Student-work folders
- Special-activities folders (Include notes of special events where others taught your child.)
- Special services (Information on services which could include a speech therapist, psychologist or other specialist)
- An end-of-the-year folder. This would be similar to a cumulative file which is kept at a regular school. List days attended, days absent and include any special testing.

This is not a complete list and you'll need to check with those in charge of home schooling in your area for specific items required by your state.

Home schooling: an opinion by the author. As a parent of home schoolers, you have a privilege I've never experienced in my many years of teaching. You can teach your child one-on-one. By being able to individualize education, you give your children a wonderful opportunity to have you serve as a tutor, mentor and loving guide in their educational program.

However, my concern as a teacher of thirty years can be expressed in one word — *commitment.* If you wish to home school, build a strong foundation before you begin. Research how you'll run your school, network with other home schoolers and be ready for the "long haul."

HINT: If and when you decide to have your youngster return to the public schools, I suggest you spend time preparing him or her. Talk with the principal of the school and arrange a time for a visit. If there's a friend in the neighborhood, check to see if your child can sit in on a class one day with the friend. You would need to ask permission first in the office.

Help to make the transition from home to public or private school as successful as possible. After the child enters, spend time talking about the "new school" each day so any problems which might develop can be settled at once.

I urge you to give your child the best education you possibly can and enjoy your time together.

Resources. Here is a brief list of resources which can help you as you consider home schooling.

Books

Home School: Taking the First Step by Borg Hendrickson
Family Matters: Why Homeschooling Makes Sense by David Guterson
The Home School Market Guide by Jane Williams. Order: (916) 622-8586
Homeschooling for Excellence by David and Micki Colfax
Better Late than Early by Raymond and Dorothy Moore
The Big Book of Home Learning, Volumes 1-4 by Mary Pride

Catalogs

Bluestocking Press (800) 959-8586
More than 1,000 items with a concentration in American History, economics and law. The catalog also includes sections on writing, critical

thinking and the arts.

Builder Books, Inc. (509) 826-6021

Great Christian Books (Discount Homeschool Warehouse) (410) 392-0800

Homeschooling Book Club (810) 685-8773

Magazines

Home Education Magazine, P.O. Box 1083, Tonasket, WA 98855

Homeschool Today, P.O. Box 1425, Melrose, FL 32666

The HomeSchool Court Report, (540) 338-5600

Newsletter

"Growing Without Schooling" (617) 864-3100

"How To Home School Newsletter," 10404 Huntsmoor Drive, Richmond, VA 23233

CompuServe

Homeschool Today can be accessed through the Christian Information Network on CompuServe.

As The Twig Is Bent...

"The important thing, we feel, is that parents consciously develop their own set of family values and work at teaching those values to their children. The home will never — should never — can never be replaced as the institution where basic values are learned and taught.

"Children may grow up and ultimately develop values different from yours and different from what you tried to teach them; but at least they will do so consciously, and with a basis of comparison — with a foundation to start from. If children start from a values vacuum — with none taught, none learned — they will float at the mercy of circumstance and situation, and their lives will never be their own."

Reprinted with the permission of Simon & Schuster Inc. from *Teaching Your Children Values* by Linda and Richard Eyre. Copyright © 1993 by R.M. Eyre & Assoc. Inc.

School classrooms are not large; the average is about 940 square feet. Put into this room as many as forty-one active youngsters as I had one year, and you have a small, often cramped mini-society living together and hopefully learning together.

Some of my students come to me happy, kind and gentle, while others enter my classroom angry, hostile, calling others names and ready to take on anyone who crosses them. In order to survive, I hold a classroom meeting at the end of each day. Here I teach my students to talk out problems and disagreements so we can begin the next day without friction.

Today we see far too many problems being settled with fists, knives and guns. I know from personal experience. One day on yard duty, a big, burly sixth grader walked up to me and said, "I've been wanting to kill a teacher, and I'm going to start with you!" Fortunately, as he held a knife to my side, his buddy dragged him off me.

Knowing the value of class meetings, I urge all parents to hold weekly family meetings at home. Teach your child to overcome anger and frustration in a respectful, positive manner. We must change our society, and the family meeting can be the training ground.

As a parent, are you aware that by age five, your youngster has learned fully 50 percent of what he or she will ever learn? Use this "fertile time" to teach a value system which will be helpful now and carry over into your child's future life.

On a personal note, I was taught values and morals early in life. I had two parents who cared about me, taught me right from wrong, and expected good manners and good behavior both at home and beyond our front door. They also made sure I attended Sunday School where I learned sound moral principles which continue to work well for me today at home and in the classroom.

In this final chapter of my book, I'll share with you some of the enduring lessons I've learned during my thirty years of teaching children. I will give suggestions on what worked for me in teaching values to my students. I'll also give you suggestions and resources on what can work for you at home as you guide your child to grow into a loving, kind and responsible human being.

Proper attitudes and behavior learned <u>early</u> are vital as a way of steering a child away from more serious problems as he or she moves into adolescence.

Books on teaching morals. When your child reaches the age of two or three, you can begin to read books about morals to him/her. Children always enjoy the story of *Pinocchio*. Another outstanding book for intermediate children is *The Chronicles of Narnia* by C. S. Lewis.

Other books are:

The Runaway Bunny by Margaret Wise Brown tells about the love between a little bunny and his mother.

Rhubarb by Stephen Cosgrove says to have a friend, be a friend.

Fanny by Stephen Cosgrove tells about being handicapped.

The Giving Tree by Shel Silverstein is a warm and loving book about sharing what you have.

Manners. During the past ten years, I've noticed a deterioration in my students' manners. At times the problem has escalated to the point where I've had to spend time actually teaching appropriate "public" behavior to my students.

As a parent, you need to teach manners to your child, model how to greet people and how to be respectful of others. Then check to be sure these skills are ongoing in your child's life.

Some of the words or phrases which help children get along peaceably with others at home, in the classroom and their community are:

• Saying, "Please" and "Thank you" to others
• Using the phrase, "May I?"
• Saying, "Excuse me" or "Pardon me" or "I'm sorry"

These simple phrases open doors to a happier world for your child. Manners are the words and actions which make a BIG difference in day-to-day living.

Honesty. Honesty develops trust and is an important principle your child should learn early. Without trust, your youngster will have a difficult time in life.

Children go through a period of lying. Don't say to your child, "You lie and you're evil." Talk about the importance of being truthful and not breaking their parents' trust, which kids don't want to lose. At the same time, don't use the phrase, "Why are you lying?" Kids don't know why they lie.

Instead, say to your child, "What happens when you don't tell the truth?" Or, "What happens when you tell the truth?" Remind your youngster, "People won't believe you when you *really* do tell the truth if you continue to lie."

I've spent hours in the classroom attempting to settle disputes over lying and stealing. Here are some of the comments I've heard.

"He took my lunch money and I can't eat lunch."

"No, I didn't. He <u>lies.</u>"

"She told my girlfriend that I was ugly and that I hated her."

"No, I didn't. She <u>lies.</u>"

"He took my baseball glove and I can prove it."

"No, he can't. He's stupid and he <u>lies.</u>"

At daily class meetings, I attempt to settle issues which are as vital as running the country to nine-year-olds. I ask for witnesses to stand; I talk with those involved in the confrontation and, at times, become a "King Solomon" settling issues so the class can go on with learning.

You, as a parent, can help your child develop the trait of honesty. Some things you can do are talk about the importance of being honest in your home, model honesty in your daily life, talk about how it *feels* when not being honest and discuss the importance of *trust* in daily living.

PARENT TIP: **Model honesty in your daily dealings with your child. If you tell your child to always be truthful and then go to a movie and tell the ticket seller, "My child is five," when the youngster is really six, you're setting a poor example.**

Self-confidence. One of the most rewarding gifts you can give your child is the ability to feel good about himself or herself. Never label your child by saying, "You're stupid" or "You're so dumb. Why can't you ever do anything right?"

Instead, raise an "I-Can" child. This means a youngster who goes to school with homework, books and a lunch without being reminded.

Children take pride when they take care of themselves. Encourage your youngster to be an "I-Can" child by saying things like, "I know you can handle this," and "You did a great job" and "It means a lot that I can count on you."

During the school years, if a problem should arise between your child and a teacher, talk it over at home first; perhaps your youngster would prefer to settle it without your being involved.

A friend's five-year-old granddaughter wasn't getting along with her teacher; she wanted to talk to the teacher alone but use her mother as a backup. The child made the appointment to see the teacher after school and the parent came and sat outside the door. Her mother said, "If you need help, I'm here." The child walked into the room, discussed the problem with the teacher and it was settled. This is an example of an "I-Can" child.

HINT: One of the best resources for a confident child is a happy family. Try to assure that your child leaves home each morning with a good feeling and returns at the end of the day to a happy home.

PARENT TIP: **Create with your child an "I-Can" poster to hang on the wall. Take pictures of your child doing things such as helping you build a porch, hitting a baseball or cooking a meal. Take a picture of your youngster helping Grandpa plant carrots in his garden. Have your youngster label each picture with a sentence such as, "I make terrific spaghetti," or "I grow BIG carrots."**

Self-discipline. As parents and teachers, one of the goals we need is to help children become self-disciplined. That means helping your child develop the ability inside to take care of himself/herself, to manage time, to become a self-starter and to learn to control temper outbursts.

To do this, we adults must model this behavior for our children. We must be an example. We know when we get angry, that it is much better to "count to ten," than explode. Share with your child the importance of doing the same thing.

If your child has problems getting up on time, buy him/her an alarm clock and show how to use it. When your youngster follows through, praise, praise, praise.

For more ideas on how to help your child become a "self-starter," particularly when doing homework, see my chapter on "Homework."

One of the most outstanding books I've found on teaching values such as self-discipline is *Teaching Your Children Values* by Linda and Richard Eyre.

Other books to have in your home library are *Golden Rules* by Wayne Dosick who tells parents how to teach ten ethical values to their youngsters such as to do good, do right and be a decent and honorable human being. *MegaSkills* by Dorothy Rich explains how to teach your child confidence, responsibility and perseverance and other qualities.

Respect. This means respect for others' views and property, but even more important, respect for oneself and for other people.

Property. My school's walls and doors have been the victims of spray-painted graffiti almost every weekend. I dread driving to work on Mondays and seeing what some uncaring and disrespectful person has done to my school.

Respect for others and for property begins at home. Children who are taught to respect themselves and others do not go out into their world and destroy property. Spend time at family meetings discussing what all family members can do to show respect for each other, for their home and community. Begin small and branch out to the world outside your door.

Talk about feelings. Say, "How does it feel when you see a child at school stuffing paper towels down the toilet?" Or, "How does it feel when a classmate walks up and kicks you?"

Show your child respect. "For every put-down your child receives," says Carol Houseman, Consultant in Organizational Development, "your child needs ten put-ups." Let your home become a healing place not only for bruised knees and elbows but also hearts and souls.

I tell my students, "You are a special person and I'm so pleased to have you in my classroom." Some weeks I write happy notes to one or more youngsters who need a little extra care, and each loves getting a "praise" note from me. All children need to feel they have someone in their corner.

SUGGESTION: For ideas on how you can write your own "happy" notes read, *Notes in the Lunchbox* by Barbara Reider.

Remember the self-respect a child develops is based on how we adults treat him/her. Make yours a positive home environment for your child to grow and blossom.

PARENT TIP: **Remind your child that he/she does not live in a perfect world, and the youngster will not do everything perfectly all the time. Neither will you, but that is all right. Explain that at times you'll give constructive criticism, for example, when homework is dashed off in a hurry and you want to work together to improve the product.**

Bullying and name calling. This is where it is vital for you to have an ongoing and open relationship with your child. Your youngster needs to feel at all times that he/she can talk with you about anything.

If you sense any problem at all, ask your child if others are not treating him/her fairly. Spend time talking about the problem and perhaps your youngster will want to settle it on his own. On the other hand, it may be necessary for you to talk with the other child or an adult. If it involves the school in any way, talk to the teacher.

Threats. I hear far too many stories about children being threatened, for example, by other kids on the way to and from school. If your child is ever threatened with something like, "I'll beat you up after school if you don't pay me a dollar now," you must intervene at once.

NOTE: Don't ever tolerate any mistreatment of your child. Also, if you wish to know what is happening at school, why not volunteer in your child's class? This way you'll spend time in the classroom and will know what is going on.

Name-calling. This has become a big item in classrooms and on playgrounds. In the past few years, I've noted an increase not only in name-calling but in the escalation of vulgarity and volume.

Children both at home and school should not be the targets of unpleasant names. One way to end it is suggested by Elva Anson, Marriage, Family and Child Counselor in Fair Oaks, California. She says, "If adults call kids names, their kids will call others names."

She suggests if name-calling occurs, you should say, "How did it feel? Tell me about it." She has found that using a hand puppet to talk through such a problem is a good way of reaching a child who might be resistant to parent-child talk. However, she recommends waiting until your child brings up the problem before you address the subject.

"In parent and child conversations," says Anson, "parents should talk *less* and let the kid talk *more*."

PARENT TIP: **Just as it helps to hold classroom meetings each afternoon before students go home, I'd suggest you consider holding a family meeting at least once a week. This is where problems can be talked about and worked out before they escalate. Remember each child has a voice, no matter how young. Anson says the family meeting at her house begins with a prayer and is followed by planning activities for the family, setting up work charts and establishing family rules. Consider holding such a meeting in your home.**

HINT: Always start the family meeting with compliments, positive thoughts and praise.

Drugs. During the past six years, the number of children entering my classroom who were born addicted to drugs has increased. No words can ever explain the sorrow, sadness and utter frustration I feel when dealing with a drug-affected child. Often the child has been given away by the mother to a receiving home, to a relative or placed in foster care. It is incredibly sad to see what these children go through each day of their lives. Sometimes to calm a child, I put my arms around him or her and the youngster will say, "Oh, (sigh) I miss my mom so much." All I can do then is hug the child and sing a little song I learned in Sunday School. Sometimes by the third chorus, the youngster will sing along with me and for a few minutes in this tiny peaceful world the small body begins to relax.

A mother on drugs giving birth to a baby can cause *big-time* learning problems for the youngster such as impulsive behavior, a decrease in attention span, emotional problems and a low frustration level.

Alcohol also has effects on the fetus. Heavy alcohol use during pregnancy can produce a youngster with fetal alcohol syndrome which leads to a child with learning disabilities.

NOTE: In a recent study conducted between 1977 and 1993, it was discovered that binge drinking among women aged 18 to 29 has *tripled*. Imagine this at a time when many young women are having their babies.

As parents, warn your children about the destructive use of drugs and alcohol. Make youngsters aware of what drugs can do to their bodies and also to the babies they might eventually conceive. I truly believe <u>every</u> high school boy and girl should be required to work full time for a minimum of two weeks in an elementary classroom which has drug-affected children. Hopefully, each young person would see the havoc that drugs can do to an innocent child's body and mind. It is simply a nationwide tragedy!

Stay in school. It is vital that your child stay in school. The life of a dropout student is bleak indeed.

Haynes Johnson, author of *Divided We Fall*, states that <u>every thirty minutes</u> across the United States the following is taking place:

- Fifty young people drop out of school.
- Eighty-five commit a violent crime.
- Twenty-seven teen-age girls give birth (sixteen out-of-wedlock).

He continues, "At the end of one year, a million students have dropped out of school, and 1.3 million have committed a violent crime, while 478,000 teenagers give birth." That's not a pretty picture, is it?

Financially, it is also a *big* loss when a youngster drops out of high school. On average, a young person will make $212,000 less dollars over a lifetime than someone who stays in high school and graduates. For students going on to college, if they drop out of college, they will suffer a financial loss of over $800,000 during their lifetime compared to those who stay in college and graduate. These figures are from a recent Drop-out Poll conducted by the Educational Testing Service.

Parenting classes. I've been pleased the past three years to see an increase in parenting classes offered by school districts, churches and social agencies. These classes supply invaluable information, a list of books to read and provide parents with a network of support. Consider attending one.

Religion. Religion can bring a sense of stability and comfort into your child's life. I have also found that Sunday School and church provide a sense of direction for a child in today's difficult times. Such attendance can also give your youngster a sense of community with other children. I still keep in touch with adults I knew as children years ago in my Sunday School classes.

Continue to motivate your child daily to stay in school and do the very best work possible. As a parent, you have the lasting influence in helping your child succeed in school. Continue by your words and actions to show your child that you have faith in his or her ability to learn and to achieve and become a happy and productive adult.

Resources

ACADEMIC GOALS FOR STUDENTS IN GRADES K-6

In this appendix you will have the opportunity to look over a general outline of the basic objectives taught at the K-6 grade level. Although it is not detailed, by reading your grade level goals carefully, you'll have a better idea of what you'll be expected to teach, and you can purchase or order supplies to fit these needs.

This typical set of objectives is from the Sacramento (California) City Unified School District.

KINDERGARTEN OBJECTIVES
READING
PHONICS

Match small letters with capital letters in random order.
Know and say beginning consonant sounds.
Tell whether words do or do not rhyme.
Tell how objects are alike and different by size, color, and shape.

COMPREHENSION

Identify objects in a picture to answer questions.
Describe pictures, actions, or activities using words or sentences.
Learn the meaning of opposites: *hot/cold, up/down, in/out.*
Put picture cards of a story in correct order and discuss sequence.
Know the colors.
Recognize first name in print.

STUDY SKILLS

Classify pictures to make categories and groups.
Identify positions such as *top/bottom, first/middle/last.*
Track objects from left to right.
Know top-to-bottom as it relates to reading and work papers.
Match pictures that are alike.

LANGUAGE ARTS
ORAL LANGUAGE

Develop a listening and speaking vocabulary by participating in:
    group discussion
    drama
    block play
    playhouse area
Use complete sentences during show and tell.
Look at pictures of people in a story:
    Tell how they may feel.
    Tell what they may do.

LISTENING

Pay careful attention when:
  others speak
  stories are read
  directions are given
  lessons are taught

WRITTEN LANGUAGE

Print first name using capital and small letters.
Dictate a story or letter for an adult to write.
Develop small muscle coordination by:
  cutting and pasting
  drawing, coloring, and painting
  tracing patterns and templates
  marking a path in a maze
  writing name, numerals, etc.
Be familiar with a monthly calendar.
Match words that look alike.

MATHEMATICS

PROBLEM SOLVING

Identify and classify objects by color, size, shape, and use.
Identify position of objects:
  in front, in back, over, under, middle, right, left, top, bottom, up, down.
Identify size of objects: *small, medium, large; short, long; narrow, wide.*

NUMBER SYSTEM

Count 0-15.
Recognize and write numerals 1-10.
Identify numbers in order from first to last.
Connect numbers in order on:
  dot-to-dot games
  graphs
  worksheets

COMPUTATION

Identify groups of objects containing: *more, less, and same number of objects.*

MEASUREMENT

Compare weights: *heavy/light.*
Compare lengths: *longer/shorter.*
Compare heights: *taller/shorter.*

SHAPES AND PATTERNS

Identify shapes: *circle, square, triangle, rectangle.*
Predict what the next shape and/or color would be in a given pattern.

FIRST-GRADE OBJECTIVES

READING

PHONICS

Recognize and identify:
  long and short vowel sounds
  number(s) of syllables in one- or two-syllable words
  singular and plural forms of nouns
  endings of action words (verbs): *plays, playing, played*
  parts of compound words: into = in + to
  contractions with n't endings: *can't*
  beginning and ending consonant clusters such as: *sh/show and st/nest*
Blend the sounds of individual letters together to form a word.

VOCABULARY

Sight-read basic vocabulary for grade one.
From a given list, select synonyms (words with similar meanings) and antonyms
  (words with opposite meanings).

COMPREHENSION

Read a story; answer questions about it.
Choose a sentence that matches a picture.
Select a word to complete a sentence.
Identify what happens first, next, or last in a story.
Select the main idea of a paragraph.

STUDY SKILLS/REFERENCES

Use table of contents to locate titles and page numbers.
Follow oral directions to locate, classify, match, compare, and contrast specific
  materials to complete a task (for workbook or homework assignment).

LANGUAGE ARTS

ORAL LANGUAGE

Use complete sentences when answering questions or speaking.
Tell first and last name, address, and telephone number.
Classify name words or action words.
Use gestures, movements, and facial expressions to portray a given character in
  a story.
Identify words that tell how, where and when.

WRITTEN LANGUAGE

Change statements to questions and questions to statements.
Expand sentences by adding descriptive words:
  The cat is big. The *gray* cat is big.
Select appropriate titles for short paragraphs or stories.
Copy names of days of week and months of year.
Copy abbreviations and titles with capitalizations and periods:
  Mr., Mrs., Ms., Dr,; days of week.
Identify important information on an invitation: *what, where, when.*
Write a thank you letter; understand its meaning and purpose.

SPELLING

Identify all capital and small letters.
Spell words using short vowel patterns: *sat, fat, cat; fan, man, can.*
Identify two-letter consonants: *that, rich.*

HANDWRITING

Print simple sentences using correct spacing, capitalization, question marks, or periods.
Print from memory without a model:
capital and small letters; first and last name.

MATHEMATICS

PROBLEM SOLVING

Answer number questions using information from a picture story.
Know when to use addition or subtraction to find an answer in story problem.
Use addition and subtraction to solve problems that require no borrowing or carrying.
Begin to use a bar graph for information.

NUMBER SYSTEM

Understand terms: *less than, as many as, more than.*
Count and write numerals to 100.
Write the numeral for a given number of tens and ones.
Know place positions: *first through fifth.*
Name fraction parts: *½, ⅓, ¼ of an object.*
Identify what comes before, after, and between given numbers: __6, 8__, 3__5.
Skip count by 2's, 5's, and 10's from memory.

COMPUTATION

Add with sums to twelve.
Subtract from numbers less than twelve.
Add three numbers with sums to ten.
Add and subtract two-digit numbers without borrowing or carrying.

MEASUREMENT

Tell time by hours and half-hours.
Name value of coins and combination of coins to 25¢.
Measure in inches and centimeters.

SECOND-GRADE OBJECTIVES

READING

PHONICS

Know sounds of words beginning with:
  all single consonants: *c, h, b*
  two-letter consonants: *sh, th, sl*
  three-letter consonants: *thr, str, spr.*
Know sounds of:
  long and short vowels: *a, e, i, o, u, sometimes w and y*
  vowel combinations: *ay, ea, oy, oi, oa, aw.*
Identify the number of syllables in one, two, or three-syllable word.
Understand how words are formed by adding a beginning and ending:
  <u>re</u> + do + <u>ing</u> = *redoing*
  making a compound word: *some + thing = something*
  making a plural word: *dog + s = dogs*
  making a contraction: *do + not = don't.*

VOCABULARY

Recognize words that have similar and opposite meanings:
higher/taller; higher/lower.
Recognize basic words and their meanings as introduced in the child's assigned reader.

COMPREHENSION

Read and follow written directions in order to perform a given task.
For a given story:
identify the meaning of an unknown word by how it is used in a sentence
recall main ideas, details, and sequences
reach a conclusion
distinguish between fact and fiction.

STUDY SKILLS/REFERENCES

Alphabetize words to the first letter.
Locate basic information in a simple dictionary and table of contents.
Group words according to likenesses or differences.

LANGUAGE ARTS

ORAL LANGUAGE

Participate in oral activities such as:
role playing, describing personal experiences, story telling, giving simple reports, and participating in classroom discussions.
Listen in order to follow directions.
Discuss ideas to gain information.

WRITTEN LANGUAGE

Learn punctuations for the ends of sentences, abbreviations, dates, words in a series, and contractions.
Learn and use proper grammar with:
present and past tense: *play, played; run, ran*
subject and verb agreement: *The dog runs fast.*
pronoun usage: *Susan is asleep; she is tired. Susan and I are friends (not me and Susan).*
Capitalize names of places, holidays, streets, people, and titles such as:
Mr., Miss, Mrs., Ms.
Write and recognize a complete sentence.
Write an original paragraph and letter.

SPELLING

Spell:
color words
number words from one to ten
Words that sound alike:
know, no; their, there.
Spell words with:
combination of vowels: *soap, cream, book*
final silent e: *cake*
two-letter consonants: *child, sheep*
combinations of ar, er, ir, or ur: *car, her, bird*
s or es endings: *dogs, foxes, dresses*

HANDWRITING

Write small and capital letters legibly and correctly.
Use correct margins and spacing.
Begin to learn cursive writing.

MATHEMATICS

PROBLEM SOLVING

Read picture and bar graphs.
Solve story problems with addition and subtraction.
Solve story problems with multiplication facts from 0-5.
Choose correct coins for a purchase: 1¢, 5¢, 10¢

NUMBER SYSTEM

Count and write to 1,000.
Know place value of: 1's, 10's and 100's.
Recognize fractions: ½, ⅓, ¼.

COMPUTATION

Know addition and subtraction combinations using numbers with digits 0-9.
Add and subtract two-place numbers, carrying and borrowing when necessary.

$$\begin{array}{r} 1 \\ 25 \\ +38 \\ \hline 63 \end{array} \qquad \begin{array}{r} 3 \\ \cancel{4}6 \\ -28 \\ \hline 18 \end{array}$$

Add and subtract three-place numbers, no more than one carrying or borrowing situation.

$$\begin{array}{r} 1 \\ 432 \\ +108 \\ \hline 540 \end{array} \qquad \begin{array}{r} 2 \\ 4\cancel{3}2 \\ -108 \\ \hline 324 \end{array}$$

Know multiplication facts through 5 x 5.

MEASUREMENT

Measure to the nearest inch, half-inch, and centimeter.
Identify liters.
Use liquid measurements: *cups, pints, quarts, liters.*
Read a calendar.
Tell time to quarter-hour.

THIRD-GRADE OBJECTIVES

READING

PHONICS

Recognize new words formed from root words using prefixes and suffixes:
   replace, untie, useless.
Read and identify number of syllables in a word to three syllables.
Recognize and use contractions with two or more letters missing:
   I'd, I would; he'll, he will.

VOCABULARY

Recognize basic words and their meanings as introduced in the child's assigned
   reader.
Learn unfamiliar words by looking for clues such as similar bases, spelling
   patterns, prefixes, suffixes, and compound words.

COMPREHENSION

For a given story, identify characters, setting and time.
Establish cause and effect relationships.
Distinguish between fact and opinion.
Draw conclusions about information, details, main ideas, character traits, and
    situations in a story.
Identify the meaning of a word with more than one meaning from its use in a
    sentence:
    This is the third act.
    Does the child act grown-up?

STUDY SKILLS/REFERENCES

Alphabetize words to the third letter.
Use a glossary or dictionary as an aid to pronunciation and word meaning.
Use a pronunciation key.
Use guide words to locate a word in a dictionary or glossary.
Read maps, charts, and graphs.
Use first and second letters to locate words in reference books.

LANGUAGE ARTS

ORAL LANGUAGE

Give examples of parts of speech: *verbs, nouns, adjectives.*
Give examples of compound words, words with prefixes, and words with suffixes.
Describe events in sequence.
Present an oral report.
Give simple directions and messages.
Listen to selected readings to develop an appreciation of literature:
    fiction, biography, poems.
Listen to an oral report for the main idea and significant details.

WRITTEN LANGUAGE

Recognize and use:
    irregular verb tenses: *eat, ate; see, saw; do, did*
    question words: *who, what, when, where, why, how*
    pronoun-verb contractions: *I'd, he's, she'll*
    comparative adjectives: *more, most; big, bigger, biggest*
Write statements, questions, and exclamatory sentences.
Write original stories, poems, and compositions.
Proofread sentences and make corrections for capitalizations and punctuations.
Classify groups of words as sentences or phrases.
Write a friendly letter:
    Place the parts in correct order.
    Address the envelope correctly.

SPELLING

Spell:
    plural forms of nouns ending in "y": *monkey, monkeys; baby, babies*
    verbs with endings added: *play, plays, playing, played*
    silent "e" words: *hope + ing = hoping; bake + er = baker*
    common synonyms and antonyms: *little, small; hot, cold*

HANDWRITING

Write from memory all capital and lower case letters in cursive.

MATHEMATICS

PROBLEM SOLVING

Learn and apply steps in problem solving:
  using addition, subtraction, multiplication and division
  using more than one computation process involving money

NUMBER SYSTEM

Use symbols: *greater than, less than, equal to.*
Know place value: *1's, 10's, 100's, 10,000's.*
Know place positions: *first through tenth.*
Know fractions that equal one: *2/2, 3/3, 4/4.*
Count and write numerals to 99,999.
Round off numbers to nearest 10.
Read and write decimals to tenths.
Find common fractions for parts of objects.

COMPUTATION

Add and subtract three-place numbers involving borrowing or carrying with 0's.

$$\begin{array}{r} 1 \\ \cancel{2}\,0\,8 \\ -\,1\,2\,7 \\ \hline 8\,1 \end{array}$$

Divide a two-place number by numbers up to 9, no remainder.

$$\begin{array}{r} 3 \\ 8\,\overline{)\,2\,4} \end{array}$$

Multiply a two-place number by numbers up to 9, no carrying.

$$\begin{array}{r} 2\,1 \\ \times\quad 8 \\ \hline 1\,6\,8 \end{array}$$

MEASUREMENT

Tell time to nearest five-minute interval.
Know value of coin combinations including dollar.
Measure length to nearest half-inch, inch, centimeter, and meter.
Recognize the difference between meters and kilometers.
Compare units of measure in feet and yards.
Measure with liters.

GEOMETRY

Recognize parallel lines, right angles, and congruent figures.
Draw lines, angles, squares, triangles, and rectangles.

FOURTH-GRADE OBJECTIVES

READING

PHONICS

Know words beginning with three-letter consonants clusters: *str, thr, spl.*
Know words with soft and hard single-consonants sounds:
  city, cent; count, cut.
Pronounce syllables in words by applying these rules:
  a syllable ending in a consonant has a short vowel sound: *cat*
  a syllable ending in a vowel has a long vowel sound: *cake*
Know the meaning of words with the prefixes ex, pre, un:
  exchange, prehistoric, undo.
Know the meaning of words with suffixes able, ment, ness, ful:
  suitable, happiness.

VOCABULARY

Understand and use vocabulary appropriate to grade level.

COMPREHENSION

Know the meanings of unknown words by use in a story.
Recall details and make inferences about a character's motives and/or feelings in a selection.
Identify a simile or metaphor in a sentence.
Answer questions for a given paragraph: *who, what, when, where, which, how.*
Select the main idea of a paragraph.
Know whether a selection or idea is reality or fantasy.

STUDY SKILLS/REFERENCES

Know the special features of a dictionary:
   etymology, pronunciation of words, parts of speech.
Know how to interpret maps, graphs, and charts.

LANGUAGE ARTS

ORAL LANGUAGE

Read aloud with expression.
Follow oral directions.
Participate in oral activities involving:
   retelling stories
   giving book reports
   reciting poetry
   sharing current events
   talking with others

WRITTEN LANGUAGE

Recognize and identify nouns and verbs in sentences.
Recognize subject and predicates in a simple sentence.
Capitalize the first word of sentences, proper nouns, story titles and the pronoun I.
Use periods in abbreviations.
Use commas in a series, dates, addresses, and direct address.
Write a friendly letter; address an envelope.

SPELLING

Know the meaning of spelling words on fourth-grade class list.
Spell words involving the use of:
   a vowel before r: *arm, hurt, word*
   consonant blends/digraphs: bl, st, fr; ch, ph, th, gh
   silent consonants letters: *mb, wr, kn*
   letter groups: *ough, aught.*

HANDWRITING

Write assignments in a legible form.
Use a uniform size, slant, alignment, and spacing when writing.
Join cursive letters properly while writing.

MATHEMATICS

PROBLEM SOLVING

Solve story problems involving:
   addition or subtraction
   three-place numbers with borrowing or carrying
   multiplication for division.
Solve two-step word problem using addition.

NUMBER SYSTEM

Write common fractions such as: $1/2$, $1/4$, $1/3$.
Recognize place values of digits in numbers up to 99,999.
Round off numbers to nearest ten.
Read and write numbers to millions.

COMPUTATION

Add and subtract three-place numbers with
   many regroupings.

$$\begin{array}{r} \overset{11}{} \\ 237 \\ +184 \\ \hline 421 \end{array} \qquad \begin{array}{r} \overset{8\,9}{\cancel{9}\,\cancel{0}^{1}3} \\ -275 \\ \hline 628 \end{array}$$

Multiply three-place numbers by multipliers up to nine.
Divide three-place numbers by divisors up to nine.
Estimate answers for addition, subtraction, and multiplication.

MEASUREMENT

Measure length to the nearest centimeter, meter, foot, and yard.
Find the areas of rectangles by counting square units.
Calculate the perimeters of regular objects up to six sides.
Know when to use appropriate abbreviations for: centimeters, meters,
   kilometers.
Know when to measure:
   weight with grams or kilograms
   volume with liters, milliliters, and cubic centimeters

FIFTH-GRADE OBJECTIVES

READING

PHONICS

Recognize noun suffixes (ist, or, ness, tion, hood, ant, er): *special<u>ist</u>*.
Recognize verb suffixes (ing, ize, ed): *giv<u>ing</u>*.
Recognize adverb and adjective suffixes (ful, ive, ly, ish): *help<u>ful</u>*.
Know the meanings of words with prefixes (ir, il, mis, in, sub, trans, anti,
   counter, en, semi, super): *<u>ir</u>responsible*.
Know the meanings of words with suffixes (ance, ence, hood, ship, tion, sion, ion,
   ation, ure, ic): import<u>ance</u>.
Read words with consonant/vowel or consonant/vowel cluster patterns (gh, psy,
   ough, squ, eight, dge):
   thr<u>ough</u>; <u>psy</u>chology.

VOCABULARY

Understand and use vocabulary appropriate to grade level.

COMPREHENSION

For a given selection:
    identify the main and supporting ideas
    identify an author's purpose
    identify the mood, theme, and setting
    identify cause and effect relationships
    form a generalization
    recognize exaggeration.
Recognize meaning and figurative language, imagery, symbols, and concrete language.
Use a variety of ways to read words including syllabication, context, dictionaries, or phonics.

STUDY SKILLS

Compile information on a topic from several sources.
Select the correct definition for a word in a sentence when a dictionary gives more than one meaning.
Summarize a nonfiction selection.

LANGUAGE ARTS

ORAL LANGUAGE

Participate in oral activities such as:
    giving oral book reports
    questioning for more information
    reciting literature from memory
    giving directions
    reading choral selections
    summarizing and dramatizing

WRITTEN LANGUAGE

Write sentences using verbs, adjectives, adverbs, pronouns, nouns, prepositions, and objects of prepositions.
Write sentences using colons, commas, question marks, exclamation points, periods, quotation marks, and hyphens.
Combine two simple sentences to make a new sentence.
Write a paragraph in logical sequence with a topic sentence and a summary statement.
Make a topic outline using two or more paragraphs.
Prepare a report with more than one paragraph.
Write a variety of personal and business letters; address envelopes appropriately.

SPELLING

Spell the most commonly used words from the fifth-grade reader.
Know the meaning of words in the fifth-grade spelling list.

HANDWRITING

Begin to write with ink.
Write neatly, legibly, and smoothly.
Write with acceptable speed.

MATHEMATICS

PROBLEM SOLVING

Solve story problems using complex addition, subtraction, multiplication, and
    division processes.
Identify what information is needed to solve a story problem when too much or
    too little information is given.
Solve story problems involving money.

NUMBER SYSTEM

Know the place value of numbers to 100,000,000.
Know the place value of decimals to thousandths.
Round off numbers to the nearest hundred.
Write a mixed number for an improper fraction.

COMPUTATION

Add two five-place numbers with a six-place answer:

$$\begin{array}{r} 98{,}764 \\ +32{,}101 \\ \hline 130{,}865 \end{array}$$

Subtract four-place numbers:

$$\begin{array}{r} {}^{8}\ \ {}^{10} \\ \cancel{9}{,}1^{1}0\,7 \\ -\ 5{,}8\,7\,6 \\ \hline 3{,}2\,3\,1 \end{array}$$

Estimate the answer for an addition, subtraction, multiplication,
    or division problem.
Find the common factors and multiples of numbers less than 100.
Divide by two-place numbers with and without remainders:

$$27\overline{)306}\quad 11\ r9$$

Multiply a three-place number by a two-place number:

$$\begin{array}{r} 246 \\ \times\ 29 \\ \hline 2{,}214 \\ 4{,}920 \\ \hline 7{,}134 \end{array}$$

Given a group of numbers, find the average.
Add, subtract, and multiply common fractions, mixed numbers, and decimals
Reduce fractions to lowest terms.

MEASUREMENT

Measure: length to nearest ⅛ inch
             length to nearest millimeter
             radius and diameter of circle
Compare lengths and weights in metric units.
Find perimeters and areas of regular polygons.

SIXTH-GRADE OBJECTIVES

READING

PHONICS

Know the meanings of words with prefixes: *centi, milli, kilo, deci.*
Know the meanings of words with suffixes: *ant, ent, able, ible, ous.*

VOCABULARY

Understand and use vocabulary appropriate to grade level.

COMPREHENSION

Identify cause-and-effect relationships.

Identify author's purpose, mood, and theme.

Answer questions for literal, interpretive, critical, and creative thinking.
  Literal example: Who discovered the remains of a serpent-like creature?
  Interpretive thinking example: What do all seven of these stories have in
  common?
  Critical thinking example: Do you think that events which are not explained
  do not really happen or do not really exist?
  Creative thinking example: Which mystery in this selection would you like to
  solve? How would you go about solving it? What dangers would be involved?

Distinguish among different types of literature: *biography, tall tale, legend,
  news article, historical fiction, folktale, science fiction.*

Express opinions, note imagery, form value judgments, and predict outcomes
  for given selections.

Identify main ideas which are implied in selections.

STUDY SKILLS/REFERENCES

Outline topics, sub-topics, and details from materials read.

Choose correct reference aids: *thesaurus, atlas, almanac, and dictionary.*

LANGUAGE ARTS

ORAL LANGUAGE

Participate in oral activities such as:
  reading choral and drama selections
  giving and following concise directions
  reciting poetry
  giving a persuasive speech on a controversial topic

Listen to a presentation; take notes and/or make an outline.

WRITTEN LANGUAGE

Use and understand parts of speech:
  nouns, personal pronouns, verbs, adjectives, and adverbs
  past, present, and future tense

Use the apostrophe in contractions and possessives.

Punctuate direct quotations in a story.

Use commas with conjunctions *(and, but, or, and so);* appositives *(John, the man
  in the blue suit, ate cake.);* interrupters *(by the way);* and subordinators
  (when, if).

Proofread material and correct mistakes.

Write several types of paragraphs: *creative, informative, explanatory.*

Organize and write creative prose and poetry, reports and research papers, and
  personal and business letters.

SPELLING

Spell the most commonly used words from the sixth-grade reader and/or speller.

HANDWRITING

Use ink for writing special projects.

Develop clarity and speed in writing.

Use cursive writing for written work and printing for labels, maps, and charts.

MATHEMATICS

PROBLEM SOLVING

Solve story problems involving:
  fractions, mixed numbers, percentages, decimals, and ratios
  graphs and tables
  computation with money
Solve story problems using positive and negative numbers.

NUMBER SYSTEM

Recognize prime and composite numbers.
Read and write numbers to billions.
Round off decimals to nearest tenth, hundredth, and thousandth.
Know the place values of decimals to thousandths.
Find the reciprocal of a fraction: $1/4 \times 4/1 = 1$; $1/2 \times 2/1 = 1$.

COMPUTATION

Add six-place numbers.
Multiply and divide with three-place numbers.
Add, subtract, and multiply fractions with unlike denominators.
Divide with common fractions and mixed numbers.
Estimate quotients for division problems.
Find prime factors of numbers below 100, decimals equivalent to common
  fractions, and the percentages of numbers.

MEASUREMENT

Find areas and perimeters of four-sided figures and triangles; diameters,
  circumferences, and areas of circles; and the volumes of regular six-sided
  solid objects.
Change liters to milliliters; grams to kilograms; millimeters to centimeters,
  meters, or kilometers.
Locate points on a grid.

MULTIPLICATION TABLES

4 X 1 = 4	5 X 1 = 5	6 X 1 = 6
4 X 2 = 8	5 X 2 = 10	6 X 2 = 12
4 X 3 = 12	5 X 3 = 15	6 X 3 = 18
4 X 4 = 16	5 X 4 = 20	6 X 4 = 24
4 X 5 = 20	5 X 5 = 25	6 X 5 = 30
4 X 6 = 24	5 X 6 = 30	6 X 6 = 36
4 X 7 = 28	5 X 7 = 35	6 X 7 = 42
4 X 8 = 32	5 X 8 = 40	6 X 8 = 48
4 X 9 = 36	5 X 9 = 45	6 X 9 = 54
4 X 10 = 40	5 X 10 = 50	6 X 10 = 60
4 X 11 = 44	5 X 11 = 55	6 X 11 = 66
4 X 12 = 48	5 X 12 = 60	6 X 12 = 72

10 X 1 = 10	11 X 1 = 11	12 X 1 = 12
10 X 2 = 20	11 X 2 = 22	12 X 2 = 24
10 X 3 = 30	11 X 3 = 33	12 X 3 = 36
10 X 4 = 40	11 X 4 = 44	12 X 4 = 48
10 X 5 = 50	11 X 5 = 55	12 X 5 = 60
10 X 6 = 60	11 X 6 = 66	12 X 6 = 72
10 X 7 = 70	11 X 7 = 77	12 X 7 = 84
10 X 8 = 80	11 X 8 = 88	12 X 8 = 96
10 X 9 = 90	11 X 9 = 99	12 X 9 = 108
10 X 10 = 100	11 X 10 = 110	12 X 10 = 120
10 X 11 = 110	11 X 11 = 121	12 X 11 = 132
10 X 12 = 120	11 X 12 = 132	12 X 12 = 144

1 X 1 = 1	2 X 1 = 2	3 X 1 = 3
1 X 2 = 2	2 X 2 = 4	3 X 2 = 6
1 X 3 = 3	2 X 3 = 6	3 X 3 = 9
1 X 4 = 4	2 X 4 = 8	3 X 4 = 12
1 X 5 = 5	2 X 5 = 10	3 X 5 = 15
1 X 6 = 6	2 X 6 = 12	3 X 6 = 18
1 X 7 = 7	2 X 7 = 14	3 X 7 = 21
1 X 8 = 8	2 X 8 = 16	3 X 8 = 24
1 X 9 = 9	2 X 9 = 18	3 X 9 = 27
1 X 10 = 10	2 X 10 = 20	3 X 10 = 30
1 X 11 = 11	2 X 11 = 22	3 X 11 = 33
1 X 12 = 12	2 X 12 = 24	3 X 12 = 36

7 X 1 = 7	8 X 1 = 8	9 X 1 = 9
7 X 2 = 14	8 X 2 = 16	9 X 2 = 18
7 X 3 = 21	8 X 3 = 24	9 X 3 = 27
7 X 4 = 28	8 X 4 = 32	9 X 4 = 36
7 X 5 = 35	8 X 5 = 40	9 X 5 = 45
7 X 6 = 42	8 X 6 = 48	9 X 6 = 54
7 X 7 = 49	8 X 7 = 56	9 X 7 = 63
7 X 8 = 56	8 X 8 = 64	9 X 8 = 72
7 X 9 = 63	8 X 9 = 72	9 X 9 = 81
7 X 10 = 70	8 X 10 = 80	9 X 10 = 90
7 X 11 = 77	8 X 11 = 88	9 X 11 = 99
7 X 12 = 84	8 X 12 = 96	9 X 12 = 108

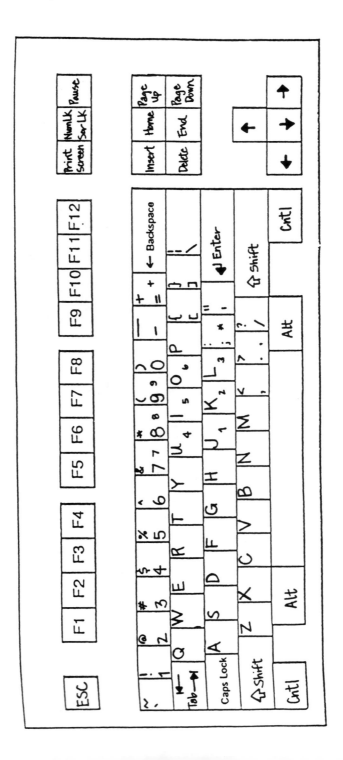

Measurement

Time

60 seconds = 1 minute
60 minutes = 1 hour
24 hours = 1 day

7 days = 1 week
52 weeks = 1 year
12 months = 1 year

Seasons

Winter = December, January and February
Spring = March, April and May
Summer = June, July and August
Fall = September, October and November

Linear Measure

12 inches = 1 foot
3 feet = 1 yard
5280 feet = 1 mile

Liquid

2 cups (c) = 1 pint (pt)
2 pints = 1 quart (qt)
4 quarts = 1 gallon (gal)

Weight

16 ounces (oz) = 1 pound (lb)
2000 pounds = 1 ton

Table of Surface Measure

144 sq. in. = 1 sq. ft.
9 sq. ft. = 1 sq. yd.
30 1/4 sq. yds. = 1 sq. rod
160 sq. rods = 1 acre
640 acres = 1 sq. mile

A section of land is 1 sq. mile.
A quarter section is 160 acres.
A township is 36 sq. miles.

Metric Measures

Length   1000 millimeters (mm) = 1 meter (m)
           100 centimeters (cm) = 1 meter
           1 kilometer (km) = 1000 meters
Area   1 hectare (ha) = 10,000 square meters
Liquid   1000 milliliters (mL) = 1 liter (L)
           1 milliliter = 1 cubic centimeter
Weight   1000 milligrams (mg) = 1 gram (g)
           1000 grams = 1 kilogram (kg)

NOTICE: Here is an outstanding resource for all parents to use. Did you know that you can order booklets on *Helping Your Child* with reading, math, science? Also, hundreds of other booklets are available on a variety of topics for little or no money. Write to Consumer Information Center, Pueblo, CO 81009, for a catalog. Keep their address handy.

Bibliography

Books
 Abruscato, Joseph, *et. al. Holt Science, T.E., Grade Six,* New York, Holt, Rinehart and Winston Publishers, 1986.

 Abruscato, Joseph, *et. al. Science - Grade Five,* New York, Addison-Wesley Publishing Co., 1976.

 Alexander, Gretchen, *et. al. Science, T.E., Grade Four,* Palo Alto (California), Scott, Foresman and Company, 1984.

 Ames, Louise Bates and Frances L. Ilg, *Your Eight-Year-Old,* New York, Dell Publishing, 1990.

 Ames, Louise Bates and Frances L. Ilg, *Your Four-Year-Old: Wild and Wonderful,* New York, Dell Publishing, 1989.

 Ames, Louise Bates and Frances L. Ilg, *Your Ten-To-Fourteen-Year Old,* New York, Dell Publishing, 1989.

 Andrews, Danielle A., *et. al., Science Framework For California Public Schools,* Sacramento (California), California Department of Education, 1990.

 Atwater, Mary, *et. al., The World Around You, T.E., Kindergarten,* New York, MacMillan/McGraw-Hill, 1993.

 Atwater, Mary, *et. al., Living and Growing, T.E., Kindergarten,* New York, MacMillan/McGraw-Hill, 1993.

 Brown, Robert, *200 Illustrated Science Experiments For Children,* Blue Ridge Summit (Pennsylvania), Tab Books, 1987.

 Canter, Lee and Lee Hausner, Ph.D., *Homework Without Tears,* New York, Harper & Row, 1987.

 Cassiday, Sylvia, *In Your Own Words,* New York, Thomas Y. Crowell, 1990.

 Cheek, Dennis W., *et. al. Science Curriculum Resource Handbook,* New York, Kraus International Publications, 1992.

 Cohen, Michael, *et. al. Science, Kindergarten,* Palo Alto (California), Scott, Foresman and Company, 1984.

 Collin, Simon, *The Way MultiMedia Works,* London, Dorling Crowell, 1990.

 Danks, Hugh, *The Bug Book,* New York, Workman Publishing, 1987.

 Edwards, Sharon and Robert Maloy, *Kids Have All The Write Stuff,* New York, Penguin Books, 1992.

 Eicholz, Robert, *et. al., Mathematics, T.E., Grade Four,* Lexington (Massachusetts), D.C. Heath and Company, 1988.

 Erickson, Donna, *Prime Time Together With Kids,* Martinez (California), Discovery Toys, Inc., 1989.

Eyre, Richard and Linda, *Teaching Our Children Values*, New York,
    Simon and Schuster, 1993.

Fennel, Francis, *et. al. Mathematics Unlimited, T.E., Grade Six*,
    New York, Holt, Rinehart and Winston Publishing, 1988.

Gardner, Robert and David Webster, *Science In Your Backyard*,
    New York, Simon and Schuster, 1990.

Guterson, David, *Family Matters - Why Homeschooling Makes Sense*,
    New York, Harcourt Brace Jovanovich, 1992.

Lorton-Baratta, Mary, *Math Their Way*, Menlo Park (California),
    Addison-Wesley Publishing Co., 1976.

Macaulay, David, *The Way Things Work*, Boston, Houghton-Mifflin,
    1988.

Markle, Sandra, *et. al. Young Scientists Guide To Successful Science
    Projects*, New York, Shepard Books, 1990.

O'Hara, Shelley, *10 Minute Guide To Buying A Computer*,
    Indianapolis (Indiana), Alpha Books, 1994.

Offinoski, Steve, *Putting It In Writing*, New York, Scholastic, 1993.

Raftery, Kevin and Kim Gilbert Raftery, *Kids Gardening: A Kids's
    Guide to Messing Around in the Dirt*, Palo Alto (California),
    Klutz Press, 1989.

Rucker, Walter, *et. al. Mathematics, T.E., Grade Two*, Lexington
    (Massachusetts), D.C. Heath and Company, 1988.

Sonna, Linda Agler, *The Homework Solution*, Charlotte (Vermont),
    Williamson Publishing Company, 1990.

Sulzby, Elizabeth, *et. al. English T.E. Grade Five*, New York,
    McGraw-Hill School Division, 1989.

Ward, Alan, *Machines At Work*, New York, Franklin Watts, 1993.

Ward, Alan, *Plants and Animals*, New York, Franklin Watts, 1993.

Wasermann, Selma, *Serious Players In The Classroom*, New York,
    Teachers College Press, 1990.

Weiss, Harvey, *Machines and How They Work*, New York, Thomas
    Y. Crowell, 1983.

Booklets and Pamphlets

Kanter, Patsy F., *Helping Your Child Learn Math*, U. S. Department
    of Education, Washington, D.C., 1992, 1-8.

Kantrowitz, Barbara, *Advice from an Educator: Getting Practical*,
    Newsweek, Computers and the Family, New York, Fall 1994, 56-59.

Seed to Seedling, produced by The Sacramento Tree Foundation,
    Sacramento (California), 1991, 3-8.

Pee Chee All Season Portfolio, © produced by The Mead Corporation,
    Dayton (Ohio), 1987.